BOUGHT,
NOT SOLD

TWO MEDIA REVIEWS

Real Estate Intelligence Report, June 2, 1998:

A new book critical of ... traditional real estate practices ... almost certainly will find a following among buyer agents, educators and consumer advocates. ... Bought, Not Sold *... is dedicated to simplifying agency concepts to the average homebuyer and seller.*

—Frank Cook, Publisher
www.reintel.com

International Real Estate Digest, June 23, 1998:

Homebuying mistakes can no longer be camouflaged by inflation, justified by irrational appreciation or absorbed by employee relocation programs, so the best defense against financial loss today is smart buying. Bought, Not Sold *provides the information necessary to be a* VERY *smart buyer.*

Dip into any page at random and you'll find a nugget worth the price of the book; read it cover to cover and you'll be better educated on these matters than most real estate professionals. Bought, Not Sold *is a gem of a book.*

Bought, Not Sold *is not just for buyers, but should be required reading for every real estate broker and agent, every state legislator and every seller of residential property.*

—Becky Swann, President, IRED.COM, Inc.
www.ired.com

BOUGHT, NOT SOLD

*Single Agency, Buyers' Brokers,
Flat Fees, and the Consumer
Revolution in Real Estate*

RAY WILSON

What every **BUYER** and **SELLER** should know
before working with, *or against,* the pros

Greenfield, Massachusetts

Published by:
CognaBooks®
P.O. Box 1108
Greenfield MA 01302-1108
(413) 772-0976
fax: (413) 772-2450
e-mail: bought@cognabooks.com
World Wide Web: www.cognabooks.com

Manufactured in the United States of America.
Cover and text design and production: Potter Publishing Studio
Text illustrations: Jeff Wilson

Library of Congress Cataloging In Publication Data:
Wilson, Ray
   Bought, Not Sold! : Single Agency, Buyers' Brokers, Flat Fees & The Consumer Revolution in Real Estate / Ray Wilson

                     p.   cm.
         Includes bibliography, glossary and index.
         ISBN: 0-9660135-0-6 (pbk.)
         1. House buying. I. Title
         2. House selling. 3. Real estate business
   HD1379.W56 1998
   333.33   97-092511
                     CIP

To the customers,

those who buy real estate

*and those who buy the services
of real estate agents;*

may they **buy** *wisely what they need
and not be* **sold** *what others need to sell.*

Contents

DIMENSION THREE
The Now

APPENDIX

Foreword

*by Thomas Early, President
of the National Association of
Exclusive Buyer Agents (NAEBA)*

WHEN I FIRST READ a draft of *Bought, Not Sold,* I called Ray Wilson to tell him that he wrote the book I always wanted to write, but never had the time. For a decade, I have been in the trenches of a battle for consumer rights, seeing a story that deserves telling. Even more important than that, there are warnings that should be sounded, and guidance given, to both buyers and sellers of real estate. Wilson beat me to the punch; but that's a good thing, because this is a good book.

This is an especially good book for real estate consumers, the buyers and sellers who should know what they are getting when they do business with real estate agents. It is also a good book for the agents, though my bet is that most traditional agents won't see it that way. While Wilson actually points to real opportunity for creative and profitable seller agency, as well as buyer agency, he sees a truth they just don't want to face — that consumers are going to know better than to trust someone working both sides of the street. They'll know it a lot sooner after reading this book.

There is one other group of people to whom I strongly recommend the pages separating these two covers — state legislators who are being pitched allegedly consumer-friendly legislation changing the rules of real

estate licensing and operations. Behind the sales pitch are the very people who have profited from the system they now propose to "reform" by,
in truth, purposely making the process so complicated as to confuse the
consumer. Their claim is that it is in the interests of consumers to redefine "agency" as something one firm can provide to both buyers and sellers. To use the language of the title, "Bought, Not Sold": I don't buy it,
Wilson does not buy it, and no responsible legislator should buy it after
reading Wilson's exposé of what is really being sold under the guise of
reform.

Ironically, the wisdom and virtue of serving only one side was the
message given lip-service by every real estate agent I ever knew when I
first entered the business in the eighties. The difference in those days was
that they all represented the same side, the sellers'! Buyers were merely
customers from whom the salespeople would work to extract the highest possible prices. The trouble, as Wilson notes, was that *buyers didn't
know that* — most often being led to trust an agent they believed was
working for them.

A small but determined group of professionals had a big problem
with that system, but we took on an even bigger problem when we tried
to give buyers the representation they needed and deserved. In 1989,
when I opened one of the first buyer-only agencies in the country, refusing to take listings, others in the industry thought I was a madman.
Reactions ranged from denial to amusement, but then, when buyers
started paying attention, I was labeled a troublemaker and ostracized.
This was a painful experience, for I went into real estate in the first place
because I value people and their feelings toward me. Fortunately, hostility came from only one direction — it was not from the buyers, and
not even from sellers who remembered their experiences as buyers. As
buyers brought their business to me, reactions of the area professionals
escalated to trumped-up charges before the association we all belonged
to, and even to threats against my license to operate. The charges never

stuck because people, most practitioners included, could not go along with the absurdity of claims that it was somehow unethical or illegal to openly represent buyers and advise them against things like high prices and leaky roofs. Still, that kind of advice did violate a tradition in which most professionals had thrived for a very long time and now saw their very survival threatened. Their acceptance was not going to come overnight, and not even over a decade.

While I was alone in the area of Columbus, Ohio, a few others were pioneering buyer agency in other parts of the country and facing the same problems. We all had to deal with social isolation and sabotage ranging from silly charges to blatant discrimination, interference with commissions, and certainly badmouthing to both sellers and buyers. Finding one another and sharing experiences gave us all both solace and a broad situational basis for developing business processes and the quality of client service.

Some, at the beginning, experimented with representing both buyers and sellers, but shared experiences, common sense, and professional tradition said that proper client service had to go one way or the other; we could be either buyers' agents or sellers' agents, but never both. So, when we formed our professional association, the National Association of Exclusive Buyer Agents (NAEBA), the word "exclusive" had very explicit meaning. No member of NAEBA can ever list homes or provide agency representation to a seller. In other words, we stay loyal to the historical and honorable tradition of the real estate industry to represent clients on one side only! We never compromise the interests of our clients with even the risk of conflicting interests; and we never deceive those on the other side with pretensions about who we really work for.

As the millennium now approaches, my business is prospering, NAEBA's membership is growing, and genuine (i.e., exclusive) buyer agency is increasingly visible and credible to consumers and consumer advocates. Consumer awareness is simply too powerful a force for the ever-present local sabotage campaigns to overcome. However, the traditionalists just don't get it, and their resistance has now gone national! Wilson points out that while certain localities are greeting their first buyer agencies with the denial and hostility I and others suffered back in the eighties, their national organization is putting on a buyer-friendly face and actually touting buyer agency as something any seller agency can do — once they legislate away certain obstacles. Confusion reigns on the traditionalist side — the price of not facing up to the simple fact that consumer awareness cannot be denied.

This book is all about what my business, exclusive buyer agency, is about: CONSUMER AWARENESS! Working for buyers, my total job is to insure that there are no unknowns about what is being purchased. That is good for everyone, not just the buyer. With everything on the table, there is no temptation for sellers or their agents to conceal or misrepresent. That means we can all sleep nights. This book puts everything on the table.

— Tom Early, CEBA
January, 1998

Preface

For awhile there, I was beginning to think that I was right and everybody else was wrong. Now that I understand the system, I see that I
had it backwards, that everybody else is wrong and I'm right.

—Overheard on an elevator crowded
with government bureaucrats.
Boston, 1971.

THE SPEAKER was only half in jest. He was fed up with a
bureaucratic system to which everyone around him conformed. The
notion that "I'm right and everyone else is wrong" is often seen as a
sign that the notion-holder has lost touch with reality.

It is not a very reliable sign....

The very harmony of activity enabled by sophisticated organizational
and cultural systems does indeed make it very possible for everyone to be
"wrong", at least everyone conforming to the system! People conform and
rely on the conformance of others because that's what gives them comfort
and security. Internal propaganda is a primary function of any organization, defining the official view of right and wrong, and the system of
rewards and sanctions to enforce conformance. "Right" becomes what
works for the individual to be successful in the system; and any real change
is necessarily "wrong". Dissidents are commanded to "get with the system"
and "go with the flow". Those caught up in the harmony of the system's

sounds and movement never notice until it's too late that the sound is of one great flushing and the movement is around and down....

Whole nations — let alone companies, industries, and professions — have gone down wrong paths with the full endorsement of citizens and members. Often it is those with most to lose who happily and righteously go with the flow of internal tradition and wisdom into the porcelain chute. In marketplace systems, the flush begins when "outsiders" (consumers) become aware of options, and "insiders" (providers) persist in denial of that reality.

A few hardy souls are not prone to denial, but they are prone to becoming outcasts as their clear perception makes the mainstream nervous. They are the revolutionaries and will be remembered as heroes by the survivors, for they sounded the warning and mapped the survival route.

History is loaded with examples, but this book's focus is on one cultural system only: the real estate industry and its mainstream profession. For consumers — buyers and sellers — the book exposes how the traditional system exploits rather than serves. It also points to options available through buyer agents and flat fee agencies, the profession's current day revolutionaries.

For traditional agents, the book is also a service — a message to those locked in denial or seeking shelter against inevitable reform with preposterous special interest legislation. It is not a message of doom for practitioners, but for certain practices. The message, for those able to heed it, is one of substantial opportunity via the same road much of American business discovered in the eighties and nineties — the road of consumer quality.

—Ray Wilson

Acknowledgments

M
Y THANKS FIRST of all to the traditionalists — not those who are simply committed to tradition, but those who wear it as a straight-jacket. This is, after all, a book about reform, something not possible without the institutions and practices which need reforming.

Above all, my sincere appreciation to the reformers, all those working on the front lines of buyer representation, represented here by the individuals specifically contributing to the accuracy and fairness of this book: the Gloria Arnebergs, Norm Bravermans, Bill Broadbents, Anne Cloys, Tom Earlys, Tom Hathaways, Ronn Huths, Mary Lawors, and Barry Millers.

Beyond real estate affairs, I am most grateful to Howard Bronstein, Jeff Potter, and Don Robb for technical advice on this business of putting a quality book in the hands of readers.

Back to real estate — In the beginning it was Bob Kelly who introduced me to the field long ago in Cincinatti, and with the critical eyes of an operationalist and reformer rather than a conformer. Perhaps the best example of a real estate businessman keeping eyes where they should be is Joe Clementi of Andover, Massachusetts, who saw it all as merely the business of men and never lost track of his Father's Business. He demonstrated to me that business is only business, good when it serves our brothers and sisters, when we remember they *are* our brothers and sisters...

And then there's Ann — for waiting patiently for me to finish this thing and get back to the business of being a husband.

Disclaimer

THE PURPOSE of this book is to provide information which, in the opinion of the author, ought to be considered when making certain decisions. It is sold with the understanding that this does not constitute the rendering of legal advice. It is expressly suggested here and in the text that an attorney be consulted in the purchase or sale of real estate and in all matters involving potentially legally enforceable obligations or liability.

IMPORTANT!

In this text, **boldface** indicates that a word may be found in the Glossary. Because it usually occurs when a word is first used, it appears very often in the introduction and may be a distraction. It is, however, necessary.

Terms so indicated have a specialized or untypical meaning — usually explained at the first appearance. This special treatment also makes repeat appearances for the same word or variations when definition is especially critical.

CHAPTER 1

Agency, Quality, Revolution, and Resistance

CRAZY! You'd say I'm crazy, if I dared to suggest that someone seeking to sell his or her home might want a good buyer's agent; you'd wonder how I missed the obvious difference between buying and selling. Most real estate agents would agree with you — and rightfully so, since, under the laws of agency, a buyers' agent must serve the interests of the buyer and not the seller. And yet, a brochure distributed by real estate agents nationwide notes the options for consumers, boasting that someone selling a home can hire a seller's agent, and that a buyer has three choices: a seller's agent, a seller's subagent, or a buyer's agent.

What is wrong with this picture? Nothing, according to most agents. It might be crazy to use a buyer's agent to sell your home, but it is somehow a rational option to use a seller's agent to buy a home. Most real estate agents see it that way because most are sellers' agents, obliged by the laws of agency to maximize the sellers' interests — but they know it is the *buyers* who have the money.

Salespeople need something to sell (Have patience; the wisdom in this book does eventually get deeper than this). Traditionally, real estate agents get to list properties in their inventories by promising owners, under formal **agency** agreements, to represent them as their exclusive (i.e., one and only) **agent** and seek the highest obtainable price. Thus, it is called a "listing agreement," and these "**listing agents**" are paid by their clients (the sellers who employ them) after the sale, i.e., after the customers — the buyers — provide the money.

N O T E :

The terms in **boldface** *are defined in the glossary* .

Of course, the source of the payroll in any business is the customer, but that doesn't make the sales people the customer's employees or agents. The difference between sales in general and real estate sales, however, is that traditional real estate operations deceive the buyer into thinking that he/she does in fact have an agent. Buyers are drawn into a listing agency by the advertised listings, then seduced by an agent's promise to "work with" them in a search of the listings of other agents. Buyers generally do not pick up on the difference between the words, "work with" and "work for"; and surveys reveal that most then think the agent-escort is their agent, since each property they visit has another agent clearly working for the seller.

IT ISN'T JUST THAT BUYERS are misled into thinking they have an agent, but that the one they trust is actually an agent of the other side! Specifically, their escorting agent is an agent of the listing agent and a **subagent** of the seller! The legally enforceable duty of these agents to their seller-**clients** is to lead buyers to them and away from competing unlisted properties, and to work for the highest price. By law, confidentiality is owed to the client, not the customer; so any information buyers confide to these "double-agents" must be revealed to the seller. For example, the agent must tell the seller when the buyer has said, "we'll try an offer of $150,000 but we'll go to $175,000 if we have to." Little wonder that they invariably "have to."

Agents, subagents, and clients

Thus, subagency — perhaps better called "double agency" — has been the method of choice of traditional real estate operations for almost all of the twentieth century. The good news is that it is doomed in an era of expanding consumer awareness, already disappearing in some areas of the country (though still entrenched in others). The bad news is that the professional subculture that spawned subagency goes on, dumping the now-outdated method like excess baggage, but keeping the tradition of working both sides of the street very much alive.

DO NOT LET THE DISTINCTION between the method (subagency) and the tradition (playing both sides) become blurred, as the **traditionalists** would have it. Leaders of the mainstream real estate profession have become resigned to the imminent demise of sub-

Method versus tradition

agency. Making the best of the inevitable, they've joined the chorus of reformers after the battle has been won, but they haven't converted. Audaciously masquerading as reformers, they now go so far as to propose state legislation to restructure real estate laws to do away with subagency and substitute allegedly "consumer-friendly" laws which are no friend to consumers.

No new legislation is needed to do away with subagency; that is being accomplished by legislation passed in the eighties. At the urging of consumer advocates, single agents and buyers' agents, "disclosure laws" were enacted which require agents to tell buyers and sellers who they truly represent. These at least opened the doors for customer awareness and market dynamics to eventually do the job; but it would take over a decade as traditionalist skirting of the disclosure requirement became an art form, ranging from blatantly ignoring it to semantic covers concealing the dangers seller subagents pose to buyers' interests. What will unfold in the coming pages is the true purpose of the pseudo-reform legislation, already passed in a few states, aimed at disrupting market dynamics and distorting simple concepts of agency established in centuries of common law and common sense. It is all to cover the ongoing shenanigans of the very forces who were the architects, beneficiaries and — until the very end — defenders of subagency.

THE READER should understand that **agency** is a well-defined legal concept, and that **fiduciary** obligations are those owed by "agents" and "subagents" to the "clients" who employ them. Real estate professionals are licensed by their states as **brokers** and **salespersons;** their behavior as "agents" is governed by the laws of agency and their "fiduciary" duties to their buyer and seller clients are legally enforceable. Simply put, agents act *on behalf of their clients.* They are legally required to act in the best interests of those clients; and that means working *against* **adverse interests**.

Adverse interests are those which inherently operate in mutual opposition. Obvious is the unique interest buyer and seller each has in the amount of the price; one's gain is the other's loss. A buyer's interest in seeing all available houses is adverse to a listing agent's monetary interest in a limited list of properties, and to a seller's monetary interest in a specific property. Adverse-interest areas go even further, encompassing all negotiable issues involving financing, escape clauses, guarantees and liabilities, matters of time schedule and effort, and well beyond.

A given agent or agency cannot represent adverse interests — a matter of both common sense and centuries of common law. This axiom was not only accepted, but preached by the mainstream real estate profession for most of the Twentieth Century. When an agent has one obligation to the seller to work for the highest price and another to the buyer to work for the lowest price, that is conflict of interest. The point of this obvious example holds true for the subtler adverse interest

Agency and adverse interests

issues present in listing, property search, and specific property negotiation.

"Dual agency" is representing both sides of a negotiation, and *it is illegal* if not fully disclosed to both parties and their consent obtained. Over the years, dual agency met with the general disapproval of most real estate professionals. The so-called **dual agent** is an agent in only a technical sense, serving perhaps as a facilitator or mediator, but precluded from "acting on behalf of" either party (i.e., as true agent) in negotiating for advantage or concession with the other. Since the adverse interests simply cannot be represented, dual agency is really non-agency.

Most real estate professionals recognized that adverse interests cannot be represented by the same person or firm, that so-called dual agency amounted to non-agency. But that does not mean it was the mainstream position that an agent should represent one side or the other. That's close, but wins no cigar. They did believe that an agent should represent only one side — but the phrase ". . . or the other" had no meaning. The one side was that of the seller; and there was simply no "other side" deserving representation. There were virtually no buyers' agents.

In 1981, new Massachusetts real-estate licensee Mary Lawor sought a position in a large and prestigious traditional agency. Her application was denied after a personality test exposed "empathy for the buyer". In 1996, Mary opened her area's first exclusive buyers' agency.

Shamefully, as already noted, most buyers didn't know that! Even after the passage of the disclosure laws intended to guarantee fair warning, buyers somehow kept getting the idea that sellers' subagents escorting them were *their* agents! While the source of the money to pay the agents was the buyer, it was as **customer** and not as employer or **client.** Thus, the seller was the only client in the picture, the only employer, and the direct source of business and income to the agents. It was, of course, a picture with a patent and compound unfairness painted over — the fact that those paying for it all not only were unrepresented, but led into trusting an agent of the other side as their own!

GOOD FOR SELLERS, AT LEAST? Not really. Sellers aren't a group of people separate and distinct from buyers, but the same people at different points in time. To be sellers, most must first be buyers, and most are in fact selling so they can buy again. Sellers and buyers are united in another way; they are both **consumers**, separate and distinct not from each other, but from the providers of the service they consume, i.e., from the agents, and they are both **customers** because they *pay* for that service.

Sellers and buyers

Thus, they have a common vested interest in keeping the providers (agents) honest and in maintaining checks and balances over adverse interests arising between them. Again, the classic adverse interest is the price of the consumed item (the service provided). What balance is there when only one side has professional representation? What check is there when the agent:

(a) tells the seller that the property price (paid by the buyer) can be raised to include the substantial commission, and then

(b) tells the buyer that the seller will pay the fee, and

(c) responds to any perceptive buyer's balking at the fee by saying it is not negotiable because it has already been agreed upon in the listing agent's contract with the seller?

When the seller's agent is balanced by a buyer's agent, the check occurs when the buyer counters (c) with "Baloney!" (or some more colorful term of choice). As property price is an adverse interest between buyer and seller, agent price (i.e., the fee) is an adverse interest between the agent on the one side and both buyer and seller on the other. In other words, as long as there is a single fee for both sides, buyer and seller have a joint interest in keeping the agent's fee down. The fee is not the only adverse interest; there is also the quantity and quality of service which pits benefits to the consumer against costs to the service provider. Without checks and balances, consumer expenses are maximized and consumer benefits minimized, all in the interests of the "service" providers.

THE BEGINNING OF THE END of such unchecked abuse of consumers emerged in the sixties. The rise of consumerism in the United States was sparked by writers like Rachel Carson (*Silent Spring,* 1962)* and Ralph Nader (*Unsafe At Any Speed,* 1965)** respectively exposing the deadly products and practices of the chemical and automobile industries. The movement took hold and grew in the form of protectionism against dangers and abuses, guided by colorful consumer advocacy groups like "Nader's Raiders"; it then evolved in the seventies and eighties to encompass consumer demands for higher quality of products and services, not just in safety but in performance and durability. Then, in the eighties, the Customer Quality Revolution exploded across industry within the internal ranks of the providers themselves, the result of the revelation that quality not only made for increased sales, but for more predictable, dependable, and less costly production and service processes; i.e., the discovery that genuine quality work meant profitable business.

This was all part and parcel of a cultural phenomenon, tied to higher educational levels of consumers and to advances in communications and media technology. Carson's and Nader's alarms weren't isolated events which would merely produce safer insecticides and automobiles and stop there. Observations, revelations, growing concerns, and accepted responsibilities over widespread and disparate market sectors were connected in the fabric of social culture. Thus it is no coincidence that about the time in the late seventies when

Rise of consumerism and the Quality Revolution

*NY:Grossman
**Boston:Houghton–
Mifflin

industry executive Philip Crosby published the precursor of the Quality Revolution *(Quality is Free),* California real estate practitioner and visionary Bill Broadbent introduced and defined the concept which would be the key eventually unlocking the forces of consumer revolution in real estate:

> **single agency:** the practice of representing one and only one side in a transaction, and being paid by the represented party.

The turning point: single agency

AT ITS SIMPLEST LITERAL LEVEL, the name "single agency" implies the functional opposite of dual agency, but the definition goes a level deeper, specifying the client as paymaster. At both levels, the concept encompassed the key values already held by a profession which publicly disdained dual agency and in fact had been providing single agency even before Broadbent put a name to it — although only to sellers. The mainstream quickly embraced the name and concept of single agency, integrating it into its publicly expressed rationale defending its tradition of seller-only agency. They would come to see (and regret) that they had unleashed the one thing that is every traditionalist's worst nightmare:

C H A N G E !

Those paying attention to what they were saying certainly realized that single agency went beyond seller agency. This time they did indeed say that agents should represent one side or the other, and clearly recognizing that the other side was buyer-agency; but for many it was a hypothetical side, not something that would really occur in any great measure. The traditionalist mind could not comprehend that any agent would actually want to provide buyer agency when seller agency worked so well; traditionalism simply does not grasp the fundamental point of consumerism: what matters is not what the providers want, but what the *consumers* want.

To such a mind-set, buyer agency, as an application of the single-agency definition, was another option for the providers, rather than the consumers, something they could use to placate individual buyers on rare occasions. Or so it seemed...

In publicly advocating single agency, the traditionalists overlooked three things:

(1) The first was the magnitude of the appeal of buyer agency to both buyers and some agents. What had been hypothetical gradually became an unsettling reality.

(2) The second was the consequence of the requirement that an agent be paid only by his/her client, which Broadbent correctly saw as essential to making true agency available to both sellers and buyers. The payroll establishes the employment structure — not only who represents whom, but who works for whom, and who controls whom. No sane employer engages workers paid by the competition — precisely what buyers unknowingly were doing under subagency and would not be doing under Broadbent's definition of single agency.

(3) The third overlooked element was the emergence of
buyer-only agency, a consequence of not only the
preference of some agents for buyer interests, but of
genuine problems stemming from the mixing of
buyer agency and seller agency in the same firms.
Introducing buyerside single agency into seller-
agency firms inevitably forces issues of conflicting
interests in direct proportion to the size of both the
organization and the listing inventory.

The reader will see in later chapters that this triple
oversight has had interesting consequences in today's
real estate industry.

- The reality of buyer brokerage has produced (a)
  panic-driven traditionalist reaction ranging from
  psychological denial to organized intrigue, and (b)
  blatant sabotage of buyers' rights to simply pay their
  own agents.

- A more benign consequence has been in the evolution of the use of the term "single agency" as a result
  of both traditionalist reaction and the emergence of
  buyer-only agency.

> *The traditionalist simply don't use it, purging
> it from their vocabulary and publications, try-
> ing to hide that they ever embraced it.*

> *Buyer-only agents paid by buyers do qualify as
> single-agents but usually self-identify as*

*"**exclusive buyer agents**" to reach their specific market.*

Those calling themselves "single agents" tend to be independent or small-firm agents using rigorously disciplined procedures designed to control against all risk of conflict of interest as they provide single agency to both buyers and sellers.

WHAT IS HAPPENING is overdue change in a system controlled not by the consumers of its services, but by those who earned their living from it. It is simply progress, not a judgment against the past or those who practiced its traditions. Well-meaning professionals, no less than consumers, simply trusted in the fundamental ethics of an institution accepted by "everyone."

Changing the system

"Everyone," in various times past, accepted monarchy, hand production, male sovereignty, and American domination of the automobile industry. The first three came to timely demises, respectively, in the American Revolution, the Industrial Revolution, and the Sexual Revolution. The fourth (i.e., Detroit) nearly succumbed to the first waves of the **Quality Revolution** as car buyers became aware of low-priced efficient Japanese alternatives to the high-priced domestic gas guzzlers. The Quality Revolution is a consumer or customer revolution, for its definition of **"quality"** is the degree to which something satisfies customer specifications. It is also a widely documented contemporary *reality*, thriving on expanding consumer awareness,

and sweeping across the industrialized world. Not confined to industry, it quickly began dislodging fundamental assumptions of management in retail and service sectors, wherever profit and loss statements
applied. Competitors learned that those who profited
and those who lost were those who, respectively,
accepted or rejected the new "customer quality" wisdom. Put simply, that meant abandoning lip-service to
the customer and restructuring philosophy, organization, and operations in not only commitment, but
obsession with customer service.

In a real estate sale, the customer is the buyer! Still,
there are other "customers" involved in the transaction.
Both buyer and seller, if they engage agents, are customers as well as clients of their agents, although the
laws of agency make the client the priority customer.
Until the advent of buyer agency (i.e., single agency on
the buyer's side) and the specific act of a buyer engaging a buyer's agent, the buyer remained only a customer and not a client.

NOTE:

Seller as "Customer"

Some texts say the seller is the "customer" of the buyer's agent.
Apparently oblivious to existence of the word "consumer," this is an
awkward attempt to classify a non-client receiving a service. Here, as in
common usage, a "customer" is someone who pays for something. The
seller is the customer of the listing agent and subagents, and certainly not
of either the buyer or the buyer's agent.

The good news, however, is for sellers as well as buyers. Just as in the pre-revolutionary domestic automobile market, real estate buyers and sellers have been captive customers. The customer quality revolution now means options for sellers as well as buyers when traditional agencies fail to meet customer needs. To survive, traditional operators will change or face the alternative, and service to both sellers and buyers can only improve.

THE BAD NEWS is that **traditionalists** (committed to tradition over progress) will always resist change. Like the auto makers, they will learn the choice simply isn't theirs. However, until the customers realize it is their choice, the traditionalists will have a certain grace period. Some will waste this period in denial and resistance. Others (like Ford, GM, and Chrysler) will survive by becoming continuously improving providers of customer quality.

Resisting the change

The reader should be very clear on what I do not mean when I refer to the traditional system or to "traditionalist" agents, subagents or agencies. My definition (Glossary) does not include sellers' agents who are upfront about representing the seller and who do not pretend a seller's agent can provide buyer service on a par with buyer agency. For most real estate agents, the relationship with buyers can be classified in any one of four modes:

WFS = working FOR sellers. This is the upfront seller agent mode just described, involving an express and emphasized declaration of agency obligation to the seller so there is no room for the buyer to misunderstand.

WFB = working FOR buyers. This is the buyer agent mode in which the agent works exclusively for a buyer, excluding any and all compromising connections to seller interests with the same level of loud and clear declaration as described for WFS.

WWB = working WITH buyers. This is the traditional seller agent mode in which the seller's agent or subagent lures buyers with a promise to work WITH buyers, distracting from the reality that they work FOR sellers. There may be the minimum disclosure effort to satisfy law or personal conscience; but it is couched in terms and tones which lull the buyer into a false sense of security and into behaving as if the agent was his/her own. This approach is inevitably doomed by expanding buyer awareness of the availability of their own agents.

WOB = working ON buyers. This is the less-than-principled way out for traditionalists who

see the inevitable end of both wwb and
subagency but want no part of wfs.
Recognizing that buyers want their own
agents; a sellers' agency simply adds
"buyer agency" to its menu of services —
despite continuing as an agency to opposing (i.e., seller) interests.

Agents following the wfs and wfb approaches will
be all that remain standing when the dust of the revolution finally settles. Actually, it is probably more
appropriate to refer to the "dust" of the *resistance* to the
revolution, for the revolutionary activity on the consumer side is very "clean," a matter of becoming aware
of options on the market and simply taking them.
Because the source of the revolution's energy is consumer awareness, the natural strategy of the counter-
revolution is to raise clouds of confusion — the "dust"
— aimed at blocking awareness of the options.
Professionals with vision will not waste time or effort
in denying the inevitable, but will simply move into the
business of meeting the new consumer demand for
agents working in exclusive wfs or wfb modes.
Traditionalists, on the other hand, won't go that road
without a struggle. An old cliche describes unwilling
participants as those who are "dragged along kicking
and screaming." In respect for their professional digni-
ty, we can substitute wwb and wob for "kicking and
screaming."

As said earlier, well-meaning people once practiced
wwb because it was simply the norm, and most

providers were no more aware of options than consumers. That changed with single agency and exclusive
buyer agency. The options have now been there for
more than a decade, and the disclosure laws obligate
agents to make them known. But to die-hard wwʙ'ers,
that only means to find the right words — a pitch — to
coax buyers into disregarding the disclosure and still
put their interests in the hands of someone legally
obligated to work in the interest of the other side of the
negotiating table. Laws of **disclosure** do not stop the
audacious claim that it is safe for a buyer to:

- engage a property search guide with both a financial
  incentive and a legal obligation to push specific
  properties;

- entrust personal financial information to someone
  required to respect only the seller's confidence, and
  to disclose to the seller anything giving advantage
  over the buyer;

- entrust the writing of the buyer's purchase offer to
  someone already contracted to negotiate the best
  deal for the seller;

- accept guidance on purchase options and value
  from someone legally obligated and financially
  motivated to work for the highest possible price.

That is what wwʙ is all about; and the disclosure
requirement for the stubborn wwʙ agent is little more
than a challenge to a baseball pitcher trying to make a
batter think it is safe to swing at a pitch out of the strike

zone. The solution is to throw a **curve.** This chapter opened with an example of such a curve, a brochure describing seller's agent, subagent, and buyer's agent all as people willing to work with buyers, something true enough but obscuring the fact that only one works *for* buyers and the other two for sellers! Implicit in any suggestion that there is anything rational about a buyer looking for buying support from a sellers' agent is the proposition that

> *when it comes to buyer service, there is no substantial difference between sellers' agents and buyers' agents.*

Such a notion is pure psychological denial, requiring the belief that there is no difference between buyers and sellers, i.e., something so absurd that you would expect it to be offered in only the most camouflaged language. Yet, I have repeatedly witnessed sellers' agents suggesting it with straight faces in the most straightforward terms. Frankly, this single element of traditionalist propaganda is appropriately classified as a "propagandumb".

A more sophisticated curve (but still a curve and still wwb) lay hidden in the subject brochure. Near to (but not quite) acknowledging the difference between buyers and sellers, it professes to help consumers understand choices present in the current real estate market, choices it admits did not exist in a traditional system which totally denied buyers the benefit of agency representation. The brochure goes on to proclaim a new enlightened system for today's fortunate

"Of course there's no difference between buyer and seller. After all, you both want the same thing — the best price! Actually, I am certified, so I don't understand why you say I'm certifable."

consumers, one which provides several new ways for agents to work "with" (that word again) buyers and sellers. These new ways are portrayed as simply evolving from the system, meaning the general population of conscientious professionals staffing it. It is a subtle curve crediting them with something really introduced by single agents, buyers' agents and other consumer advocates who forced laws which now require sellers' agents to disclose who they really work for, and providing buyers with options, making them no longer a captive market. The curve extends the credit from the small minority of reformers to the very people who continue the practices of the allegedly reformed traditional system.

This fiction still allows the wwb pitch to naive buyers who, even after technical satisfaction of the disclosure requirement, miss the point that the "choice" is between protection and no protection — in other words, no real "choice" at all. At a deeper level, it disarms even the buyer who is aware of the general risk of one-sided representation, but finds assurance in the illusion that the agents themselves have made the choices available. There is, after all, a professional code of ethics, likely on the agency's office wall; to some degree, the professional and personal ethics of such agents would appear as some protection against sellers seeking too much. The deceptive trick of this curve is in taking the buyer's eye off the reality that protection may be needed not so much from sellers as from their *agents*.

Revising the history of the mainstream profession's role in the evolution of consumer options has still another consequence. When a seller agency matures beyond denial and faces up to the certain end of an era in which buyers can be sold on the notion that "working with a sellers' agent" is even an acceptable rational option, it is left with one of two operating strategies:

- stick with historical principle, and provide agency to only one side, i.e., wfs or wfb mode;

- abandon the historical disdain for dual agency, and offer alleged "agency" service to buyers as well as sellers, i.e., wob mode.

The historical revision provides the self-deception and rationalization needed for the second approach. WOB firms may superficially appear non-traditional, or even progressive, but they are hard-core *traditionalists.* Their response to buyer agency is to merely choose between two traditions: full agency service, which they boasted as the very heart of their professional ethics, and the practice of working both sides of the street, which they see as the heart of their profitability. From the beginnings of the real estate profession in this country, the WWB mode went unchallenged; both lip-service to lofty principle and self-serving business practice co-existed in support of both self-respect and bank account. That changed with the appearance of agents who saw that buyers, like sellers, are entitled to agency. Their shift into the WFB mode was a giant step forward for principle. For those in the business, it is a choice between principle and practice.

For most of the Twentieth Century, spokespersons for the real estate profession consistently preached the common sense and common law axiom that true agency simply cannot be provided by one office or company to both buyers and sellers. In a sudden turn-about, these same voices now support traditional firms outrageously claiming to provide exclusive buyer agency through one agent and exclusive seller agency through another. The WOB pitch alleges that the "exclusive" buyers' agent at one desk has no personal interest in the property sales bringing income to his/her supervisor and the seller-agent colleagues at surrounding desks. The very presence of such adverse interests both defies common law definition of exclusive representation and exemplifies common sense understanding of conflict of interest.

If you go no further into this book, then at least fix this critical bit of knowledge firm in your mind:

> *An exclusive buyers' agent (EBA) is one who works exclusively for buyers, never accepting listings or other obligations adverse to buyers' interests, and who is not part of any firm or agency which provides agency to sellers or accepts listings or other obligations adverse to buyers' interests.*

Rather obviously, the term "exclusive buyer agency" refers to the function of an EBA or to a firm including only EBA's. This meets the standard of the National Association of Exclusive Buyer Agents (NAEBA), and every buyer should apply it to anyone claiming to be an exclusive buyers' agent. *Sellers should be just as cautious,* for agencies in the WOB mode cannot provide true exclusive agency to either side; the curve of the WOB pitch is designed to work on sellers as well as on buyers.

Traditionalists are taking this double-agent route because it seems safe. The traditional WWB mode was profitable; and they think the profit had more to do with playing both sides than with the principle of true agency. It appears simpler and safer to change the principle than the operations — a matter of market over service, economics over principle.

Actually, the apparent safety is an illusion. The double-agency gimmick is a sand-wall against the rising tide of consumer awareness on many fronts beyond real estate. Increasingly enlightened consumers (buyers and sellers, clients and customers) will understand their options and *buy* those that are in their individual and varied best interests.

Caveat IN FAIRNESS to a certain few individual exceptions, it is important here to recall that I introduced these four classifications (WWB, WFS, WFB, and WOB) noting that they applied to *most* real estate agents. There are always those who are borderline, perhaps at a point in their own personal growth or decision making where they have not fully transitioned from one to another. I am also concerned about giving a "bad rap" to the exceptional individual in the mixed-agency setting who is stubbornly committed to buyer agency despite the conflict of adverse (to the buyer) interests. The WFB mode includes not only true exclusive buyer agents who have severed institutional and procedural ties to seller interests, but people of strong character and radically idependent personality who work out their own ways for keeping such ties from interfering with their agency obligations. That almost inevitably requires that they be either independent practitioners or in very small firms where institutional complications and pressures are minimal. The key for the consumer is to realize that these individual **single agents** are not just exceptions, but rarities on the professional spectrum; that picking this "wheat" from the professional "chaff" requires some depth of understanding of the system dynamics described in the following chapters.

THE CONSUMER QUALITY REVOLUTION is already a well-documented successful world-wide phenomenon. This irresistible force totally focused on empowering buyers is overtaking a business sector — real estate — which has totally *de*powered buyers; and its foothold has been established in the form of genuine exclusive buyers' agents. Revolutions are always resisted by those committed to the traditions being displaced. Some resistors are simply in blind denial, others in open defiance and subversion; and all are casualties in successful revolutions. The first level of resistance, *denial*, has already failed, though many still cling to it (i.e., the WWB mode). The second level, *defiance and subversion*, is underway in buyer lip-service campaigns, and clever "spins" put on traditionalist explanations of agency (i.e., the WOB mode). In a few states, traditionalist lobbyists have won legislation creating buyer-friendly disguises for traditional operations that are no friend to buyers. I reflected above* on the American Revolution, Industrial Revolution, and Sexual Revolution and on the impact of the Quality Revolution on the automobile industry. The final result of the Real Estate Quality Revolution is just as inevitable as democracy, industry, women's rights, and 200,000 mile odometers.

Inevitability of the revolution

*pages 13–14

Inevitable in real estate are "exclusive buyer agency" (as defined above) and its parallel, "exclusive seller agency." We cannot group these two forms under the umbrella, "exclusive agency," because that particular term already has another specific meaning in real estate jargon (to be explained in later chapters). Instead,

"**dedicated agency**" will be used here since, as opposed
to those wob firms claiming a mix of buyer and seller
representation, these are openly dedicated to one or the
other. Each will be either a dedicated sales agency
which exclusively represents sellers of specific properties, or a dedicated purchasing support agency which
represents buyers entitled to consider all available
properties.

Also inevitable are **flat fees** for itemized services,
displacing the packaging of all services for a single
commission(usually sale price percentage). Aware
consumers will know precisely what they are buying
and what it is worth to them. It logically follows that
counter-reform interests in keeping the old double-
agency operations will try to obscure that growing consumer awareness. Thus, the inevitable includes traditionalist legislative lobbying to redefine common law
concepts of agency and now legitimatize the **mixed-
agency** practices once sanctimoniously abhorred.

This book is written for sellers as well as buyers. It is
not about one class of people versus another, for while
roles of buyer and seller are indeed adverse, the people
in those roles at different points in time are nevertheless one and the same. Substantial focus is indeed on
buyers, but because buyer agency is at the crux of the
cultural phenomenon in which both buyers and sellers
have common vested interest — the spread of the **customer-quality revolution** into real estate and the dis-
placement of a traditional system that served neither
buyer nor seller well. This book is about that phenomenon, and about the anti-reform tactics which add to

consumer pitfalls, especially for the unaware. It is about awareness, the thing that will mean the eventual triumph of the revolution and, most important to readers, how they can make the system work for them today. The good news of this book is that *neither buyer nor seller has to wait for the reforms* — for the traditional system traps people only through misinformation, and has absolutely no power over those who know what is going on.

THIS IS *NOT A BOOK* on how to buy or sell a home; but about dealing with agents and agency in the buying and selling process. It is about the difference between buying and selling (i.e., between "bought" and "sold") and about engaging, or not engaging, the very different professional services supporting those disparate activities. Buyer or seller, your choice to use or not use an agent should be based upon what you know after reading this book. Having read this far, you already know the questions of which agent to use, and how to use one, are more complex than the traditional agent is likely to tell you. Going solo will avoid only those agents on your side of the table; so you'll need what's here to prepare for the agents on the other side.

Putting the agent to work for you...

Buyer or seller, if you select the right agent and use him/her the right way, then you'll be hiring all the expertise and experience you'll need, and minimize the amount of research you'll have to do in the subject areas of buying and selling property. That doesn't mean you should not do some, to both evaluate and assist the performance of those you hire. It does mean that your back should not be against the wall, requiring instant self-education on sales techniques, appraising, financing, market values, law and liability, land, and building structure.

...or going without an agent

GOING SOLO IS ANOTHER MATTER. If you are selling and choose not to use a sellers' agent, then you are strongly advised to be solidly up-to-date on the details and ramifications of selling, and should dive into books on that subject the moment you finish this one. If you're buying and choose not to use a buyers' agent, then to help insure that a sellers' agent will not be using you, detailed reading on the subject of buying is critical. Knowledge is power. Professionals have knowledge; so do some of the laypersons with whom you may be negotiating.

With or without an agent, a good book or two on the appropriate subject will serve you well, for easy reference or serious study. Some are referred to in the text and recommended in the last two chapters.

There are three dimensions to what is happening in the real estate industry — essentially the matters of (1) where things have been, (2) where they're going, and (3) what it means for you as a buyer or seller today. So, I've organized the rest of the book according to these broad dimensions, entitled "The Traditional", "The Inevitable", and "The Now."

Dimension One (Chapters 2-4) exposes the traditional real estate system for what it is — a frog masquerading as a prince. With the kiss of disclosure, the

facade of nobility falls away, and with inevitable consequences.

Those inevitable consequences emerge in
Dimension Two (Chapters 5 - 9). They include the
frog's predictable scrambling to restore its seductive
power over the consumer (Chapter 8), and its sudden
lobbying for laws which confer respectability on practices it publicly reviled when it was prince. These laws
enable new disguises and new promises, things the frog
needs to ward off new suitors for the affections of buyers and sellers, legitimate suitors whose courtship gifts
are not traditional lip-service, but simple straightforward customer quality. These are the buyer brokerages
and flat-fee seller agencies portrayed in Chapters 6
and 9.

Dimension Three (Chapters 10 and 11) provides
insights for for today — the "now" — for buyers and
sellers. If you are a seller, here is a special insight: do not
rush to Chapter 11. If you are a buyer, do not just jump
to Chapter 10, and do not ignore Chapter 11. The very
purpose of this book is based on the principle that fairness and optimum gain for everyone depends on both
buyer and seller being fully informed, not of one
another's confidential affairs, but of the rules of the
game. So, settle back and read it all.

DIMENSION ONE

The Traditional

CHAPTER 2

Working Both Sides of the Street

I N THE TRADITIONAL SYSTEM of real estate sales and purchase, homes enter the market through a **"listing agent"** hired by the owner to **"list"** the home, advertise it to attract buyers, make it available to buyers brought by other agents and, in general, do all that is necessary to sell the home at the best price and terms for the owner. The home is advertised with the listing agency's telephone number. Interested parties call, and are shown not only the advertised home, but others on the agency's list and — finally — homes on the lists of other agencies. This cooperative arrangement among real estate agencies is called **"co-broking"** and made economically possible by the listing agency sharing its commission with the agency qualifying as **"procuring cause"** (the one procuring the buyers). Co-broking is facilitated by many agencies actually

NOTE:

*Terms in **bold-face** are defined in the glossary.*

pooling their lists in one computerized list maintained by a **"multiple listing service" (MLS).**

The subagency deception

In the traditional co-broke situation, the agent who brings the buyer to the listing agent represents the *seller* and not the buyer! Nevertheless, the buyer is very often under the illusion that he/she is this agent's "client". This selling agent derives a commission share directly from the listing agent, is contractually employed by the listing agent, and is a *sub-agent of the owner-seller!* By law, the buyer is merely the *customer* and not the client of the agent. Under the law, agents owe all loyalty and confidentiality protection to their clients and not their customers. The law requires the agent to convey to the real client (the seller) any and all information about the buyer which might work to the seller's advantage — including anything the buyer reveals in imagined confidence. This is fair if the buyer is forewarned, unfair if the buyer is unsuspecting, and scurrilous if the buyer is led or allowed to believe that he/she is the client.

* Residential Real Estate Industry Report

A 1983 FTC report* revealed 71 percent of buyers believing they were represented by an agent who was actually a subagent of the other side of the transaction — confiding in someone required to keep the confi-

---

The phrase "merely the customer" is in striking contrast to the primary lesson of the customer quality revolution, which, simply put, is that putting customer first is what best serves the interests of the employer (here, the client).

dence of the seller and not the buyer! The classic example is the buyer who says to the agent "I'll go to $205,000 if I have to, but I want to offer $175,000 first and see if they accept that."

The agent's legal responsibility to the seller requires the agent to inform the seller that the buyer will go to $205,000. This not only makes a mockery of the buyer's trust in the agent, but costs the buyer an extra $30,000 (of which the percentage-earning agent will get a slice).

Law of disclosure

TO PUT AN END to this victimization, the law in many states now requires every real estate agent to immediately disclose to potential clients and customers whether he/she is a buyers' agent or sellers' agent, or acting as a "dual agent". That is also a requirement of the **National Association of Realtors®** (NAR) as expressed in its "Code of Ethics." Nevertheless, the traditional system survives with buyers still drawn into it by the ultimate lure — an advertised home — bringing them right into the office of a sellers' agent rather than one representing *their* interests. As a matter of logistics, the legally-required **disclosure** cannot take place until after the buyer has physically entered the domain of the sellers' agent, probably not even aware that there is even such a thing as a buyers' agent. So, the sellers' agent beats the buyers' agent to the buyer with the traditional pitch (except in the case of buyers fortunate enough to first read this book).

page 16   As said above, one dead giveaway of the traditional sellers' agent is the repeated pitch of "working WITH
buyers", or even the cozier, "working with *our* buyers".
They never say, "working FOR buyers"; for that would
be legally dangerous.

The "No Difference" Curve

BUT WHAT ABOUT the law requiring that they disclose
themselves as sellers' agents? One might think buyers
entering the office of a sellers' agent, whether drawn by
house ad or by the WWB pitch, would be fairly forewarned by the legally required disclosure. That would
be so if the disclosure wasn't quickly neutralized with a
follow-up something like "... but in practice, it really does-
n't matter because there is actually no real difference
between the two." Of course, such self-serving contention of "no real difference" contradicts the very
premise of the law which was instituted precisely
because the differences are very real (as is the massively
unfair disadvantage to buyers unaware of the difference).

The cornerstone of the "no difference" fantasy is the slogan that "neither seller's agent nor buyer's agent gets paid if
a transaction isn't made." It is offered as a meaningful
premise in private conversations, public presentations, and
published documents (including the above-cited
brochure). What nonsense! In the first place, not all buyers' agents are paid contingent on the transaction, but even
in the case of those who are — still pure nonsense! The
conveyance attorney, lender, and maybe a contractor or
two also won't get paid if there is no transaction; but that
doesn't mean their roles are all the same! Neither the buyer
nor the seller will get what they are looking for if the trans-

action isn't made; so, does that mean there is no difference between buyer and seller? If there is a difference between buyer and seller, there is necessarily a difference between those who represent them as their good-faith agents.

The "straight answers" brochure tosses its own curve in support of the traditionalist theme of sameness. It is closely aligned with this "no sale — no pay" pitch and follows the one about a buyer working with a sellers agent, subagent, or buyers agent:

> *"Remember the goal of all real estate agents is the same — to help bring about the sale or purchase of a home."** *

Maybe this pitch is more of a slider than a curve, for it is very subtle, gently slipping past the reality of a very big difference between a "sale" and a "purchase"****. A key premise in this book, from the very title through its back cover, is that buying something is not the same as being sold it, a difference cunning sales professionals always strive to veil. The reality dodged here is that one goal of a buyer's agent is actually to *prevent* the purchase of a home not best meeting the buyer's needs, while any buyer's money meets the seller's needs.

The notion of "no real difference" works to the advantage of those who profess full service to both buyers and sellers (traditional agents and dual agents). It is not impossible for both sides of a transaction to be adequately served by the same agent, provided there is both (a) *fully informed* consent on both sides and (b) a definition of "adequacy" on at least one side which allows surrender of certain rights normally considered

* Gooder Group brochure, 1993, AGENCY: *Straight Answers About an Agent's Role*, page 12, columns 1–2

See the glossary definitions for **buy and **sell.**

essential in the bargaining process. The illusion of "no real difference" undercuts any capability for *informed* consent. Your decision as a buyer should be based upon full understanding of the genuine differences and whether they matter in your particular circumstance.

In most circumstances, they do matter, as will be evident in the Chapter 6 discussion of what a buyers' agent does for a buyer. Prior to that, however, it is necessary to say a little more here about those who work both sides of the street (i.e., traditional and dual agents).

Before the Chapter 6 discussion on buyer agency, we will also look at why agents "list" properties (Chapter 3) and at how traditional commission practices affect both sellers and buyers (Chapter 4)

Dual "agents"?

Dual agents are truly "agents" only in a technical sense. Representing both buyer and seller, they cannot act in behalf of either one in dealing with the other (the crux of being an agent). To the degree that there is not already a single mindset between the parties, the dual agent can help with mediation, but cannot step in as either side's agent in negotiation. Their role would seem to be most suitable when there is little of significance to negotiate between the parties, as in a simple transfer of property within a family. The meeting of minds necessary for a **purchase and sale agreement** to be **valid** develops outside of what the agent does, *if* the agent stays within the boundaries of appropriate dual agency. There is too much opportunity for self-interest to operate at both conscious and subconscious levels, too much difficulty in reliable detection of it, and too much room for suspicion to arise with later regrets. There is simply too little opportunity for adequate controls. Thus, observing the biblical wisdom that no one can serve two masters, consumer advocates tend to disapprove of dual agency.

Undisclosed **dual agency**, even before the new disclosure laws, was and is illegal. It is fraudulent to agree to represent both buyer and seller when one or both are not aware that you are also representing the other guy. Undisclosed dual agency can still occur even when the prescribed disclosure terminology is given lip service, if other words or actions nullify or compromise the intent of the required disclosure. If those words or actions make both sides believe they are being served as a client by an agent, that is dual agency; and if either side doesn't know the other side is receiving a client's privileges, that is undisclosed dual agency.

It should be clear certain possible consequences of the "working with buyers" (wwb) pitch crosses not only into undisclosed dual agency, but even into further violation of client rights where the perpetrator deserves the more accurate title of "double agent".

IF:

the "working with" approach implies to buyers:

- that what the agent learns about buyer's financial capabilities or personal business won't be used to the seller's advantage,

- that the agent will work for the best **price** and terms in the buyer's definition, or

- that the agent will write the buyer's **offer** to maximize the buyer's negotiating leverage,

THEN:

"working with" means "working for" and an agency agreement has been made with the buyer in opposition to seller agency obligations. The last two promises cannot be met even in dual agency which, by definition, does not assist one side in taking advantage of the other (no such restriction on double agents, who are not constrained by promises).

A traditional sellers' agent working with you as a buyer has legal obligations and financial incentives to

"You need us to sell your home because, as your agent, we put ourselves in your shoes, knowing you want top dollar. We'll actively promote it and get buyers to make you an offer before they are tempted by other homes on the market. Then, we'll help you find your new home, examining everything on the market to find you the best house at the best price."

seek the highest possible price and terms *favorable to sellers!* That applies to any and all properties listed by his/her own agency plus any properties listed by any other agencies which are even made known to you. To the degree that such an agent may in fact serve any of your needs which compete with any interests of any of those sellers, the agent is either compromising the client's interests (in violation of the law) or accomplishing some net gain in the seller's advantage over the buyer. Seller wants the price up; buyer wants the price down. There are only two ways to go; one's gain is at the other's expense — the classic example of adverse interest.

CHAPTER 3

Why Listing Agents List

W HEN AN AGENGY "lists" a property, it adds it to its inventory (list) of properties to be sold and agrees to market it for a commission, payment of which is usually contingent on a successful sale within a specified time. Types of listing agreement vary, but the usual is the **"exclusive right to sell"** listing which gives sole marketing rights and guarantees the commission to the agency no matter who actually produces the buyer. This provides the agency with security to expend both agent effort and advertising dollars, and also to involve other agencies on a co-broke basis* in the promised effort to find a buyer for the property. An **"exclusive-agency listing"** differs from the exclusive right to sell in that the owner retains his/her own right to sell without paying a commission, but all selling agencies must deal though the listing agent as co-broking subagents. By contrast, **"open listing"** agreements offer no

Listing: definitions and types

*(page 31)

such guarantees, promising only to pay a commission to whoever brings a buyer (i.e., the procuring cause). Spending effort and money on an open listing runs square against the risk of a competing agency collecting the whole commission.

One might suppose from this that agency expenditures on an open listing are necessarily losses when another agency sells the property and collects the commission — or for an exclusive-agency listing when the owner finds a customer and there is no commission. Such logic is often part of the pitch when a listing agent is trying to convince an owner to grant an exclusive-right-to-sell. In most cases, the exclusive right to sell might well be the best arrangement for both owner and agent, but this particular logic is not totally valid, for it does not take into consideration all the reasons listing agencies list.

On the face of it, it does appear that the whole reason for listing is solely to develop an inventory of stock to sell, and that exclusive rights are simply the protection needed to set about marketing the stock. However, something very fundamental is still missing.

What listing agencies get from a listing

THE REASON FOR any activity, by simple definition, is to achieve the expected outcome. As an example, there are three apparent possible outcomes for the listing of a specific property by "The ABC Agency":

1.0 Full commission to ABC from sale of the listed property to a buyer attracted directly to ABC (internal sale);

2.0 Partial commission to ABC from a sale of the listed property to a buyer brought by a co-broking agency;

3.0 Expiration of the agreement without sale or commission.

By limiting our focus to what happens to the listed property, there are only three apparent outcomes for ABC (internal sale, co-broke sale, no sale). However, if we consider *all* the things one listing can bring to a listing agency, we see that ABC has much more to gain:

1.0 Full commission to ABC from sale of the listed property to a buyer attracted directly to ABC;

> **1.1** Full commission to ABC from one or more internal sales of other ABC listings to buyers attracted directly by ABC advertising of the subject property;

> **1.2** Full commission from ABC sale of one or more unlisted properties to buyers attracted directly by ABC advertising of the ABC-listed property (**For-Sale-By-Owner** properties — "FSBOS"* — are often sold with commission through an agent who procures an interested buyer);

*pronounced fiz´-bos

2.0 Partial commission to ABC from a sale of the listed property to a buyer brought by a co-broking agency;

2.1 Partial commission from a co-broking sale of one or more properties listed by other agencies to buyers attracted directly to ABC by advertising for the ABC-listed property;

3.0 Expiration of the agreement without a sale of the listed property, and no commission.

3.1 Expiration of the agreement without a sale, but not before realizing income via 1.1, 1.2, and 2.1;

4.0 Future listings, prompted by visibility of the advertising to future sellers and subsequent future income.

The real reason for listing

THE SHORT LIST included two commission possibilities, but there are actually *five* ways a given listing, even when expired, can bring income, involving one or several sales. Most significantly, four of the five (1.0, 1.1, 1.2, and 2.1) income routes have one element in common, one element that physically brings money into the agency, one element that is the basic reason, the sum and substance, of why listing agencies list — a *buyer* attracted by the property's advertising.

Listing agencies list to **attract buyers!**

* p. 44

They do not, as postulated above,* list "solely to develop an inventory of stock to sell," for there is plenty of stock to sell, including that listed by other agencies, and even FSBOS. Access to all the stock in the world means nothing without access to *buyers*; and a traditional real estate business cannot survive without listing because that is what it uses to attract buyers. That is how it has been ever since some early entrepreneur had the revelation that houses somehow attract people who are looking to buy houses.

Consider the point made that it is not necessarily bad business to spend money on an open listing. Agencies will sometimes get an owner's permission to advertise a home without an exclusive-right-to-sell contract simply because they don't really care whether they sell that home or *other* homes to buyers attracted by the ad. If there are several Mediterranean-style homes for sale in the Multiple Listing Service, and many buyers in the area committed to that particular style, then an agency better advertise a Mediterranean-style home to attract those buyers. If one is not listed by the agency, then it has to get one. It will try for the exclusive-right-to-sell, but, if necessary, settle for the open and advertise it.

The point of all this is that advertising a home is far more an advertisement for the agency than it is for the seller. While the listing agent may pitch advertising a seller's home as an agency expense on the seller's behalf, the seller might well suggest foregoing the expense and reducing the commission.

IT FOLLOWS THAT it is not necessarily a good thing to sell a listed home if it happens to be the only one of a particular type. The same home advertised over a long period loses its attractive power, but the optimum is to have it around long enough to draw as many buyers as possible before being sold. For this reason, the tendency of owners to overprice their homes can have an

Overpricing and agency interests (the "upsides")

upside for the agency, preventing the "premature" sale, letting the home attract buyers for other sales until the owner adjusts to its real value.

There is another upside to overpricing (for the agency, not for sellers or buyers). Both homes and homebuyers differ not only according to house-style (Mediterranean, cape, ranch, etc,) but also according to price range. An advertised eighty-thousand dollar house attracts eighty-thousand dollar buyers. An eighty-thousand dollar house advertised for a hundred-thousand dollars attracts hundred-thousand dollar buyers!

Most agents dislike overpricing as a matter of both professional ethics and personal pride, and do try to avoid it. Working against that, however, is the agent's fear of losing the listing to a competitor who will cater to the owner's inflated view of the property's value. The two "upsides" of overpricing are very rarely cause for strategic overpricing, but they can combine with the satisfaction of a secured listing to overcome the bad taste.

Listing agencies do not want to resort to advertising open listings or to tolerating overpricing in order to include all the home types and price levels needed to attract buyers. What is simply called for is a good strong, consistent, and focused listing effort. That need is real not only at the agency level, but at the agent level, for even in a large "well-stocked" agency, buyers come to individual agents according to their individual listings.

THUS, though the end reason for listing is to attract buyers, all focus in the traditional system is upon listing, upon the means rather than the end, upon listing property rather than finding or servicing buyers. The entire system is driven by listing activity — recruit listings, advertise listings, service listings. Buyers are not "forgotten", because they do sign the paycheck, but they are regarded not as the reason for it all, but as an ultimate consequence of the listing activity. It is often observed that the most successful agents are listing agents, with both agency principals and top-producing agents preaching, "Get the listings and the sales will follow".

Danielle Kennedy, author of *How To List and Sell Real Estate in the 90s,* advises that

> **Listings taken and listings sold are the heart of this business.** *

Kenneth Edwards, in *Your Successful Real Estate Career,* cites the old real estate profession adage:

> **If you list, you last.****

Both Kennedy and Edwards are writing for real estate professionals, teaching them essentially how to *sell* their services to real estate consumers (buyers and sellers). Kennedy, who sales guru Tom Hopkins describes as "America's Master Teacher on Real Estate Skills," even has a chapter entitled "How to Capture the Consumer."

Misplaced focus on listing in the traditional system

*Prentice-Hall, 1990. Page 167.

**Amacom, 1993. Page 43.

Listing focus is a disservice to sellers

IN CONTRAST to Kennedy and Edwards, Robert Irwin writes *for consumers* of real estate agency services, and is the author of a pair of excellent books *Tips & Traps When Selling a Home* and *Tips & Traps When Buying a Home*.[4] Rather than teach agents how to sell their services, he teaches potential clients how to select and buy, or not buy, agent services. In *...Selling A Home,* like Edwards, Irwin also refers to the "If you list, you last" adage. However, unlike Edwards, he is not emphasizing the importance of listing, but warning of the mentality the slogan represents — a focus on the gathering of listings rather than servicing the need of the consumer. He adds:

[4] Both works: McGraw-Hill, 1997

[5] Irwin, Selling: page 22.

> *The last thing you want to do is list your property with an agent who "gathers" listings.*[5]

The problem is that the traditional system is built upon listing. The fact is that those who preach, "Get the listings and the sales will follow," have historically been absolutely right! Prior to the advent of the buyers' agent, and even today while buyer agency is still in the "toehold" stage, agencies and agents who list are the most successful in terms of their own security and profitability.

Emergence of buyer agency and traditionalist reaction

NEVERTHELESS, history has taken a turn. The sacrosanct assumption that listings are the only way to attract buyers has suddenly been torpedoed by buyer-agents who attract buyers by recruiting and servicing them directly! It just does not seem right to traditional agents whose experience tells them buyers are "supposed to" go to the listing agency. Buyers' agents just aren't doing the "right" things (in their view). The next step for some traditional agents is to openly complain that they cannot even imagine what buyer-agents do to earn their commissions. Some actively work to limit buyer-agent commissions to one-half or even a smaller fraction of what they would pay a **sub-agent** bringing a buyer.* Such reaction is clearly an admission of what level of time and effort these traditional agents actually give to buyer-service in their own work experience. Something deeply ironic occurs when such people also advertise how they "work with" buyers. **

*Below, pages 63–64, 90–92

**Above pages 2, 16, 17–18

Nothing better depicts the antithesis of client-service than exploitation of the traditional "open house" to turn a seller's property into general buyer-bait. An advertisement and signs invite all comers to "drop in" without appointment or pre-screening and tour a property. Ask yourself why the listing agent would put copies of the multiple listing book on the kitchen table so buyers can look at properties competing with the property of the person who is not only everyone's host, but the agent's client. Far more probable than finding a buyer for the host property is that the agent will gather a fistful of names of buyers to "work with" in the search for other properties. It is a strategy widely promoted in the listing agent manuals. Often, buyers not interested in a visited property want something "better" — i.e., "more expensive" — and that means a higher commission. That is especially the case when the house is overpriced; then both seller and property are working exclusively for the agent. Even with a reasonably priced property and a real sale potential, host clients are not served if "their" agent ignores arriving visitors to pitch the "working with" script to prospects for other properties.

Working *for* their client, ethical agents will spend no time with a disinterested visitor about to leave while there is a genuine prospect on the premises. But, even for an ethical agent, there is room to rationalize — to believe just a few more moments are needed with the departing but prosperous shoppers before getting to the young couple with the old Chevy. The employing owner is not usually present to point out that a sales agent is employed to **sell** the employer's property, and to tell the employee to stick to business. Fortunately, a more effective incentive already exists when visiting buyers have contracted with buyer agents. Such buyers routinely disclose that fact; and they will not be pursued by listing agents adverse to violating either the law or the Realtors® Code of Ethics prohibition against interfering in the contracts of others. Sadly, neither law nor ethics deters everyone.

When targeting uncontracted buyers, the "working with buyers" pitch may be sincere (however rationalized), and it is certainly a smart tactic in the competition for the cash controlled by buyers. Nevertheless, Chapters 4 and 6 will expose the lack of substance in seller-agent claims of buyer service:

- Chapter 4, dealing specifically with the chase after commission dollars, will reveal distinct selectivity regarding which buyers get attention (let alone "service");

- Chapter 6, getting to the heart of buyer agency, reveals that the legal and ethical duties of listing agencies does not allow them to give buyers the full-service and agency representation of exclusive buyers' agencies.

Traditional Commission:

What it Does to Buyers and Sellers

C OMMISSION RATES are not set by law, and must not be set by agreements among agencies or their associations. Any agreement to set uniform commission rates is a violation of **antitrust laws.** Even seemingly innocuous conversation relating to commission levels can be taken as **conspiracy to fix prices.** Fees are supposed to be a function of a free and open competitive market.

Commissions are negotiable

In a free competitive market, any business is free to set its own prices and must of course consider the prices of the competition. Thus, for any commodity or service, there can be some price consistency without conspiracy among the price makers; i.e., a **"going rate"** can develop. So if the ABC company has been charging one price for a certain service and hears that the XYZ company has been successful in charging more, then ABC may increase its price, perhaps matching the

The phrase "going rate" is a proper observation of market patterns. However, it is improper as an agency's explanation of its fees to a potential client, for it implies a *set* standard, and no client options. Such a marketing practice does in fact reinforce a standard, crossing the line into "price fixing."

XYZ price — unless the action will drive enough customers away to wipe out the net gain of the extra money from each of the customers who remain. By the same token, one company may deliberately slip its prices under those of another (competitive pricing) to gain competitive advantage, i.e., to add enough new customers to more than make up for the unit price loss.

The freedom of pricemakers to charge what they want is limited only by customer response. With raised service prices, people can dicker the price down, comparison shop for the best price among competitors, postpone getting the job done, or maybe perform the needed work themselves. For a price lowering to work, people have to be assured that what they are getting for their money is as good as the higher priced competition. For any price differences to work, people have to *know* about them and about their available options — often not the case in the matter of real estate commissions.

In real estate affairs, one of the above response options — *postponement* — very rarely is feasible. The timing of the decision to sell or shop for real estate is often determined by personal events and needs which are simply not postponable. Another of the options, however, does exert strong counter pressure on any urge to raise commission fees — i.e., the willingness of owners to sell their own homes expressly to avoid commissions. Agencies are well aware that charging an unacceptably high rate prompts owners to try it themselves; the FSBO option* does more than most things to put an upper cap on commission rates.

*above, page 45

As FOR COMPARISON SHOPPING or dickering in the selection of an agency, these basic "supply and demand" dynamics are confounded in several ways. The "price" is not easy to comparison-shop or dicker because it is a *percentage,* not a fixed dollar number, and really depends on the house's ultimate selling price. What matters to the owner is not the commission rate, but *an unknown* — what will be left over after the commission and other charges are paid. Further clouding an owner's discernment may be an agent's contention that higher commissions are necessary to finance the advertising that will produce the best sale price in the shortest time. Implied is that a lower commission may limit the advertising and thus net the seller less rather than more money. Thus, owners are led to downplay differences in commission rates and may hesitate to dicker.

Things clouding the fee picture for owners

The result of the weakness of price dickering and comparison shopping is that the base level of commission rates is not far below the ceiling in a given area (which, as shown, is capped by the FSBO option). Thus, evolving out of pure market dynamics can be a fairly uniform pricing structure in a given area; i.e., a "going rate" but with some individual variations, since (or "if") it is not imposed by clandestine collaboration. Thus, in New England, homes are most often listed for either 5% or 6%, and a few at 7%, with 6% prevailing in the great majority of cases. Here and there, 5.5% or 4.5% will show up, the result of dickering, or on the spot competitive pricing — signs that the free market is alive and well and available to aware consumers.

The commission rate should have no bearing on whether a home is advertised (outside the MLS) or not. No seller should accept the inflation of a commission rate to cover advertising, or the claim that advertising the home is for the seller's benefit. To the degree that the commission adds to the price demanded, it in fact works against the likelihood of a timely sale. The process of using listings to advertise and attract buyers was shown in the previous section ("Why Listing Agencies List"); the XYZ Agency's purpose in advertising John and Mary Smith's property is not to sell the Smith property, but to attract buyers for *anything* it is able to sell. Buyers attracted by other homes XYZ advertises will be shown the Smith property, and buyers drawn by the Smith ad will be shown other homes. Furthermore, if it is listed in the MLS, the Smith home will also come to the attention of buyers who've come to other agencies. In short, advertising the Smith's home will do more for XYZ's general profitability than anything specific for the Smiths. Even if the ad directly attracts a buyer, it won't be much sooner or necessarily with more money than with buyers from other agencies, but it will mean that XYZ gets the whole commission. If a listing agent suggests that advertising requires a higher commission, then an owner should simply pass on the advertising and take the lower commission.

COMMISSIONS DIRECTLY IMPACT buyers and sellers in two ways: (a) in taking money out of the purchase price that might otherwise have gone into the seller's pocket, and (b) exerting upward pressure on the price and resisting the promptness of sale. The first one is a matter of negotiation between owner and agent, and the second between the selling side and buying side until the price comes into line with what some buyer is willing to pay.

Real effect of commissions

Commissions indirectly impact buyers and sellers by how they effect the behavior of selling agents and subagents. That agents are indeed motivated by commission size is a matter of common sense. It is also illustrated in a story Robert Irwin tells of a house-shopping experience when he discovered a list of houses he was not being shown by the agent working "with" him. What the houses on the hidden list had in common was a commission lower than those of the houses being shown.*

*Irwin, ...*Selling a Home.* Page 53.

Percentage commission is not real incentive for higher selling price

THE MOST FAMILIAR EXAMPLE of how a commission motivates agent behavior occurs with the common purchase price percentage (PPP or "**three-P**") commission. The idea is that since a higher price to the seller means a higher commission to the agent, there is a natural incentive to work towards the highest priced sale (perfectly honorable, as long as there are no illusions about who is working for whom). However, the effectiveness of this incentive is not as straightforward as the simple percentage logic, for the agent's motivation involves other factors. Consider the case of a 6% commission of a $100,000 sale evenly split four ways among listing agent, listing agency, selling agent, and selling agency. Each will net 1.5% or $1,500. A thousand dollar difference in price will mean only fifteen dollars to an individual agent (1.5% of $1,000). A thousand dollars (or two) can kill a sale; and $15 (or $30) is no real financial incentive for an agent or an agency to risk losing the whole $1,500 commission share by pushing for an extra thousand or two for the seller. A former sellers' agent for one of New England's largest brokerage firms testified at a 1997 Boston seminar that the firm's agents were taught, as a matter of policy, to never tell a seller considering an offer how high a buyer might actually go if the offer was rejected. Quite aside from the illegal violation of fiduciary responsibility to the seller, the weakness of straight percentage as incentive is clear; while the higher return might be worth it to the seller to risk a sale, it is not worth it to the agency or agent.

A caveat is necessary. In the case of upper-bracket home sales where differences in price may approach tens of thousands with commission differences in the hundreds, agent incentive for raising price becomes obviously more real.

AGENCIES WILL GENERALLY MAINTAIN that how they divide their commissions should be of no real concern to their clients. On the contrary, the structure of commission splits has profound impact on the interests of both buyers and sellers. Owners in particular should make it their business to understand how splits work, and *dictate* in the listing agreement a sharing structure that will facilitate rather than hinder the selling and buying process.

Fee-sharing between agents is legitimate concern of buyers and sellers

The above example of the four-way **commission split** reflects the fundamental dynamics of commission-sharing within and between agencies. Consider a hypothetical case involving a traditional 6% listing and even splits (50-50) between all parties. John Brown of "Listor Realty" lists the O'Malley home, and it is sold for $100,000 to a buyer brought by Mary Green of "Sellit Realty". Listor Realty will receive a 6% commission check for $6,000. Listor will then send $3,000 (3%) to Sellit Realty and pay $1,500 (1.5%) to its own agent, John Brown. Sellit Realty will keep only $1,500 (1.5%) of its 3% share, paying $1,500 (1.5%) to its agent, Mary Green.

If, instead of the co-broke situation, the buyer was obtained by John Brown, then he and his agency (Listor) would have each wound up with $3,000 (3%).

If Jane Adams, a fellow Listor Realty agent, procured the buyer, then Brown and Adams would each receive $1,500 (1.5%), but Listor Realty's share would be $3,000 (3%).

In reality, payouts within agencies tend to be more complicated than simple 50-50 splits. They might well be 60-40 or 40-60 or other arrangements tending to reflect differences in experience and skill level among an agency's agents. They might even involve bonuses for volume or quality of service, and adjustments for expenses. Even with a 50-50 split between Listor Realty and Sellit Realty, where each receives $3,000, what Brown and Green each get has nothing to do with the other or the other's agency.

The convention among traditional agents is that these internal commission-sharing methods are no one else's business. That misses the point that it is all quite literally O'Malley's (the seller's) business, for Listor is O'Malley's agent; and Sellit, Brown, Green, and Adams are all his *sub-agents*. Before he agrees to hire Listor Realty and the whole gang of as-yet-unknown subagents, O'Malley should know that the performance incentive system he is agreeing to finance is focused on **selling** and not on listing. He might want assurance that what will be delivered is exactly what Brown is promising — i.e., a system geared to **sell** his property for the best price in the shortest time. He might well question the sincerity of such promises if listing shares are greater than selling shares. He might well be concerned about all of these things *if he was aware of them* — but he probably won't be concerned about any of them because the self-interest of the traditional system is not served by making sellers aware of such matters.

DATA DRAWN IN LATE 1996 from an Eastern state MLS exposes much about the dynamics and underlying motives of commission structuring. Due largely to geography, one county — we'll call it "Benjamin County" — has existed in a certain amount of political, social, and economic isolation. As a result, many of its institutions, including its local real estate market and practices — have evolved in relative independence from the rest of the state. Like most other places, the outside world is now beginning to make its incursions: new highway, outsiders moving in, the Internet... Specific to real estate, local MLSes have been replaced by a computerized statewide MLS and, in 1996, Benjamin County got its first buyer-agency.

Listing data reveals level of self-service

The convention in the state outside Benjamin County — and generally nationwide*— is for listing agents to split their commissions evenly with subagents. With 96% of the subagency commissions indicated in the MLS at exactly either 3% or 2.5% (52% of cases were at 3%; 44% of cases were at 2.5%), it appears that the statewide "going rates" are 6% and 5%, depending on locality. As a matter of direct observation, the going rate in Benjamin County is 6%, *but 95% of the subagency fees offered are at 2%!* While most of the state's listing agents share commissions evenly with subagents, Benjamin County listing agents keep twice as much for themselves as they give to subagents.

*H.I. Sonny Bloch and Grace Lichtenstein. *Inside Real Estate.* Grove Weidenfeld, New York, 1987. Page 275.

This is not a matter of "greedy" listing agents taking advantage of subagents, for the listing agent in one sale is the subagent in another sale. So, among the agents working with one another in the county, things tended to balance out. The justifying rationale is the traditionalist belief that the listing agencies shoulder the greatest expenses (chiefly advertising) — but, of course, there is no reason to believe that advertising nor any other kind of listing expense is any higher in Benjamin County than in the rest of the state.

What is really going on here is a straightforward result of the listing bias that exists among traditional agencies everywhere, including those who split evenly with subagents. It just happened that the unique isolation of Benjamin County provided an environment which allowed the lopsided approach of traditional agencies to naturally reflect itself in the inequitable *pages 49–51 commission split. As stated above,* the traditional agent focus is so occupied with listing that there is little appreciation of what buyer service — let alone buyer *agency*— is all about. That is why traditional agents in Benjamin County will give only a third of the commission to a subagent (and some even less to a buyer's agent — a point addressed in Chapter 3).

FATTENING THE LISTING AGENT'S share at the expense of the sub-agent's commission has a direct impact upon buyer services. It became evident as I participated in a buyer-agency booth at the Benjamin County Fair when several people separately came forward with the same complaint about traditional agents. First, a young couple asked if I knew why area agents didn't seem to want to sell them a home! They told me they had good credit, down payment, and sufficient income, but that, after a few visits, the listing agents seemed to not want to spend any time with them. The "after a few visits" should have been the clue, but it didn't register until the next couple told me the same story. Then there was a third and a fourth!

These frustrated buyers all had one thing in common: though serious about buying a home (i.e., not just "lookers"), they were not moved to buy any of the first homes they were shown and thought it was perfectly appropriate to keep looking until they found the best home for them — i.e., they were *fussy* buyers. When they first walked into a real estate office, they represented a potential full 6% commission for the agency as they were first shown the agency's internal listings. Declining those, they then became potential 2% commissions as they were shown the listings of other agencies. In business language regarding potential reward to the agent, they went from "high reward" potential (6%) to "low reward" potential (2%). There is also a risk factor involved in working with buyers, for, unlike homes, buyers are not under contract to listing agencies, and can at any time buy a home through

Disserving owners by ignoring buyers

another agency. For obvious reasons, the "fussier" the buyer, the higher the risk. To use a common business school phrase, these buyers meant **"high-risk low-reward"** activity for the agents.

An agent's time spent with these high-risk, low-reward buyers is time made not available for potentially high-reward buyers (i.e., "six-percenters") and for listing activity; and listing activity is *low-risk, moderate-to-high-reward*. It is low-risk because it contractually obligates, and it is moderate-to-high-reward because it brings at least the 4% piece of a co-broke or the full 6% on an internal sale. It is a choice created by the system, a choice between high-risk, low-reward activity on the one hand, and low-risk, moderate-to-high-reward activity on the other. It is a choice that contemporary jargon calls a "no-brainer."

While Benjamin County peculiarities provide an extreme case illustration, the logic and dynamics apply beyond the county borders even with the 50-50 commission split. Fussy buyers are still high-risk, and listing is still low-risk. The still "no-brainer" choice is between high-risk, moderate-reward activity on one hand, and low-risk, moderate-to-high-reward activity on the other. Inside and outside Benjamin County, there are buyers the traditional system neglects, and it is not in the interests of sellers to neglect buyers.

DIMENSION TWO

The Inevitable

CHAPTER 5

About Inevitability

WHENEVER someone asks you if it is going to rain, there is always one safe answer:

Yes.

Technically, the answer is inevitably true, though not in the real time context in which the question is asked. Usually, it is a shared joke in which both the questioner and the joker implicitly acknowledge a broader reality encompassing more than the "here and now".

There is a parallel to an even greater reality — eventually it will snow and there will be hurricanes, tornados, floods and droughts. Given a broad enough timespan, not only do these events happen, but so do massive systemic changes (i.e., oceans and continents move). Things we think of as "never happening here" actually do happen — some actually recently, just beyond our memory. Our "never" really means "not in our limited personal experience" or, at the longest, not in *recorded* history.

It is not yesterday that is inevitable

MOST OF US KNOW THAT; and we see the foolishness of ignoring forecasts of floods and volcanic events because it's "never" happened in that place. And yet, when it comes to things more subtle than natural disasters, many of us follow the same pattern of taking false security from a relatively short pattern of events. We know that yesterday's sunny weather does not mean it will be sunny today; but several days of sunshine still spoils us, and we arise each morning expecting another. We get into the habit of going off to work without the umbrella we'll inevitably need.

Habit has a function in our lives. We habitually do what we did yesterday and the day before because, usually, that is what will work today and tomorrow. But humans need not be enslaved by habit. We're smart. We can monitor and forecast not only weather and seismic events, but also social and economic activity. We can change our habits and grab our umbrellas or move our butts out of the suddenly dangerous comfort zone. Or we can stay comfortable, sheltered in denial...

Today, tomorrow comes much faster than it did yesterday

THERE IS, OF COURSE, a difference between weather and real estate, between the physical and social/economic worlds. In the physical world, we step outside and discover that our expectations of sunshine were "all wet." But, in our social and economic worlds, even the systemic changes are often so fast and so subtle that people feel comfortable denying that

they're coming long after they've arrived. Some village blacksmiths were still teaching their sons how to
shape a horseshoe, even while others were scrapping
their forges and installing gas pumps.

We recognize the naivete of the blacksmith who
was sure that his proven method of forging a horseshoe would guarantee generations of economic
security for his family. Business analysts now recognize the same naivete in the American automobile
executives in the 1970's who were certain that their
proven methods of production would guarantee
continuing American dominance of the automobile
market. Both the village blacksmiths and the Detroit
industrialists who replaced them knew what *they* did
to make things work, and knew that such things
"always" worked.

BOTH FAILED TO ACCOUNT for the force underlying
all markets — i.e., *consumer choice* — and to envi-
sion any consumer options other than what they
produced. The horseless carriage made the blacksmith extinct, and high-quality low-cost autos from
Japan did the same thing to the domestic gas guzzler.

Consumer choice drives today and tomorrow

Detroit survived, just barely, but only through
belated acceptance and adapting to the inevitable.
The lessons learned unleashed what has become
known as the **quality revolution** through the world-
wide industrial community, now pouring into the
service sector and even government (there called
"reinvention"). **"Quality"** is the key word with a

very technical definition loaded with enough meaning to change the structure of the economic world:

> *the degree of conformance to standards deter-*
> *mined by customer specifications of perfor-*
> *mance, utility, and price.*

The Quality Revolution is very much a customer revolution; the "specifications" would no longer be set by sellers, but by *buyers*. Both the movement itself and newly quality-conscious organizations are driven by aware consumers who know the options available and their economic power, which they are willing to use. In hindsight it is easy to see it all as a consequence of increasing education and communications technology. For those who refuse to see, there is no need to argue the logic. The research is plentiful; in competition, companies adopting the new quality philosophy demolished their traditional competitors.

What keeps consumers aware are competitors willing to put consumer-quality first, consumer advocates, and most recently, the media who are themselves caught up in the quality competition. As a case in point, television network consumer reporters brought buyer agency into the national spotlight with highly supportive reports on *NBC Nightside News* (January 1993), *Good Morning, America* (April 1993), and *The Today Show* (February 1996).

Buyer agency is in the forefront of the quality movement in real estate because even a cursory view
through the quality perspective (i.e., customer specifications) reveals that the customer who pays all the bills
— the buyer — has been left out in the cold.
Dedicated agency* (purchase or sales) becomes part
of it because, as consumers (buyers *and* sellers)
become more aware and discerning, they will put their
trust only in agencies which have no risk of infiltration
by opposing interests, agencies in which all agents represent only their side of the sales counter. Finally, tailoring service to customer specifications means recognizing the difference not only between buyer and seller,
but among buyers and among sellers! One does not
require the same services as another, nor the same
agent time and attention, and these differences occur
irrespective of offering price or sale price. Thus, flat
fees (Chapter 9) based on specific services or time rendered are inevitably part of the new era.

This chapter opened with an observation about
being asked if it is going to rain, and about the
inevitably true answer being "Yes". Suppose, instead,
that the question was, "Is it raining?" The same safe
answer — "Yes" — could be given. It is always raining
somewhere.

In fact, most often, your local weather forecast for
rain is based on the fact that it is raining somewhere,
and that the stuff is moving your way. (Yeah, yeah.
Sometimes it forms right there where you are.) Buyer
agency is happening somewhere whether it is falling on
your house or not. Both buyer and seller exclusive

Buyer agents and flat fees are inevitable

*Above, page 26

agency is happening somewhere. Yes, it is flat-feeing out. These weather systems are moving into the local region. In some low spots flood waters will rise causing extreme discomfort and worse for those who have their heads stuck in the sand.

In the rest of these pages on The Inevitable, we will concentrate mostly on buyer agency (Chapter 6). Then we'll briefly (Chapter 7) revisit the dynamics of the quality revolution to see just why it is all so inevitable. and why die-hard traditionalists cannot accept that. The last gasp of traditionalism, rewriting laws to legit-imatize double-agents, will be given more attention than the maneuver deserves (Chapter 8) only because it is a bad weather cloud on the otherwise inevitable dawn of a bright new day of consumer service. Chapter 9 — "Flat Fee Seller Agency "— looks at a future of seller agency with one absolutely certain pre-diction: that the great majority of seller agents reading it will not believe it. These are the same people who refused to believe that buyer agency would have the impact it is now having. Flat fees are the future for both buyer and seller agency, with people paying only for what they get, and fully getting what they pay for.

CHAPTER 6

Buyer Agency

We're one-sided and listless, and proud of it!

T HIS BOAST in a newspaper ad I once wrote for an exclusive buyers' agency was not about closed minds and a lack of energy. The point was that the agency represented only buyers and never took listings. This is the concept of **"exclusive buyer agency"**,* — *dedicated* agency on the buyer's side — refusing listings to avoid not only the **conflict of interest** inherent in representing sellers, but the appearance of it. For a listing agency to meet such a standard, it would mean never indulging in activities which give the appearance of buyer representation (i.e., both WWB and WOB charades).**

*Above, pages 23, 25

**Above, pages 15–17

> A ctually, as will become more clear in the discussion on fixed fees that follows, listing is a service separate and distinct from providing agent representation to a client. Thus, a buyers' broker could list without being any kind of sellers' agent, but it is probably not good business because appearance as well as substance is integral to a successful business.

To promote itself and the unfamiliar concept of buyer agency, the agency for which I wrote the ad staffed a booth at the county fair, and used a free prize drawing to attract passers by. Among them were homeowners happy to enter the drawing, but most stressing that they had no interest in selling their home or having it listed. When the agents said they had no interest in either listing or selling, the owners were first disbelieving, then curious, most pausing to hear more about this unheard-of idea of a "buyers' agent". They had all been through the buying process at least once, and several responded to what they were now hearing with some version of the same revealing rhetorical question:

"Where were you guys when I needed you?"

Approval was universal among owners, including sellers, and nearly everyone stopping at the booth. Even without the details of exactly how buyers' agencies work, the simple concept of the buyer having the same rights to agent representation as the seller was seen as fundamental — especially by those who remembered buying a home through a subagent they mistakenly thought was "their" agent.

The "buyer agent" label

SIMPLY ENGAGING A "BUYERS' AGENT" doesn't resolve all problems of representation. Responsible professionals are trying to quickly establish terminology consumers can depend upon; but clever traditionalists know how to turn trust-evoking terms into handy self-stick labels...

Informed buyers will seek an *exclusive buyers' agent* — one who represents only buyers in any and all transactions, and never sellers, and who is not part of a firm in which associates, supervisors and/or owners are obligated to sellers (i.e., they work in organizations that do no listing). True exclusivity dictates that all of an agent's personal, social, economic and other attachments are exclusively in synch with the buyer's interests. In truth, exclusivity is indispensible to agency itself; and to the degree that an "agent" is tied to any interest **adverse** to his/her client, agency is not merely "limited" but nullified. A true agent renders full **fiduciary** responsibilities. That is why I said dual agents are "agents" in only a technical sense.* Frankly, "nonexclusive agency" — for buyers or sellers — is an oxymoron! As we will see in Chapter 8, one traditionalist approach to keep working both sides of the street is to claim to provide "limited agency" to each side. Limited agency is like limited pregnancy...

*Above, page 6

The "exclusive" label is a desirable marketing device; and some listing agencies will paste it on in-house "agents" despite the fact that they cannot be exclusive of powerful workplace ties to seller interests. The touted rationale is that these agents do not list property, nor represent sellers in any transactions. But this is just another **curve,** teasing a buyer's eyes off the ball, away from who and what truly holds the agent's loyalty. Every member of a listing agency — even one contracting only with buyers and not listing property — works with and for those who do list and whose income is very much affected by where and in what amount the buyer's money is spent. They do not operate exclusive of personal, social, economic and other ties to seller interests; thus, they are non-exclusive buyer's "agents" despite claims to the contrary.

Fear of commitment

NON-EXCLUSIVE BUYERS' AGENTS are real estate practitioners who want the right to claim to work "for" rather than merely "with" buyers, but are unwilling or unable to divest themselves of their sellerside security blankets. Making the leap to full exclusive buyer representation does not offer these agent the best deal; consequently, they are not the best deal for buyers if their exclusive equivalent is available in the area. Some fit the old political definition of "mugwumps" who fence-sit with mugs on one side and wumps on the other, giving full commitment or service to neither buyer nor seller.

The few exceptions

*Page 24

OTHER NON-EXCLUSIVE TYPES, exceptions to whom I alluded in Chapter 1*, are on a higher intellectual and moral plane; they believe that in their own set of narrowly defined circumstances, they can provide full **single agency** service to their clients, controlling the acknowledged risk of adverse interests. These include buyer agents in listing agencies who do not pretend to be "exclusive buyer agents" and "single agents" who will represent a buyer here and a seller there, but never in the same transaction. What distinguishes them from the traditionalists masquerading as agents is that they do not pitch limited or dual agency, but acknowledge what true agency requires and work to provide it; they admit to areas of potentially adverse interest, enact procedures to keep them in control, and provide clients with options for dealing with conflicts that may arise. It also means they *must* be in a situation where they indeed can exercise control; and that almost assuredly requires them to be independent agents or, if part of any firm, that it be a very small organization imposing few institutional pressures and with very few clients on the other side. Holding equal things like personal ability, resources, and experience, the exclusive buyer agent who is simply detached from such potential conflict is the better choice for a client; but non-exclusive agents meeting these tests should indeed be the preferred choice where there are no exclusive agents.

Above, I likened limited agency to limited pregnancy. There is another parallel between pregnancy and agency: *false pregnancy* is a medical reality — the illusion of pregnancy when the status is actually "non-pregnancy". "Non-agency" is no more inherently unhealthy than "non-pregnancy" if it is a matter of choice and not an illusion. It is appropriate for a real estate firm to offer its customers limited services, or even "limited representation", provided the customers know they are not clients, — i.e., that the service or representation is "limited" because it does not meet the requirements of agency. False pregnancy is not deliberately induced for profit; and prevention and cure are a matter for the medical profession. *False agency*, as opposed to mere non-agency, is a quite another matter; prevention is a matter for lawmakers, and cure for the courts.

The term "single agent" in its literal sense means one who practices single agency, i.e., represents only one side in a transaction, which does of course describe exclusive buyer agents and exclusive seller agents. In *practice*, the term refers to those who will represent either buyer or seller, but under agency contract and paid by the client.

Seller agency service to buyers

DISCLOSED NONAGENCY SERVICES can, in some circumstances, be provided by an exclusive buyer or seller agency to those on the other side. The classic example is a selling agency working in the WWB mode with uncontracted buyers when the buyer knows both that he/she is not the client and that the seller is. Though likely not the best deal for the buyer, it is not technically unethical when it does not violate the concept of agency. Required is that the seller's agent takes on no interest in the buyer that creates an interest **adverse** to the seller; thus, the agent is free to promote the seller's property to the buyer and at the best price for the seller. "Gray areas" here involve just how aware the buyer truly is, even with technical disclosure, and the sheer magnitude of what the buyer has at risk. The bottom line is that very much is at stake in almost any given real estate deal, with no one ever fully aware of all elements of the interplay of personal interests, motives, and rationalization.

Buyer agency service to sellers

ON THE OTHER SIDE, exclusive buyer agencies might provide services to uncontracted sellers such as "FSBO registries" — data banks for home searches which include properties not in the MLS. This seller service is a clear benefit to buyers who are clients of the agency, provided the agency has no obligation or incentive to motivate any buyer toward one of these properties. Some innovative buyer agencies go so far as to provide free or low-cost advertising for its registered FSBO homes (after their buyer clients have seen them); the chief gain here is openly for the agency, enabling it to promote itself to the buyers the homes attract — all with full disclosure and permission of the sellers. It is critical that neither the agency nor anyone in the agency act as an agent for the seller, nor take on any interest adverse to the buyers' interests. But still, there are those "gray areas".

WORKING BOTH SIDES of the street has its roots in traditional seller agency, and the pure size of the traditionalist agent population and its market control sometimes force buyer agents to do the same as a matter of survival. Among buyer agents, even those practicing it, it does not rest well; and they go to painful extremes to provide disclosure and insure consumer awareness. But there is still the appearance of conflict, and others believe that appearance is enough reason to ban the practice. So, there is dissension in the evolving profession on this matter which the agents and consumer advisors are working to resolve.

UNLESS CLEARLY INDICATED otherwise, whenever I refer to "buyers' agents" in this text, it is to exclusive buyers' agents in an exclusive buyers' agency. The most scrupulous and honorable non-exclusive agent, performing acrobatics to avoid profiting from adverse interests, still dilutes the full benefits that genuine agency provides clients. Worse, the halo effect of the honorable non-exclusive agent provides a cover for you-know-who to don sheep's clothing. It is no great leap from the "working-with-buyers" mentality to the "yeah-I-can-do-that" mindframe when a traditional agent sees an opportunity for a previously unreachable prize — a buyer signed to a contract. Thus, someone totally immersed in seller service, and maybe even traditionalist bias (i.e., anti-buyer

True buyer agency

agency) is magically transformed into a "buyer's agent". Even the nobly-intended, really believing they "can do that", cannot be expected to have the commitment and focused buyer-dedication demonstrated by the agent who has fully forsaken seller-side security.

One misuse of buyer agency contract

A REAL-LIFE EXAMPLE of non-exclusive buyer agency being motivated by factors opposed to buyer interest arises from the legitimate concern of one New England sellers' agent for his seller-client. One negative aspect of the traditional system for sellers is that the seller actually engages a network of largely unknown individuals through sub-agency and picks-up expanded liability risk for any number of things they might do while in the seller's employ. The listing agent bears this same risk of liability. One particularly astute non-traditional listing agent protects himself and his seller by refusing to work through subagents; he mandates that any agent — *including traditional sellers' agents*— bringing buyers to him first sign them up under a buyer-agency contract. If that seller's-sub-agent-turned-customer-agent should then misrepresent the property to the buyer, the buyer will have no recourse against the sellers' agent or the seller because the error will have been made by the buyer's employee and not the seller's employee. This **"seller's customer-agent mandate"** (**SCAM**) is what the acronym implies, for buyers are "scammed" into thinking they are signing something for their own protection that is really a device to limit their recourse and protect the other side.

EARLIER IN THIS TEXT I suggested three possible implications in a sellers' agent's offer to work "with" buyers:

Revisiting WWB

- what the agent learns about buyer's financial capabilities or personal business won't be used to the
  seller's advantage, or that

- the agent will work for the best price and terms in
  the buyer's definition, or that

- the agent will write the buyer's offer to maximize
  the buyer's negotiating leverage.

While nevertheless attractive to a buyer, these are
false implications. The first is passively inconsistent
with a seller's agent's responsibility to his/her client,
and would require a seller's express waiver of rights. It
would, however, be something a dual agent could
appropriately promise, for a dual agent does not do
anything to give one party advantage over the other.
The second and third implications, of course, are
directly contrary to the interests of the seller, and violate the responsibilities of both sellers' agent and dual
agent — and also those of anyone claiming to be a
neutral "facilitator" or "intermediary" rather than
agent.

The good news is that while these buyer-benefiting
functions are simply not available in the traditional
system, they are still available to buyers. They are fundamental to the role of buyers' agent. In Chapter 2, we
reviewed the traditional system of real estate "sales and
purchase." In contrast, our interest now is in "purchase and sale" — i.e., the process from the perspective

of the **buyer**. We will first examine the agency relationship created by a buyer employing (not "working
with") a buyers' agent, and then each of the steps of the
purchase (not "sales") process:

A. Agent/client relationship (representation, work,
compensation, agreement);

B. Purchase process (financial preparation, property
search and qualification, acquisition).

A. AGENT/CLIENT RELATIONSHIP

Revisiting "agency"

IT IS IMPORTANT HERE to revisit this all-important
concept of agency, remembering that real estate brokers and sales people are licensed by their respective
states. A given state's real estate licensing law may or
may not identify them as "agents"; but when they present themselves as agents — expressly or implicitly —
they are governed by laws specifically defining that
term and its express obligations. Remember that a sellers' agent must work for the best interests of the seller,
that the seller is his/her client and the buyer is merely
the customer. Remember also that any real estate agent
who brings a buyer to a seller's agent, and who has not
properly entered into a buyers' agency agreement with
the buyer, is a subagent of the seller with fully binding
obligations to the seller.

In the traditional system, the seller hires the listing
agent, and the listing agreement is the employment
contract. The listing agent hires subagents via standing

To create agency liability, it is not necessary to expressly state that one is an agent or represented by an agent. "Implied agency" occurs when one's behavior leads another to act on the belief that agency exists.

agreements and/or offer of a specified commission-share in the MLS listing data on the property. Using money earned from the sale at the closing, the seller pays the listing agency (actually processed at the closing). The listing agency then pays the co-broke share to the selling agency (if there is one). Both agencies then pay their own agents out of their respective co-broke shares. It is an *employment hierarchy*, with authority flowing along the lines of hiring and payroll, with the seller "officially" at the top. The underlying rationale is that of the traditional work organization in America:

He/she who does the hiring and pays the wages calls the shots.

The premise accompanying this rationale in the traditional real estate mentality is, of course, that the *seller's* money is paying the wages. It is the same misguided premise that led American automakers and other manufacturers to near ruin by losing sight of who was really paying the bills. The quality revolution and its customer-focused definition of **"quality"** came to the rescue when it reminded even those doing the hiring where the money was really coming from. There, as well as in the purchase and sale of real estate, the payer of all bills and all wages is the buyer!

Traditional elements that can continue

THERE ARE TWO ELEMENTS of the traditional system which many buyers — perhaps most — do not want to see changed:

- the paying of brokerage fees only when and if a property actually changes hands, and

- the inclusion of all brokerage costs in the full purchase price and mortgage loan.

These things do not need to change when a buyer engages a buyers' agent. The buyer's purchase offer to the seller may specify, as a condition of the offer and purchase agreement, that the offered price encompasses full brokerage fees including the fee to be paid at the closing to the buyer's agent. Accepting such an offer will make no monetary difference to the seller. The only change effecting the seller's agent should be that, instead of a subagent share, there will now be a buyer's agent fee. The buyer's agent fee could be less than the expected subagent fee, with the seller's agent profiting from the difference (though I personally believe such profit should be returned to the seller). The only way the seller's agent might actually net less-than-anticipated money is if he/she had been relying on the leverage of the traditional employment/payroll structure to pocket some of the commission earned by those working "with" or for buyers (eg., the Benjamin County subagent fees*). However, for the listing agent to advise non-acceptance on the basis of lost opportunity to skim off some buyer-side earnings would be in direct conflict

*Above, pages 63–65, See also matter of buyer agent commissions below on pages 91–92.

The full commission rate set at the time of the listing agreement is premised upon there being "buyer side" and "seller side" effort and expenses, with the seller-side money guaranteed to the listing agency, and buyer-side money reserved for whoever brings the buyer to the table. The listing agent should not profit because the listing presentation overestimated the actual buyer-side payment from *the seller's* money.

with the seller's interests and counter to the agent's fiduciary responsibility. Such misconduct would in turn place the listing agent's entire commission at risk. Thus, it is in both the seller's and the listing agent's interest to accept a fair offer which includes buyer agents' fees in the purchase price and mortgage loan.

THE LISTING CONTRACT is the employment agreement between seller and seller's agent, specifying obligations and compensation, and it is fully binding upon **subagents**. However, it has no *binding power whatsoever over buyers,* nor over buyers' agents who, by definition, act on behalf of their buyer clients. Buyer and buyer's agent establish their own "buyer agency agreement" specifying obligations and compensation. *This is the defining point in the break with the traditional system.* For real estate professionals to survive and thrive, it is vital that they learn to accept it, understand it, and *respect* it.

Formal agency agreement

An indication that acceptance, understanding, and respect is far from current reality emerged in the abovenoted analysis of the statewide and Benjamin County MLS data. I noted above that the hiring of subagents sometimes involves a listing agent's offer of a specified commission-share in the MLS listing data on the property. Since buyers, and not listing agents, hire buyers' agents, *no listing agent should be making offers of money to buyers' agents.* Yet, the MLS data sheet entry next to the listing agent's offering to subagents is one to buyer's agents. It is not an act of generosity, nor of accepting buyer agents. At best, it is a matter of someone "just not getting it." At worst, it is specifically to envelop the buyers' agent in the listing agent's employment and control. An example of that is in the National Association of Realtors® Standard of Practice 16-16 which imposes restrictions upon both subagents and buyers' agents as to what may appear in a purchase offer — apparently oblivious to the fact that a purchase offer is an act of the buyer and not of the agent!*

*Discussed more fully below on pages 139–144

For a while, as buyer agency first began to evolve, and even today as individual agents first venture into buyer agency, buyer agents have and do accept such listing-agent dictated commission shares. It is a mistake, for it disenfranchises an exclusive fiduciary right of the person who truly does hire the buyers' agent. Increasingly, buyer agents are now startling traditional agents with a formal statement that they will not be participating in the offered share. (As we will see below,** that does not mean that the listing agent is being given license to put those declined dollars into his/her own pocket. Nor does it mean that the buyers' agent's fee will not be coming out of the purchase price or mortgage loan money.)

**Pages 100–101, 145, 284–285

THE BUYER'S AGENT belongs on the buyer's payroll, and not the seller's payroll, as a pure matter of tightening up the buyer's control over his/her own affairs. The money originates with the buyer, even if the seller or seller's agent is to be the conduit; and the amount and terms of the buyer compensation to his/her own agent are simply no affair of either seller or seller's agent. There is no better place to establish compensation than in the buyer-agency employment agreement, which will both pre-date even contact with sellers' agents and be clearly recognized as outside their purview. If it is the buyer's intention to utilize a seller-side conduit, the agreement should stipulate that all offers to purchase will clearly communicate that to sellers.

Buyer agent fee no concern of seller or seller's agent

IDEALLY, the buyers' agent fee for services will not be a purchase price percentage (PPP). The problem with the **"three-P"** commission is not what obviously first comes to mind — i.e., that it is an incentive for agents to maximize price. As we saw earlier, a $15 to $30 individual agent incentive per thousand dollars of increase is not all that powerful. The upward incentive is totally offset by a far more powerful reward to the agent for securing a lower purchase price: the ability to show future potential clients a track record of homes purchased at a percentage of asking price that is lower than the area average.

Nevertheless, for reasons other than the upward-incentive issue, the three-P commission is still far from the ideal method of compensating a buyer's agent, especially if the seller or seller's agent is to be its con-

Buyer agent incentive inconsistent with three-P commission

duit. Ironically, the thing most wrong with it is the very reason some buyers' agents use it, i.e., that it is the traditional method of compensation. The usual well-intended but misguided rationale is to avoid adding unnecessary waves to the disturbance buyer agency has already brought to the local traditionalist-occupied pond. Actually, this yielding to the status-quo for the sake of "peace" accomplishes the opposite, creating two problem sets which set the stage for battles far more serious than the minor splash of abandoning the traditional three-P commission.

Myth of seller agent authority

THE FIRST OF THESE two troublesome problem sets is that combining the seller conduit with the traditional percentage commission perpetuates the traditionalist mindset of an employment hierarchy and payroll from the seller through the listing agent to the buyer's agent. Anything supporting the illusion of the buyer's agent being on the seller's or seller's agent's payroll invites conflict every time the buyer's agent acts like he/she is working for the buyer.

The second problem set is that, with the basis of both listing and buyer's agent commissions being percentage of purchase price, the image is created of one overall commission being divided — i.e., one "pie" — providing the temptation for one to cut a bigger slice at the expense of the other. One example of that has already been shown in the case of the Benjamin County subagency commissions.* The same study of MLS data showed an even broader propensity —

*Above, pages 63–64.

beyond Benjamin County — when it came to cutting into a buyers' agent's slice.

WHILE NO MONEY OFFER at all should be made to buyers' agents by sellers' agents, to make such an offer with less than that offered to subagents, or for zero dollars, is blatant discrimination with antitrust overtones. Nevertheless, the MLS study revealed that offers to buyers' agents were often less than to subagents — statewide in 24% of the cases, and in 36% of the cases in Benjamin County. Overall, buyers' agents were offered an average of 12% less than subagents statewide, and 30% less in Benjamin County. Moreover, 21% of Benjamin County cases specified *zero* percent to buyer agents, something that occurred in *none* of the statewide cases sampled. Again, it should be noted that, while the extreme may prevail in Benjamin County (likely because buyers' agents are brand-new there), the discrimination is statewide.

Traditional agents have tried to justify the lower offering to buyers' agents by claiming that their *sellers* insisted on it; but in no case was the insisting seller deducting it from his or her overall commission payout. The monetary gain is thus to the listing agent and not the seller. Still, monetary gain cannot be the whole answer, for equally vulnerable subagents are not being equally exploited. If the reason for decreasing the payout for an action is not simply to pocket the difference, then it must be to decrease the incentive — i.e., as a deterrent to the action. To discourage buyers' agents from bringing buyers to a seller is certainly never in the

Evidence of boycott activity

seller's interest, so, by pure logical deduction, it must be perceived as being in the interests of the seller's agent. Such apparently deliberate deterrent is also not in the interests of a free and open market. Practiced publicly under the cooperative auspices of the MLS, it is not far removed (if at all) from the group boycott activity outlawed by antitrust legislation.

Solution: remove seller agent from buyer agent compensation channel

NEITHER BUYER NOR SELLER should have to tolerate agent commission squabbling or, even if they are not aware of it, the distractions it causes from the agents' work. The solution: no common "pie" — or appearance of one — to squabble over; and no simulation of the simply inapplicable agent-to-subagent payroll. Set the buyer's agent fee, or formula for it, in the buyer's agency employment agreement. Also provide in this agreement that any purchase offer to a seller may require that the seller, *but not the seller's agent,* serve as a conduit. Finally, provide there that any offer will state the buyers' agents commission amount only if the seller conduit is used, and then *only as a flat fee with no mention whatsoever of percentage!*

Structuring the buyer agent employment agreement

A HOST OF PROBLEMS can be avoided early through appropriate structuring of the buyer agency agreement. Obviously, its primary function is to clarify issues and agreements between buyer and buyer's agent, but an appropriate secondary function is to set a basis for clear signals to those eventually on the seller side of the table. Traditional listing agents are accustomed to citing their agency employment agreement (the listing contract) to justify certain things as "out of their hands" and beyond negotiation; so the buyer agency agreement is a good place to do that on the buyer's side.

A common approach to explaining the buyer agency agreement, is to compare it to the listing agreement, and even to say that buyers' agents "list" buyers. Actually, the expression is not accurate because the whole business of "listing" is to place the home on a **public list** of properties for sale. That is the nature of sales. The consistent theme here (even implied in the title) is that purchase is of a different nature than sales. While selling necessitates public marketing, buying is something often best done **privately**, even at times anonymously; so part of the function of the buyers' agency contract is to protect the privacy, and sometimes the anonymity, of the buyers.

The buyers' agency agreement commits the agent to protect the confidentiality of the buyers, giving sellers only what they need to know to be assured the buyers are legitimate. The buyers' agent is specifically forbidden to disclose, not only information irrelevant to the transaction, but especially facts which sellers' agents and subagents would actually be obligated to reveal to the seller and use in the seller's interest. These are things about needs, motivation, or even affluence which the buyers must sort through with their agent and keep out of the hands of the other guy's agent. It is a nuisance at best, and dangerous at worst, to enable a seller's agent to selectively exploit those elements in favor of the few properties which put the commission in his/her pocket. Buying through traditional agents without buyer-agency protection makes it almost impossible to avoid this pitfall.

One thing listing agreement and buyer-agency agreement have in common is that they are both **employment** agreements. Through them, both sellers and buyers become **clients** of the agents they hire for specific purposes, identified periods of time, and for specified compensation. Both gain full client rights to the loyalty, confidentiality, and professional capability of their respective agents. On the downside, they both also accrue a certain amount of liability for errors, omissions, or misrepresentations such agents might commit while working in their principal's (buyer's or seller's) name. However, such liability is far more serious for a seller than for a buyer; only the seller's agents, with incomes contingent on the sale of specific properties, are generally the ones to gain from misrepresentation.

An essential element of the buyer agency agreement, to be detailed immediately after identification of the parties, contract term (period), and termination particulars, is the nature of agency being contracted. Note that a document entitled, "exclusive buyer agency agreement" does not guarantee that the agency is an exclusive buyer agency, i.e., that it does not also represent sellers. In this context, "exclusive" usually means that the *client* will deal exclusively through the identified buyer agency. Rather than rely on interpretation of the jargon, a buyer seeking exclusive buyer agency representation should require the contract to detail an agency promise to not represent sellers.

THE **term** OF A BUYER AGENCY contract may be for any length of time from a day to several months, depending on the specific buyer's purpose. The contract may even be for a specific piece of property the buyer already has in mind, with the term of the agreement ending with the purchase, the rejection of the buyer's offer, or the decision not to offer. The term is usually far from ironclad, with "bail-out" clauses often permitting either party to terminate the agreement at any time without penalty.

The reason for the easy bail-out lies in the inherent differences between selling side and buying side. By the very nature of the selling function, a listing agent works with a piece of property, with other agents, and with customers far more than with his/her client. The owner-client is really only a partial observer, and normally makes a performance-based judgment to renew or go elsewhere only at the end of the listing contract term. On the buying side, by contrast, the buyer's agent works closely with the buyer on a day-to-day basis; and that quickly becomes what binds or dissolves the agreement between them, more than the ink on the contract. Even if the term of the contract was "cast in cement," a dissatisfied househunter could simply hold back on the househunting — there is simply no way to force serious shopping. Agents who will be successful in this business are those who will actively perform for clients and who, consequently, will be happy to let performance rather than contractual obligation be the tie that binds.

Term and termination of the agreement

Fees   BUYER'S AGENT FEES might be fixed for itemized services or for time charged, or calculated according to the value of properties searched or purchased. Payment might involve advanced retainer, regular billing, or be totally contingent on sale and due at closing. Fees paid directly in return for services and/or involving an advanced retainer can be expected to be measurably lower than those contingent on sale. It is perfectly appropriate for the buyer's purchase offer to include cash refund to the buyer for all such prepaid brokerage expenses, or payment to the buyers agent for fees due, and to include that amount in the mortgage loan; and the buyers' agent employment agreement might specify that at least the fees-due condition will be included in the offer. *

*More on this below, on pages 145–147

When payment is contingent upon a property sale, the contract will usually be worded to include the purchase of any property which came to the buyer's attention while the contract was in effect. Often, the time it takes between an accepted offer and actual conveyance of the property will extend beyond the term of the agency agreement; and the easy bail-out clauses are not intended as opportunities to default on earned commissions.

Whether or not the agent's idea of payment is due at closing, up-front retainer, or pay-as-you-go, the buyer should remember that until the contract is signed, *everything* — payment method, fee amount, work required, term — *is negotiable.*

The local area's going rate for listing commissions is a good place to start developing a perspective for judging the equitableness of a given buyers' broker fee. As indicated earlier, the "going rate" for full (both sides) brokerage commissions in the traditional system really does seem to have emerged in free market competition, with a fairly consistent ceiling and base legitimately explainable.* It appears reasonable that total brokerage costs encompassing both sides of the table should not exceed the general area going rate because a buyers' broker is employed. That typical going rate across the nation, encompassing both selling side and buying side brokerage, is 6%, and half of that (3%) strikes me as a reasonable ballpark measure for full buyerside brokerage in a "typical" transaction. Again, I offer this as a guideline only, and for a transaction that is typical in terms of the service requirements upon the agent. Thus, in this text, **"typical"** merits its own place in the Glossary, and definition here:

*Above, pages 55–58

> When applied to brokerage on either buyer's side or seller's side, or to full brokerage (both sides), it means that all usual service elements are required, in the usual quantity, with no unusual elements or extreme demand (or near absence of demand) upon the agent's time, effort, or expense, or and that payment for service is contingent upon sale and due at closing.

For buyers who require the full run of services from finding purchase money to finding property and negotiating the purchase, fees that average about 3% of the purchase price are probably fair — *on average.* However, an average is not something that necessarily can be fairly applied to even most of the *individuals* in a population. Work required of a buyers' agent will vary from one buyer to another, and the work contract —

the buyer agency agreement — should be specific to the individual buyer. For those requiring the full service spectrum for a $200,000 home, perhaps $6,000 is the right fee; but should the fee be $12,000 for a $400,000 home for a buyer who needs no help with financing? Some buyers, particularly those purchasing upper bracket homes, will have their financing in place. Others will have located their own property. Still others will require the agent to personally examine prospective purchases before taking valuable time for their own visits. Accordingly, a buyers' agent should have a schedule of charges which vary with the nature and amount of service required. The 3%-for-the-typical-job rule, at best, provides a handy reference point for judging the equitableness of the overall agency compensation schedule *on both the buyer's side and the seller's side.*

Understand that in the traditional system, there is no such standard as "typicalness" to serve as a reference point for varying compensation for varying services. Should a buyer walk in off the street with an acceptable offer before the ink is dry on the listing contract, the listing agent will expend untypically low time, effort, or money and still receive the entire 6%. Traditionalists will defend the ethics of that by noting it is usually agreed upon by all parties before signing. It does, however, require a level of consumer naivete that will disappear, by definition, as the consumer quality revolution displaces the traditional system in real estate.

THE TRADITIONAL JUSTIFICATION is that an agency may get "lucky" on one deal, but will lose on another that does not materialize in a sale even after considerable agency effort and expense. The acceptability of such rationale relies on consumer unawareness of the profit dynamics of listing and of the real reason agents list. * It also means that a seller who has properly priced his/her house for prompt sale is paying for sellers who have failed to do so, as well as for agents who allow that to happen. It also means that the *buyer* will have to pay the seller to pay the agent, for, as pointed out already, the buyer pays for everything in the purchase price.** And that is the Achilles' heel of the traditional system....

The arrow to pierce that heel is *customer awareness,* the driving force of the customer quality revolution! If the seller in a case such as that just described is not aware of the lack of listing-agent expense, a buyer advised by a conscientious buyer agent *will* be. The aware buyer will also know, and make the seller know, that one way to narrow the gap between buyer's offered price and seller's asking price is to eliminate the unearned commission dollars from the listing agent's side.

This straightforward observation of the inevitable will be viewed by some as no less than a *double heresy,* because it violates two commandments for **buyerside** behavior cast in the cement of traditionalism:

I. Thou shalt not touch the listing agent's commission (even though the research cited above*** indicates the commissions of both subagents and buyers'

Seller agent fee an appropriate concern of buyer and buyer's agent

*Above, pages 43–46.

**Above, page 85

***Above, pages 63–64, 91–92

agents are considered fair game for the listing agent).

II. Thou shalt not go around the listing agent to communicate with the seller.

Preaching these as absolutes, traditionalists will cite both the **REALTORS'®** Code of Ethics* and simple professional courtesy to point out that no agent — or principal for that matter — should be interfering in the relationship or agreements between another agent and principal. I personally agree with that notion, but with two caveats, the first of which is supported, and the second not disputed, by the Code of Ethics:

*Article 16. The Code applies to all members of the National Association of REALTORS®, i.e., all "REALTORS®".

1. The client's best interest takes precedence over the code's call for cooperation among agents ;**

**Code of Ethics, articles 1 and 3.

2. The buyer is bound by no agreement in which he/she did not participate (including listing commission agreements and professional association rules) and has every right to directly contact anyone for any reason, including the seller, and to do that with and/or through his/her agent.

The first means an obligation upon the buyer's agent to advise the client of all things in the client's interest. It includes any opportunities to reduce price, and necessarily includes any legitimate potential reduction of seller's expenses. Most important, the listing agent's duty to put his/her client's best interest first dictates an absolute obligation to cooperate with, rather than resist, a buyer's attempt to reduce seller expenditures for services never provided.

THE SECOND CAVEAT means that listing agents must recognize, not only that buyers' agents simply do not work for them, but are in fact the agents of those who will be dictating their requirements to the listing agent's employer. That is a hard reality for traditionalists accustomed to being in control, that the customer is now in the driver's seat. Still, it is a healthy reality, and one accepted by America's best management minds and most powerful executives:

Authority flows from the buyer, not the seller

1 9 8 0

"[Needed is] an approach where the entire focus of your definition of quality is driven by the customer, and the customer's wants and needs."

—Ford Chairman Donald E. Petersen, beginning the effort that would bring Ford and lead the entire American auto industry into recovery from the "Car Wars" disaster of the 1970's.*

*Gabor, Andrea. 1990. *The Man Who Discovered Quality.* Page 219.

1 9 8 2

"[The traditional approach] has arguably led us seriously astray.... It doesn't command that we overspend on quality, overkill on customer service...."

—Tom Peters and Bob Waterman, denouncing the traditional structure of American business organizations, in *In Search of Excellence,* the enormous best seller which catapulted the quality revolution into the national popular arena.

1 9 8 7

"A quality revolution means eating, sleeping and breathing quality.... And, as always, the customer must be present — as the chief definer of what's important."

—Peters again, in *Thriving on Chaos:* handbook for a management revolution.

1 9 9 0

"There is emerging at GM a concerted and remarkably centralized quality strategy that takes its vision from Deming and that is attempting to create a framework for institutionalizing a customer-driven vision of quality throughout GM."

—Andrea Gabor, former Senior Business Editor at *U.S. News and World Report,* writing in *The Man Who Discovered Quality: how W. Edwards Deming brought the quality revolution to America* — the stories of Ford, Xerox, and GM.

1 9 9 3

"In business, there is only one definition of quality — the customer's definition."

—George W. Bush, President of the United States, quoted on the cover of the *1993 Award Criteria for the Malcolm Baldrige National Quality Award.*

Evolution of the inevitable

THE BALDRIGE AWARD raises a good point here. Despite the learned and powerful people who've put aside the old "wisdom", it might still be said it will take an "act of Congress" to change the minds of stubborn traditionalists. That is exactly what "The Baldrige" is all about; it was in fact established by an act of Congress — the National Quality Improvement Act of 1987, specifically to bring about a customer-focused change in American businesses of all sizes, in manufacturing and *in services*. It was not a matter of government interfering in business, but a response to a call by business leaders who were distressed at the decline in American productivity, quality, and profits as foreign competition and markets were on the obvious incline. The language of the Act specifically noted that other countries had galvanized their own national economies with such award programs, naming Japan, Australia, France, and England. The first and most successful award after which the others were modelled was Japan's — named not after any Japanese hero, but after an *American:* W. Edwards Deming.

During World War II, Deming was a leader in this country's productivity and quality efforts. When the war ended, there was no international competition for American industry, meaning that American customers were captives of the producers. Busy with filling orders for the burgeoning post-war buying, the concern was for production rather than for productivity (which would have limited waste and contained costs) or for quality. Thus, there was little use for Deming in the United States; and Japan with its bombed-out production capability did need him. In short, while America was forgetting the lessons of quality and productivity that made her great, Japan was listening and learning. Thus, defeat in the great war in the forties led to victory in the Car Wars in the seventies.

In the eighties, America began to rebound by remembering. And it was its customers who remembered first, reminding the producers, by buying from the competition. The difference was that the customers were no longer captive, and were aware that *they* could call the shots. The irony is, that despite the bumper stickers denouncing the customers for buying the better quality, lower priced products of another country, the upshot was a strengthening of American quality and productivity power — at least by those flexible enough to take on the new quality approach. And the lessons spread to services (e.g., in the seventies, pizza was not a home delivery item).

In the nineties, American real estate buyers are no longer captives of sellers' agents. The customers are becoming aware, and so will sellers, of options to the traditional approaches. Real estate professionals flexible enough to develop approaches for aware consumers (buyers and sellers) will prosper at the expense of those with the bumper-sticker mentality described in the last paragraph.

B. PURCHASE PROCESS

THE TRADITIONAL SYSTEM in real estate is a sales process, not a purchase process. The table compares the stages of the purchase process (financial preparation, property search & qualification, acquisition) to those of the sales process (buyer qualification, property showing and sale, conveyance). It is more than semantics; the differences between buying and selling perspectives have profound practical implications for both buyer and seller.

SALES PROCESS	S1 Find and qualify prospect (buyer).	S2 Show and sell property.	S3 Convey property and liabilities.
PURCHASE PROCESS	P1 Prepare buyer.	P2 Find and qualify prospect (property)	P3 Acquire property and benefits.

In the traditional sales process, it is the responsibility of the seller's agent is to help prepare the property for showing and sale (S2) and to "qualify" the buyer (S1), i.e. establish that the individual is financially qualified to indeed buy the property. However, in a **purchasing process**, the task of the buyer's agent is to help prepare the buyer (P1) and find a property qualified according to the buyer's needs (P2). The final stage of a sales process is conveyance (S3), which translates into "moving" the product, delivering it and thus ensuring the payment. In real estate especially, it also means getting rid of it along with all the problems of possession; the buyer acquires more than the property. "Conveyance" reflects getting *out* of something and the attitude it prompts is simply one of relief. "Acquisition" (P3), on the other hand, is getting *into* something, calling not for relief, but caution. That necessitates far different work tasks and mindset for the buyer's agent than those facing the seller's agent.

B1. Financial preparation

Peeking in the buyer's wallet

THE ONE THING both buyer and buyer's agent owe to the seller and seller's agent from first contact is the assurance that the buyer does have the capability to purchase the seller's property. However, the seller side is entitled to know nothing beyond that assurance about the buyer's financial condition.

In the traditional system, the seller's agent gets a far better look into the buyer's financial condition than that, usually through the device of "assisting" the buyer with finding mortgage money. Even when a buyer needs no assistance, the seller's agent gets to justify the peek into the buyer's wallet with the seller's need for assurance of purchase capability. But there are two other reasons for a sellers' agents "curiosity", both of which are directly opposed to the buyer's interest:

- to be able to advise the seller when to hold out for a higher offer;

- to identify a buyer who can be steered toward higher-priced houses yielding higher commissions.

What the seller does need

THE FIRST OF THESE is fully legitimate, for the agent is duty-bound to work for the seller's interest. However, the second is another matter... The sellers' agent works for more than one seller; the so-called "exclusive" contract does not give them any exclusive rights to the agent's loyalty, and the sellers of higher-priced homes are paying more for the agent's interest. Worse, knowing the buyer can afford more than the home being considered opens the agent's financial interest beyond just those who've entrusted him/her when they signed over their own selling rights. When a subagent is faced with the decision, seller loyalty is a greatly diminished factor, if it exists at all in this context. Thus, a sellers' agent's "qualifying the buyer" is not always to a given seller's benefit.

Whether the information beyond purchase capability is being used in the seller's or the agent's interest, it is not being used in the buyer's interest. The point is that it should not and need not happen; it is avoided with the employment of a buyers' agent who is not on a percentage of price commission. The buyers' agent also needs assurance of buying capability, but is strictly forbidden by the law of agency to relay anything more than that to anyone else (without the buyer's permission). It should be sufficient assurance for the seller to be told that the buyer's agent, as a business person, would not be wasting his/her time with a buyer who couldn't deliver.

In the case where a 3-P commission applies and the difference in house prices approaches tens of thousands, the second problem (steering) may in fact be a cause for concern. The solution, of course, is a fee that does not vary with price.

Even a buyers' agent does not necessarily need to look at financial records for the preparedness assurance. A buyer who has the purchase money, prefinancing, or a preferred lender need only have the lender or banker communicate that fact to the agent. However, when properties are to be shown before a loan commitment (i.e., a lender's promise contingent on a qualified property) is secured, the agent will need to assure sellers that the buyer's credit and income are sufficient to obtain a loan. The buyer's agent is, of course, liable for representations made in this regard, and buyers should be willing to cooperate in the necessary credit checks and income verification by the buyer's agent — who will give assurance, and that's all, to the other side.

Never involve seller's agent in buyer financing

CLEARLY, a buyer with money in-hand has a clear advantage in any purchase negotiation process. At the same time, the first stop for most househunters is more often a real estate agency than a lender. Thus, for many buyers, the real estate agent (buyers' or sellers') does get involved in finding the financing — and, for reasons already made evident, it is far better for the buyer that it be a buyers' agent. The buyers' agent is legally bound by the confidentiality rule from the first moment of initial inquiry by a potential buyer, before and despite whether or not a buyer agency agreement is ever signed. By contrast, sellers' agents and subagents owe disclosure of relevant information to their principals, i.e., to any and all sellers or listing agents to whom they have agency or subagency obligations.

Pitfalls in finding the right professionals

A GOOD BUYERS' AGENT is prepared to personally shepherd his/her clients through the entire process, at least to the degree they require, or bring them to financial experts who specialize in such things (eg., mortgage brokers, money managers, credit specialists). A word of caution — this is no guarantee that all buyers' agents are "good" — and there are pitfalls in this business of utilizing other people, whether the shepherd is a buyers' or a sellers' agent. Used properly, and with appropriate buyers' agent guidance, other service professionals (not only in finance, but property experts, lawyers, ...) can provide far more in-depth support than any one talented individual. However, they can be selected for reasons other than what they will do for the buyer.

REFERRAL FEES are a case in point, paid by service professionals to the agent for bringing them business. No matter what path the money takes, the source is always the service charge paid by the buyer and the fee exerts upward pressure on the charge. Referral fees should always be disclosed and, as a general rule, declined by the agent in favor of a discount in the charge to the buyer. When a service professional stubbornly holds to a fixed charge, but still offers a referral fee, the agent can accept it and simply rebate it to the buyer.

Referral fees

None of this is to deny legitimate or even substantial income to the agent. He/she can set the above-board agency fee as high as a client will accept for all the effort made in the client's behalf. But it must be in the *client's* behalf and referral fees are given for favors on behalf of someone else.

In some cases, the agent or agency will actually perform the service and charge the buyer directly. A real estate agency may be in the mortgage brokering, insurance, or even well-drilling business. All may be quite appropriate, if a buyer is aware of all alternatives and feels the agency's package of services is worth the price.

The problem is that it is usually the job of the buyers' agent to help the client find the best services at the lowest price, so there is some potential conflict of interest there. It is, however, also possible that there is also shared interest between agent and client, if the agency is actually able to provide a cost-effective package. It comes down to a buyer being on the alert for such issues before engaging an agent.

Other referral incentives and factors

THE SELECTION OF A LENDER (or other services) can be consciously or subconsciously biased, not only by a referral fee, but by social and/or business relationships formed between service professional and agent. These relationships naturally occur in the course of normal human interaction. They are also sometimes deliberately cultivated either by agents building a reliable network of service for their clients or by the service professionals simply "drumming up" business. Regardless of why or how the relationships are established, the problem is that they become *comfortable*; and comfort in itself can be an interest of the agent that is not in the interest of the client. An agent may not be comfortable with facing the fact that someone he/she has come to like is a little too-high priced or under-performing for his/her clients. An agent should provide buyers with a broad list of competing lenders (and other services) with objective measures of current performance to consider. The agent can certainly tell a client about the human qualities of a given professional; i.e., that he's a nice guy, extremely helpful, hard working.... However, the bottom lines of performance, price, and availability should be paramount and clearly laid out for the client's decision. Again, as with referral fees, full disclosure of relationships is the key, with the buyer being aware beforehand of benefits and drawbacks in this area.

B2. Property search and qualification

THE PHRASES, "qualify the buyer" and "qualified buyer" (above) are revealing indicators of traditional market systems getting off-track. What any market is all about is providing products and services that are qualified to meet the buyer's needs; i.e., **quality** products and quality services. To speak of "qualifying buyers" is to view buyers as something to control; to speak of qualifying the purchase item — an automobile, a service, a house... — is to acknowledge the buyer's control. It is the difference between pre- and post- quality revolution. In real estate, it is the difference between seller's agent and buyer's agent.

Sellers' agents have a fiduciary obligation to their clients (sellers) to steer buyers into properties under exclusive contract, a privilege their owners purchased by granting exclusive rights. When an agent has appropriately disclosed him/herself to a buyer as a sellers' agent, that buyer should have no complaints about that agent not showing unlisted properties. Sometimes, a particular unlisted property might offer a faster or bigger commission than a co-broke share, tempting a sellers' agent to show it before exhausting all listed

Keeping the buyer in control

prospects — but an agent so casual about client obligations is not one either a buyer or seller should trust.

Purchase prospects should be unlimited

BUYERS' AGENTS are obligated to include in the property search any and all qualified properties, listed or
unlisted, on the market or not on the market. To do
that effectively, they must indeed have access to the
MLS, which is most likely the biggest single source of
prospective purchases; but that does not limit the
search to the listed properties nor give those priorities
any preference or priority. The priority is simply the
needs defined by the buyer.

It might be surprising that I have included homes
not on the market, but because a home has not been
offered for sale does not mean someone isn't willing to
sell it at the right price. A buyer may tell an agent they
want a home "like that one on top of Sawyer's hill."
The agent immediately knows where there is a home
exactly like it — on top of Sawyer's hill. If that's the
dream house, go for it!

There are two reasons you, as a potential buyer, may
not want to personally approach an owner of a property not offered for sale. The first is the personal discomfort inherently involved in the uncertainty, the
possibility of rejection, or of intruding on people for
something you might ultimately not want to buy. A
second reason is that the very act of coming forward
on an unoffered property indicates strong interest, giving some negotiating leverage to the owner. A buyers'
agent can remove some of the uncertainty through
records research on the house, would take on the dis-

comfort of the approach, protecting your anonymity, and avoid giving an impression of a "hooked" buyer.

The scope of the search through the buyers' agent should also not be limited to a narrow geographic area, except as specified by a buyer. Residential listing agents, except those specializing in unique property types (eg., large rental complexes, mansions) tend to concentrate in clusters of communities, as the only practical way to operate. A buyers' agent invested in the buyer, and perhaps expensing travel, may not be so limited. This is important because what the buyer seeks may be less location-specific than even the buyer realizes. A good buyers' agent will belong to at least one statewide MLS, subscribe to widespread publications which advertise homes, link to the Internet, and have available current local quality of life detail for the broadest possible range of communities. Subjects detailed will include economic conditions, schools, taxes, society, sports and health activities, health care, entertainment, youth organizations and amenities, shopping, public safety, government, proximity in time and miles to "wherever and whatever"....

The buyers' agent should have some catalog of all homes for sale outside the MLS, containing information gleaned on a daily basis from newspapers and other publications, the Internet, For-Sale signs, direct seller submissions, and other sources. The agency may actually participate in a FSBO registry or listing service and even assist sellers in the preparation of property profiles and descriptions for the agency use, provided there is no intimation of agency representation for the seller, and that the seller fully knows the agent is a buyers' agent.

Vulnerability of the relocating buyer

THE BUYER probably most in need of a buyers' agent is the one relocating from outside the area, and unaware of local factors like those just alluded to in the previous paragraph. Having left a four bedroom ranch which was sold for $190,000, a buyer may delight in now finding a similar home for $175,000 — without ever realizing the price is $25,000 over the local market price. Perhaps the local house-hunting began in one community because of proximity to the new job — without an understanding of local driving realities which make more suitable communities just as close in terms of travel time. Local sellers' agents probably won't be going out of their way to suggest that a community beyond their payoff range is a better fit for the buyer.

Beware the advertised "relocation specialist", a self-bestowed credential which, if touted by a sellers' agent, is a spin on the "we work with buyers" pitch and means *especially those buyers combining a pressing need to buy with a lack of local knowledge.* Remember that the most ethical sellers' agents, by virtue of their client responsibility as sales agents, are indeed "relocation specialists," i.e, specialists at relocating money from the buyers' wallets to those of seller and agent. Relocation needs are absolutely genuine, but they are buyers' needs and sellers' advantage! Professionals can serve those needs, or exploit them. Each approach is a simple matter of who is working for whom; the relocating buyer should be mindful of the differences between buying

"As relocation specialists, we are totally focused on your needs and circumstances, since you are newcomers to the area. Now, the first thing we have to do is take a look at your finances..."

and selling, between buyers' and sellers' agents, and of the ploys to downplay those differences.

Cultivating buyer awareness is fundamental to true buyer service. It is the sellers' agents' legitimate job to **sell** specific properties, and to steer buyers into them, limiting exposure of the buyer to competing options. The buyers' agent works in the opposite direction, pointing to all options, including the option of *not* buying, at least until the time is right according to the individual buyer's circumstance.

Some buyers, of course, are already fully aware of all needs and options, and do not need to be educated or have their consciousness raised in that regard. The

Buyer awareness: whose job is it?

problem is that, to work together effectively, both buyer
and agent really need to know that; thus, in the beginning, the full scope of needs and options must be
mutually questioned and explored. The truly professional agent, like the truly loyal employee, will indeed
question his boss' wisdom, provide new information,
and suggest alternative paths — and then follow directions. But the directions will be counterproductive if
both buyer and agent do not know where they are
leading, and that comes down to a very tangible element — the specific target of the property search.

The capable agent has a lot of information to provide, and some handy tools for sorting it all out. The
least technical buyers' agent has worked out some sort
of structured "Buyer Awareness Development" (BAD)
process (In this case, BAD is good). The best buyers'
agents will keep the BAD process dynamic throughout
the property search, something that should become
evident as we consider the following BAD phases:

BAD Phase I: Disclosure and More

This is the first half of the "getting-to-know-each-
other" stage of the buyer-agent relationship. Since the
cornerstone of successful buyer agency is *buyer* awareness, the agent goes first. Except for the usual amenities of greeting, and making sure the person is there
because of interest in property purchase (i.e., he/she
isn't looking for street directions), the agent should get
right to the **agency disclosure,** which is required in
some states, but not all. It might begin with a question
about what the buyer does know about real estate, as a

foundation for making the disclosure clear. In states with strong consumer protection laws and traditions, the buyer may be asked to sign a form containing the disclosure information and acknowledging that it has been explained. It is a legitimate request, with no obligations to the buyer, and merely evidences that the agent has done his/her duty.

There's more. Disclosure of the differences in definition and duty between types of agents is the beginning. The point of it all is that the buyer's eyes are open regarding the *entire* process (again, awareness is the name of the game). (If you have read this far into this book, you already have much of the "more" regarding the general use of agents.) Before the buyer starts revealing significant personal information, the agent should say more about the overall process, and describe the specific process in his/her agency for a "typical" buyer. The description should include visual display of the physical documents, materials, and equipment involved, and should certainly cover compensation.

Growing comfortable with the potential match of the agency's resources to his/her needs, the buyer can discuss those needs with the agent, particularly pointing to any variances from the "typical" or expected. The buyer should be aware of the context of the discussion, keeping two points in mind: (a) while the agent is a buyers' agent, during this stage, he/she is a *seller*, selling the agency service; and (b) everything is negotiable. The agent is human, and though facts may be presented from an honest perspective, it is nevertheless the *agent's* perspective. The buyer should go home with all materials, most especially the unsigned agency employment contract, mull things over, and be sure he/she is fully aware of the whole process, benefits, costs, and bail-out options before signing on. It is not so much to avoid being trapped in a bad deal (actually unlikely) but to establish that full awareness and perhaps improve the proposed agreement or understanding to ensure the best possible deal.

BAD Phase II: Profiling

Since I described Phase I as the "first half of the getting-to-know-each-other stage," and since Phase I was mostly about the buyer getting to know the agency, you might expect Phase II to be about the agent getting to know the buyer. You would be half right — it is not only about the agent getting to know the buyer, but about the *buyer* getting to know the buyer! There are usually subconscious notions of the worth of certain potential property features which have not been fully examined, especially by both members of a buying couple. So, the topic here is about raising buyer awareness of wants and needs, about bringing notions and predispositions of worth* to a conscious level for fully informed discernment and action. *Buyer* awareness is always what BAD is all about; we certainly want *agent* awareness too, so he/she can earn his/her money.

*See box, top of next page

Both sellers' agents and buyers' agents use a similar form, a "Profile Sheet," to record essential information about the buyer. After all, the phone number has to be written somewhere. So does other basic personal

Worth differs from **value.** *Worth* refers to the desirability or utility of something to you personally, and may be measured in money, or in comparison to quantifiable knowns, or simply described in unquantifiable terms such as "like," "dislike," "want," "love." *Value* relates to what something can command on the market — usually in dollars.

information regarding financial purchase capability and basic property features (eg, preferred locations, number of rooms, yard size, general house style). However, needs go far deeper and are more complex than reflected on the traditional profile sheet. Over the years, traditional agents have been so misled into "wasting time" showing the wrong properties that they often caution new agents with the catch phrase, "buyers are liars."

The traditional form contains the common-sense categories of contact information, financial information, and buyer need information — usually all on one piece of paper. But the form developed in traditional seller's' agency is really a *sales-prospect* profile, rather than a true *buyer's need* profile; it is geared to making a sale, i.e., to fulfilling *sellers'* needs for relocating buyers' money.

Since buying differs from selling, buyerside and sellerside profile sheets reflect different objectives. The sellerside sheet is legitimately targeted toward finding an *acceptable* house (a sale), for that is the sum and substance of what is owed to the clients (the sellers). The buyerside objective is not a *sale*, and not even the purchase of an "acceptable" property, but the *best pos-*

sible match to the buyer's needs — i.e., the greatest **worth** to the buyer — again reflecting what is owed to the clients (the buyers). Consequently, a buyers' agent's profile of buyer's need should reflect far more depth than the sellerside counterpart; and the form to record it should provide more space than just what's left on a single sheet after contact and financial information.

Detail about what each family member will individually gain or lose from each potential property feature — i.e., the personal *worth* of each feature to them — should be explored by the buyers with the agent as a guide.   Rather than pose questions which assume known answers, the form should provide a checklist of life-quality issues aimed at helping the buyer consider and understand what they really seek in a given property attribute. For example, instead of asking buyers to list their preferred communities, or even to ask what type of communities they prefer, one might encourage more reliable responses by calling for discussion of the following issues (among others):

- ties to family, friends, job, organizations, and activities which have bearing on proximity to a particular location in terms of time and distance;

- aspects of the buyer or buyer's family which could benefit from certain amenities in any given area such as churches, fraternal and civic organizations, a nearby golf club, youth athletic leagues, academic resources, theater, active night life....

There are other issues regarding this one matter of location, and whole aggregates of issues around aspects of property from the style of kitchen to social entertainment areas that a buying couple may never have discussed with each other, let alone reveal to an agent without inducement. But when they come to stand in the wrong style kitchen, or even the right kitchen in the wrong community, the issue comes to bear. There, standing in the home they've described on the traditional profile sheet, they realize it is not *worth* considering. No wonder frustrated agents relying on the inadequate traditional sales-prospect profile come to the belief that buyers are liars!

The problem is that the traditional approach, using the traditional form, is to profile the *buyer*, rather than the things that are meaningful in the buyer's decision making. To say the traditional form legitimately evolved in the sellers' interest is not to say that it did a good job of actually *serving* sellers' interests. Outside real estate, the defining lesson of the quality revolution has been the importance of specifying exactly what the customer wants — inherent in the revolutionary definition of **quality**. It is shortsighted to think that effective selling can happen without full understanding of the reasons for buying. Put another way, you cannot effectively sell if you don't know what makes your merchandise *worth* buying. It makes even less sense to think that an effective search in the *buyer's* best interest can take place if even the buyers don't have a clear idea of what various property features are worth to them. Profiling is all about helping buyers map out the relative worth to themselves (and each other in the case of a buying couple) of various features of property. It is not so much to give the agent a profile of the buyer as it is *to give the buyer a profile of the complex maze of relative worth* for any number of possible configurations of features and required tradeoffs.

BAD Phase III: Developing Buyer Perspective of Value

Contrary to traditionalist fiction, the market value of property is not set by owners, tax assessors, banks and other lenders, real estate agents, or even by professional appraisers. It is established exclusively by buyers. Simply put, "value" is the ability of an item (here, real estate) to command a price (here, in dollars). An owner can *de*mand, but never *com*mand a price, as evidenced by properties sitting unsold on the market until the price drops to a point a buyer cannot resist.

Tax assessors, real estate agents, and appraisers make *estimates* of value, specifically, market value; i.e., the price they believe a property will *likely* command among *informed* buyers in the market. What the property will command is a function of one thing, and one thing only: the perspective of buyers regarding what they would have to pay for a competing property of equal worth to them.

It is important to not confuse **"value"** (as used here) with what a property is **"worth"** to either buyer or seller. If property is worth more to an owner than what it commands on the market, then he/she won't sell it. A buyer may fully acknowledge that a property's market value is $250,000, that the seller will indeed find other buyers at that price, but also decide it is not *personally* worth it to spend that much — especially if another property worth as much to the buyer is selling for less. Worth and value are linked: value is the dollar level at which, under normal circumstances and within normal market time, purchase will be worth it to *some* informed buyer.

There are situations that are not "normal," i.e., when a property may sell above or below market value. An obvious case would be one involving an *uninformed* buyer or seller. A FSBO may move within hours of coming on the market because a naive owner priced it well below value. Something priced over value could be bought by a buyer relocating from a high-priced market with no local market knowledge. Sometimes an informed seller "dumps" a property below value because it is simply worth it for personal reasons. An informed buyer may see some personal opportunity in buying above the market value — perhaps a way to raise the value, once acquired. Regardless, sales under other-than-normal conditions, or involving uninformed buyers or sellers, do not indicate market value.

In a given negotiation, sale price is a function of one thing only — the *buyer's perspective* on worth and on value. The seller has two strategies:

(a) find a price low enough to conform to the buyer's perspective, or

(b) try to influence that perspective.

Strategy (b) can be done honestly, making a buyer aware of legitimate facts and circumstances that were depressing perceived value or worth. In the case of a fully-informed buyer, the seller could well be the one to be made aware and realize that strategy (a) is the appropriate choice. An informed buyer, aware of both worth and market value, will either make the fair offer in the first place, or accept a fair counter offer from an informed seller. Ideally, a property will be put on the market when worth to the seller is below value, a purchase offer will be made when worth to the buyer is above value, and final purchase price will be right at value — a net gain to both seller and buyer. This is the **ideal deal,** with the highest probability of happening when both seller and buyer fully are aware of market value and what it is worth to them. An other-than-ideal deal is most likely to occur in the absence of consumer awareness, resulting in a good deal for one side, perhaps even a *great deal* — but at the expense of the other ("other" generally being the side most short on awareness).

What might seem to be a chance on one side to exploit unawareness on the other, may be less of an opportunity than either side sometimes thinks. Except in the case of brand new or relocating buyers without the protection of a buyers' agent, buyers do not stay unaware of market value long. An overpriced house will simply not sell to buyers who have been shopping and have seen the competition. Unaware sellers seldom create advantage for the buyers because the unaware seller usually overprices his/her house. The *aware seller* puts a house on the market at market value, above what it is worth to him/her; and the *aware buyer* knows that it is priced at fair value and below its worth to him/her. They come to the table ready to do business, without having spent months looking for someone to exploit, or having to deal with would-be exploiters.

Thus, both buyer and seller are generally served by awareness even on the part of the other, at least in terms of the other's realistic approach to value. The good news is that with the move of customer quality philosophy into real estate, the traditional resistances to such mutual awareness are inevitably doomed. However, the customer awareness reforms that are part and parcel of buyer brokerage by definition, may be slower in coming to seller service due to the deeper hold there of traditional practices and practitioners.

FOR EXAMPLE, consider how a seller might develop perspective on his/her property's value:

Developing value perspective

(a) Decide the value him/herself, using anything from wishful thinking through real knowledge and rigorous research, running the risk of underestimation of personal bias and overestimation of technical ability;

(b) Rely on the listing agent to do a **"competitive market analysis"** (CMA), a standard agent service which compares the property to comparable others in the current market. This runs the risks of underestimation of the bias of traditional business interests already described, and of overestimation of technical abilities not guaranteed by an agent's license.

(c) Hire a professional appraiser, technically trained and certified in the business of doing what he/she is being hired to do, and without a financial interest vested in the dollar outcome of the appraisal.

Option 'c' is by far the more reliable choice, but probably the least used on the selling side. Professional appraisals just don't fit into traditionalist strategy for landing listings, which either requires catering to the owner's price demand (a) or offering a CMA (b) as one of the agency's "benefits" to the seller.

Worst option is the most used

THE *LOGIC* OF A CMA is sound, basically involving comparison of the subject property to a handful of similar properties on the market (the **"comparables"** or **"comps"**) and pricing it accordingly. In actual practice, the process is highly flawed and fraught with the possibility of bias and error, being performed by people with a personal interest in the outcome of their "measures" and who may be inadequately trained, prepared, or supervised. At its worst, the supervison's very purpose may be to ensure that the CMA produces the dollar value desired in the *agency's* business interest.*

*See above, pages 46–53

The comps themselves may be unrealistically priced and selected precisely because they support the price the agent thinks the seller wants to hear. To prevent this in my agency, I required agents to include *three* distinct sets of comps: currently *For-Sale* properties, recently *sold* properties, and properties which *failed to sell.* The last category included those taken off the market and those reduced in price, indicating unrealistic price levels. However, even these precautions were flawed, for some properties do get sold above market level, and identifying ridiculously-high prices doesn't say at what level they become reasonable. Then, there is the question of just how genuine a match the comps are to the subject property. Location cannot be the same, neighborhoods and communities differ, as do the features and conditions within homes — complications compounded by insufficient checks on agent and agency competency and bias. The bottom line is that CMAS can be performed badly, or, consciously or subconsciously, to support a predetermined value rather than a reliable objective estimate. The credibility of a CMA-established value is revealed at mortgage application time when the lender, at the buyer's expense, sends out an *appraiser.*

All this is not to say that a competent unbiased CMA cannot arrive at a reasonable estimate of value. It is to say that the structure of traditional real estate dynamics removes all guarantee of a competent unbiased CMA on the sellerside of the market — i.e., it cannot be trusted. However, the basic concepts of the CMA process have legitimate application on the buyerside. A sellerside CMA is an estimate of the collective buyer perception of value and of where a particular piece of property fits in that aggregate. Its fundamental weakness lies in the specific property interest. However, when CMA is applied to establishing general comps *without a specif-*

ic subject property — i.e., without the undermining special interest — the comps become reliable reference points for buyers to use in their personal assessment of property.

Buyer Market Analysis proposed

A BUYER IS FAR MORE DISPOSED than a seller to rigorously compare properties, so while a sellerside CMA is solely an agent task, property comparison on the buyerside is primarily a client task. The buyer's agent is certainly involved, but more as a guide, and active client involvement greatly reduces both opportunity for and effect of unobserved agent bias or error. With this source of bias and error neutralized, CMA theory provides a basis for a method of **"Buyer Market Analysis"** (BMA) which should more efficiently organize the property comparisons buyers inevitably make.

As observed earlier, buyers do not stay unaware of market value long, but it is often in that period of unawareness that the risk of bad decisions is high. The standard precaution is to resolve to *not* buy any property early in the househunting, i.e., to get out and look at houses until there is a solid understanding of value and of the process. But the "right" house can come along in that period; and — right house or wrong house — there is also a convincing seller's agent who knows how to convert "lookers" into buyers. Fortunately, double protection is available in the form of a buyers' agent and the buyer's own value gauge developed through BMA.

A buyers' agent should maintain a "base list" of current comps for standard type houses in the areas he/she serves, cultivating and updating the list at least weekly. The buyers' agency might even engage services of a certified appraiser in the maintenance of this base list. The list should contain two types of properties:

- **"Anchors"** which are actual properties in actual locations, fully documented with accurate measures and photographs;

- **"Variants"** which are variations of the anchors, with features added or subtracted (eg., dormers on a Cape), with adjusted values.

"Location factors" can be developed to show the differences in value for a specific property if it were set in different neighborhoods and communities. (See box, below.) Thus for any buyer, a set of comps should be available which applies to his/her price range and can be mathematically adjusted to the locales he/she visits.

With properties provided by the agent from the base list, each buyer should develop a "value stack" — a list of properties arranged in order of increasing value. Properties being considered for purchase (**"object**

> I f identical ranch houses in neighborhoods A and B are worth, respectively, $100,000 and 125,000, and that difference holds for other identical properties, then the value of any B property can be estimated to be 125 percent of the known value of a similar A property. Likewise, the value of any A property can be estimated to be 80 percent of the known value of a similar B property.

properties") can be slipped between property pairs of lower and higher value. This is where worth and value can come together, in the mind actually being faced with the purchase decision, even to fine-tuning the exact position of object property between the two **"flanking properties"**

The purpose of the BMA system is to provide buyers with a value perspective that is more organized than the one carried inside their heads and more trustworthy than the one being *sold* by the sellers' agents. It is a perspective needed in the search, and certainly before making an offer, but not intended as a substitute for the final formal appraisal upon which actual purchase should be conditioned (see below, Chapter 10).

"Drive-bys"

BUYERS' AGENTS do something that was unheard-of in traditional agencies, i.e., they encourage buyers to go out on their own, *without being accompanied by an agent*, and scout out prospective properties. It is common to provide the buyers with a list of **"drive-bys"** — homes in the right price range and locations, *loosely* meeting the buyer's described wants and needs — for the buyers to literally drive by and look over. It is then up to the buyers to tell the agent which houses they'd like to see up close.

This drive-by system helps the buyers develop their personal sense of property worth and value, without contamination by agent bias. It ultimately focuses in on the right house from among the broadest possible array of choices. It even serves sellers and their agents by taking up their time only for properties in which there is some real interest. The buyers' agent can afford to "turn his clients loose" in the world, because they are under agreement. Traditional agents will accompany buyers, calling it "buyer service"; but shielding them from hungry competitors is the primary motive.

Escorting buyers takes time, and time is money for both a buyers' agent and a sellers' agent. The sellers' agent's only way to reduce costs is to *sell* the buyers something, and quickly. That means reducing the time-consuming options, avoiding routes that show the drawbacks of locations, and "cutting losses" by dropping fussy buyers.* The *buyers'* agent's time is paid for   *Above, pages
by the buyers, so it is in their interests to reduce the   65–66
"escort service." Even for those agents who do not charge directly for time, time costs must nevertheless factor into the establishment of their fees. So the drive-by system serves buyers by cutting costs as well as broadening options and honing their value perspective.

BAD Phase IV: Tailoring

There is a tendency among both buyers' and sellers' agents to "get the paper work out of the way" early, then get on with the "real work". Thus, the buyers' perspective at the beginning of the whole process may be carefully explored and documented, but be neglected as it changes with evolving awareness. On the seller-side, time and change is the enemy; and the "real work" is to sell a house before minds change. On the buyer-side, the real work is to match a property with the buyers' needs on the day they take title, not on the day they walked into the office. Time is on the buyers' side. The buyers' agency system must "go with the flow" of time and change; its "paper work" is not something to get out of the way, but to keep current with the changing awareness, perspective, and needs of the buyers.

Essentially, that means that the Buyer's Profile and value stack must be examined regularly, as a part of the schedule of activity determined between buyer and agent. As in the original profile development, that does not mean simply going down the list of desired features and asking if they still matter, but *revisiting the issues* behind those feature choices.

Buying logically rather than emotionally

THE BAD PROCESS, as formulated here, deals with awareness of general things like worth, value, and market dynamics. That creates the framework against which a *prospective purchase* is judged. These words are italicized to emphasize a difference between traditional brokerage and buyer brokerage, for a "prospect" in traditional brokerage is the *buyer*, and not the house. But, it is the buyer who is making the critical decision at this point; and it is the house which must meet the qualifying standards of the buyer, and according to the buyer's logic. Yes, I said, *"logic!"* Consider the traditionalist approach to the buyers' decision process as reflected upon by one of the gurus of traditional real estate sales people, Tom Hopkins, in his best-seller, *How to Master the Art of* LISTING & SELLING *Real Estate:*[10]

*Prentice-Hall.
New Jersey: 1991.
Page 6.

**People don't buy logically.
They buy emotionally.** *

Hopkins goes on to advise his sales agent disciples not to try to convince their "prospects" logically.

Wise buyers will recognize that Hopkins is probably right in his observations and that, even allowing for an occasional logical buyer, the advice to *sales* agents about buyers in general is not only right, but proper. *After all, that is what sales people do — they* **sell** *things, and if they didn't know what aspects of their prospects to appeal to, they would be misrepresenting themselves as sellers' agents to their clients.*

There is a difference, however, between the buyers Hopkins wrote about (in the 1991 but still-current best seller) and those accompanied today by a *purchasing* agent. Hopkins is a brilliant sales trainer with all the answers to the question of how to sell. But buyers' agents change the question to how to *buy!* The Quality Revolution replaces the old ideas about pandering to a buyer's emotions with respect for the new aware buyer's definition of **quality**. The prospect becomes the house, and not the buyer. If it is the right house, according to the buyer's *logic*, it will be *bought and not sold*.

In terms of what a buyers' agent does, he/she is not a sales agent, but a purchasing agent. In all states, real estate agents are licensed as "salespersons", or "salesmen" if political correctness hasn't caught up with the terminology. What the legislative terminology really needs is a shot of *operational* correctness; for true buyers' agents not only do not sell, sometimes it is their function to actually *stop* the sale!

The purchase approach

THE CONCEPT of **due diligence** requires agents to aggressively and proactively root out anything indicating a possibility of their clients getting something different than they expect from a deal.   Since a seller is usually expecting one very straightforward thing — money — this task isn't especially tough for a seller's agent: make sure the check is good and in the right amount. By contrast, a good buyers' agent will poke at beams, read boiler inspection tags, verify measurements, watch for water marks, examine floor plans and survey reports, check out the neighborhood (perhaps a "Megan's Law"* inquiry at the police department) and, for condominiums, research the quality of management. *After all, that's what purchasing agents do — they help **buy** the right things, and if they didn't know what aspects of the prospective purchases to investigate, they would be misrepresenting themselves as buyer agents to their clients.*

* see box, next page

B3. Acquisition

Once an acceptable property is located, the process of acquisition involves two general steps:

- a meeting of the minds of buyer and seller, set in writing, regarding the price and particulars of the property transfer;

- the actual passing of title to and possession of the property, payment or settlement of all acquisition costs, and entry of the transaction and related documents in the legal records.

egan's Law is the law in some states requiring convicted sex offenders to register addresses with police. Some jurisdictions may make the information available only at the request of a current neighborhood resident or owner. In such cases, if it is an issue to the buyer, the offer might require the seller to inquire.

The first of these is the most critical. The agreement/contract determines what is supposed to happen at the passing of title and payment. Problems can still happen, but a properly prepared and valid agreement will not only go far to avoid them but provide recourse when they do occur.

All real estate agreements must be in writing to be legally binding. A buyer and seller can come together verbally, negotiating back and forth before setting it all down in writing. My wife and I sold our first house that way. We priced it right at market value and put an ad in the paper. A couple dropped by, and offered the full price, which we accepted. The next day, we met before a lawyer who wrote up the agreement between us, without either couple trying to "nickel-dime" the other.

All the things that could have gone wrong did not go wrong. Two couples who had never met trusted each other. The buyers had no problem in getting a fast mortgage, and both the house and neighborhood were just as we said they'd be. The lawyer, who we hardly knew, was honest and competent and, given the simplicity of the deal, reduced his rate.

Sometimes it happens. Sometimes it doesn't. In the years since, I have seen the times when it does not, and

I know how very lucky we were. Considering both the amount of money involved and the overall complexity, there are just too many ways in which even the most well-intentioned people can run afoul of one another. And then there are those who are not so well-intentioned....

Offer and acceptance process

THIS IS ONE PROBLEM where the solution developed in traditional real estate is not only conceptually and fundamentally sound, but fair to both buyer and seller:

- It begins with the buyer submitting a *written offer to purchase* which details what the buyer wants in price and terms. The offer form includes a place for the seller's signature in acceptance *in all its particulars*, and that makes the document a binding contract between the two parties.

- If the seller "accepts" it, but with any changes at all, it actually becomes a *counter-offer* from the seller to the buyer. Then, it is up to the buyer to reject or accept, or accept with changes. Again, any changes create a new counter-offer, setting-up another cycle. At any point where one accepts the offer of the other *in all particulars*, it becomes a binding contract.

- Often, the same document does not travel back and forth through a series of counter-offers loaded with changes and changes to the changes. Rather than counter-offer on the original form, the buyer will often write a new offer closer to what the seller might accept.

Usually, the person making the offer or counter-offer is not present when the other receives it, at least not when agents are involved. The agents act as the couriers. All things being equal, with each client having their own agent to explain what's before them, neither party should have to worry about misinterpretation on the other side. Of course, all things are *not* equal if only one of the two parties has a true agent; and it is, of course, *inexcusably unequal* when one side's imagined "agent" is actually an agent or subagent of the other side.

The myth of 'negotiation'

THE BENEFIT TO EACH PARTY is that each, writing or reading, has the opportunity to consider the exact words of the proposed agreement without deliberate or inadvertent distractions caused by the other's presence. They can step aside even from their own agent to go over the document, or to consult an attorney or other advisors. The decision can thus be based on known elements, without side pressures. Everything is as clear as possible, and it is relatively painless. Ironically, what has been removed from the equation is one thing agents on both sides will cite as a reason for hiring them — i.e., *negotiation,* as "negotiation" is generally understood.

What people think of as "negotiation" — face-to-face confrontation, involving point and counterpoint, balancing pressure and comforting reassurance, word-artistry blending logical and emotional manipulation — is simply not present. That is as it should be, for such negotiation does no more than obscure facts and obstruct *informed* decision-making. It has no place in transactions where people are investing so much of their lives. Under normal circumstances, both buyer and seller are served by simply being able to consider an offer (or counter-offer) away from the influence of counterposed or masquerading third-party interests. Such a favorably enabling environment is most assured when both seller and buyer are competently and ethically represented by their own agents specializing in articulate *presentation*, rather than the "negotiation" often implied. At times, bargaining is necessary, the on-the-spot trading of concessions.

Pitfalls in standard offer forms

NEEDED FAR MORE than "negotiation skills" is the ability to detect and maneuver among the traps and snares lurking in the language of standard forms and phrases originating in traditional real estate. Consider that the originating system was so oblivious to buyers' needs that it openly declared as a matter of "virtue" that every agent in it represented sellers. Consider that this system was so much in the control of sellers' agents that the standard offer allegedly from the buyer requires that the sellers' agent gets paid for getting the buyer to offer the most while demanding the least. How can anyone imagine that a system so totally one-sided in favor of sellers, and so totally controlled by seller's agents, would produce an offer form written in the buyer's interest? And why would reasonable buyers expect sellers' agents to violate their client responsibility by helping the buyer negotiate around the clauses and phrases giving advantage to the seller?

The problem is not reserved exclusively for buyers putting themselves at the mercy of sellers' agents; buyer brokerage evolved from traditional brokerage, and many of the more subtly biased conventions — in forms,* phrases, concepts, even attitudes — continue on in buyer agency, sometimes escaping detection even by buyer agents.

*Already discussed above regarding Profile Sheets on pages 118–121.

It gets even more complex, compounded by the fact that the agents themselves see an opportunity to protect, even serve, their own interests via these documents....

THE ROOT OF CONTINUING PROBLEMS is an *attitude* that the offer is an instrument of real estate brokerage, i.e., one of the forms that makes the business work. What that attitude misses is that the offer is *not an instrument,* and it is *not a form!* The offer is an *act of the buyer!* It is an *expression of the buyer's will* which should be fully and accurately reflected in the paper and ink that comprise the document. The form (i.e., the words) may properly serve legitimate secondary purposes (with the fully informed consent of the buyer), but its primary purpose is to communicate the offer. It is incumbent on the agents to remember whose offer it is!

What an offer is, and whose it is

If you look up "offer" in the Glossary of this text, you will not find the definition there. Instead, you will find a reference to the "*buyer's* offer to purchase." The definition has been placed under that entry because it is too easy to think of the offer as a piece of paper, something separate from the buyer. Then, when agents consider how the paper can address *their* concerns, they literally begin to forget whose offer it is and what it is all about.

The primary function of an offer is, of course, to establish the buyer's side of an agreement, but there are strategic reasons why a buyer would put things in the offer that cater to interests of others, specifically the seller, and any agents involved. Obviously, the offer is worthless if the seller won't sign it; so, along with an offered price, the buyer will make certain covenants as seller inducements. Also, both in fairness, and because there is still work the buyer and seller want the agents to do, the offer may often include acknowledgment of the agents' roles and what they are owed, and make payment part of the proposed transaction.

Such strategic catering to seller and agent interests in the buyer's offer is simply common sense because it serves the buyer's interest to do so. But, here's the rub: that common sense acceptance of a legitimate rationale provides an excuse for not looking deeper into whether or not the buyer's interest really is the beneficiary.

Reshaping forms and processes in the buyer's interest

THE ESSENCE OF the **customer quality revolution** is a refocusing on procedure from the customer's perspective, away from the standpoint of the needs or existing procedures of the business. Taking on the mantel of buyer agency, however sincerely, is not a full revolution until the procedures (including the forms) are built according to the buyer's perspective *from the ground up*. It is not enough to merely reshape instruments conceived in the interests of everyone but the buyer.

A major point should be made here. The traditional instruments evolved in an unfairly one-sided system.
They provide no justification for the same kind of
unfairness in documents now originating on the buyerside. These new documents are coming into being in
a balanced system, with professional representation on
both sides; the sellers are not defenseless as were the
buyers under the old order. The tables have not been
turned, giving the buyers the advantage once held by
sellers; rather, the playing field has been made level.
The old-order instruments were conceived in the interests of *everyone but the buyer;* the new-order instruments will be in the interests of *everyone.*

My entrance into professional real estate back in the
seventies was not as an agent, but as a buyer and devel-
oper of investment properties (apartment complexes).
The purchase offers used by my partner and me were
business proposals — i.e., tools of *our* business, not the
business of sellers or their agents — and we created our
own. In that sense, we were no different than other
investment buyers. A long-time agent thanked us for
one thing in our standard offer that was not generally
in other non-agent-originated forms; ours stated for
the record the name of the agent who had brought the
property to our attention. The point being made here
is that any such considerations in a buyer's proposal are
by the grace of the buyer and *not the right of the agent!*
This point is not altered by the fact that a buyers' agent
may acquire that right as a covenant of the buyer
agency employment contract — it is still a right grant-
ed by the buyer.

Agents knowing their place

IN A CONVENTIONAL HOME SALE, the buyer can at least see the agent-protective covenants in the standard offer form before he/she signs it (too often not seeing the document until the last moments). In itself, and done properly, it is not unreasonable to provide such covenants in the standard form and to expect the buyer to willingly allow that. The problem is underscored here by the word, "allow", i.e., the evolved attitudes of agents that they somehow have possessive rights over what is included in the buyer's offer. Some standard forms even make the agents *signatories* of the offer and ensuing purchase and sale agreements with apparent equal status with buyers and sellers. Other standard forms provide for agents to sign as witnesses, something at risk of legal challenge due to their obvious personal interest in the outcome. In short, agents have lost sight of their place, and more importantly, the buyer's place.

Agent intrusions on buyers' rights

NOT KNOWING THEIR PLACE in the minor matter of if and where their name appears in the offer, agents move on to major error, assuming rights that are plain intrusions upon the rights of the buyer. The insidiousness of the displaced focus is exemplified in its surfacing in what is normally a bedrock of appropriateness, the Realtors'® Code of Ethics. Consider Standard of Practice 16-16:

> Realtors®, acting as subagents or buyer/tenant agents, shall not use the terms of an offer to purchase/lease to attempt to modify the listing broker's offer of compensation to subagents or buyer's agents nor make the submission of an executed offer to purchase/lease contingent on

the listing broker's agreement to modify the offer of compensation. (Amended 1/93)

In actuality, agents shall not use the terms of an offer for *anything,* since it is *not their offer to use.* One might defend Standard 16-16 by claiming it really is a restriction against improper *influence* by the agent upon the offer, but that is just not true. There is no explicit or implicit mention or indication of "influence." The clear presumption is that the offer is an instrument of the agent.

THE OTHER MISBEGOTTEN PRESUMPTION of 16-16 is that there is something not only legitimate, but worthy of protection, about a payoff from a seller's agent to a buyer's agent. It is perfectly appropriate for the buyer's payment to his/her agent to pass through any **conduit** the participants agree upon, including the listing broker, and to be in any amount the buyer and buyer's agent agree upon. That is the obvious intention of any buyer passing money to the seller with a direction to give some of it to the buyer's agent. Any language indicating compensation "from" the listing agent usually comes either from a standard offer form created by listing agents or from a naive buyers' agent trying to work within local compensation customs enforced by listing agents.* Ironically, 16-16 purports to be about preventing one Realtor® from interfering in the agency of another; and, yet, it is itself a tool for the listing agent to throw a monkey wrench into the buyer-agency payment agreement which usually predates any contact between the buyer and the seller.

Listing agent interference in buyer agent compensation

*Above, page 88

Listing agent limiting seller awareness

PERHAPS THE MOST OFFENSIVE THING about 16-16 is that it supports the seller's agent in limiting the seller's awareness of options. The buyer's offer is, in fact, only an offer. The seller is free to reject it. However, the buyer's offer is also a source of *information* about brokerage possibilities the listing agent perhaps did not reveal to the owner at the time of the listing agreement.

Most importantly, it is the *buyer's* offer. The buyer is not bound by the listing agreement which he/she did not sign, nor by 16-16. The buyer is, after all, the employer of his/her agent, and the buyer's money will pay both seller and all agents. It is appropriate here to recall the principle cited earlier*:

*P. 85

He/she who does the hiring and pays the wages calls the shots.

Buyer notice of agent status and roles

THIS IS THE PLACE for the first shots of the customer revolution. The following clause in an offer represents one way to apply mortgage money toward the buyer agent fee, using as a conduit either principal, seller's agent, or even "the transaction" (explanation to follow). It clarifies and protects the buyer's relationship as employer of the buyer's agent and sole definer of his/her responsibilities. Finally, it serves notice about something else the seller has a right to know, and buyer has a right to communicate, i.e., the facts about "procuring cause". These facts are necessary to insure that seller can see the straightforward fairness in the buyer's offer.

Be it herewith known that beyond publishing the availability of Seller's property, all brokerage assistance and guidance to Buyer normally associated with "procuring cause" was provided by an agent of Buyer, employed by Buyer, whose brokerage fee has been determined in prior contractual agreement with Buyer, and whose compensation is provided by Buyer in the offered purchase price. Inclusion of buyer-agent compensation in the offered purchase price is consistent with conventional practice, specifically the convention that market value encompasses the cost of brokerage and agency services on both selling and buying sides of the transaction (reflected in standard listing agreements). *Accordingly, it is a condition of this offer that the transaction encompassing acceptance of title and conveyance of purchase monies will not take place without payment in the amount of $_____ from the purchase price to [buyer or buyer's agent] for payment of brokerage services to and in the employ of Buyer.* Buyer's employment agreement with Buyer's agent precludes said agent from accepting or participating in any commission or fee structure set by any agreement to which Buyer was not a party, including Seller's employment agreement with Seller's agent.

This wording allows the buyer agent fee payment to take any route (any conduit) through seller, seller's agent, and/or buyer — or through *none* of these with the buyer agent simply being written a check from "the transaction", signed by the administrator of the transaction/conveyance proceedings. This wording would also allow for the buyer to receive the subject payment and, in turn, either make payment to the agent or *keep* if payment has already been made in the form of a pre-paid retainer.

Clearly, this latter method (payment to or through the buyer) is more consistent with the employment structure and fiduciary responsibilities of buyer representation. The other alternatives — payment from "the transaction" or from the seller — are needed because *lending institutions* are saddled with their own traditions which may not have kept pace with consumer reform. At the time of this writing, most of these will balk at cash to the buyer, and some (perhaps goaded by seller agents) will shy away from the transaction payment. When such lender restrictions apply in a given circumstance, the seller conduit is a less suitable but still workable approach (but the clear statement of agency employment obligations is all the more important).

Lending institutions are legitimately concerned with the value of the loan collateral (the property), but the restrictions are based in confusion about the effects of buyer agent compensation methods on value. One error is the formula approach dictating that value is the price paid, less any cash back to the seller; the second and major error is the fear that buyers will be tempted to offer prices inflated above market value when the excess funds are funneled back into their own pockets. Both cases fail to account for the buyer's *cash outlay to the buyer's agent*, cancelling out the cash back in the formula and the "excess" in the temptation scenario. The fact is that cash for the buyerside fee exists in the long established traditional method embraced by the same institutions. If neither effect upon value nor inflation opportunity exists there, then these things don't suddenly materialize because the fee now passes through the buyer's hands, nor do they occur when the buyer is rebated an amount verified as a prepaid agent retainer.

An enlightened local lender may in fact be fully willing to pay the buyer agent directly, or rebate to the buyer, but still must acquiesce to the regulations of **"secondary market"** institutions which will purchase the loan from this **"primary market"** lender. The secondary market is insulated from the loan customer by the primary market, and thus will be slower to respond to customer demanded reforms.

Nevertheless, reform is inevitable, beginning with enlightened primary market lenders who recognize that a significant change is taking place in their long - time source of customers. Their customers, after all, are *buyers, not sellers,* and the appearance of buyer agents means a decline — if not the disappearance — of seller agents as a source of buyer customers.

When agent compensation is to be made on either side by the respective principal, there is nothing intrinsic in the essence or purpose of an offer that necessitates naming the agent; that is a convention coming from traditional agency in the interests of agents. Separate written agreements between agents and clients on both sides can give the agents all the commission protection needed. It is the buyer's offer; and it is the seller's choice to accept it or reject it. It is an affair of the **principals** and not their employees. Keeping the roles clear makes it smoother for everyone, agents included.

Offer as the statement of buyer specifications

THIS BOOK is about the impact of the customer quality revolution on traditional real estate operations, with **"quality"** defined as conformance to customer specifications. Of course, that is exactly what the buyer's offer is, an explicit statement of the buyer's specifications. Thus, fundamental errors about definition and purpose of the offer, and about the related roles of agents needed to be addressed. At this point we're ready to look at some examples of concrete issues between buyer and seller with respect to the offer.

The offer will, of course, include a price for the owner and some timeline within which the money and the property will change hands. One of the requirements of a **valid** contract is that each of the parties surrender something of value in **"consideration"** of the other's signing. The buyer's consideration will be a money deposit to be held in escrow as insurance for the seller against buyer default, and either returned to the buyer or applied to the purchase price at closing *(see box below)*. The seller's consideration is taking the house off the market and passing up chances for better offers. Seller default is automatically insured against by the ability of the courts to force performance if the seller tries to back out.

Some unknowns usually exist when the agreement is first made; the house may not be all that it is pictured or represented to be, and financing may not be as avail-

This deposit is also referred to as a "binder," "earnest money," or "deposit." What the buyer has surrendered to meet the consideration requirement is the use of the money while it is being held.

able as believed. Thus, the offer will generally include some no-default escape clauses giving the buyer a brief time-period in which to secure financing and have the house professionally inspected. If the buyer cannot obtain financing during this period, the deal is terminated; if serious problems are discovered in the property inspection, the buyer has the option to terminate. There being no default under these conditions, the buyer's deposit is returned, and the legal positions of both buyer and seller are restored to what they were just before the agreement.

The financing escape clause in a typical traditional standard offer form might be as follows:

> Sale is subject to Buyer obtaining a commitment for a ___Conventional, ___VA, ___FHA, mortgage in the amount of $\$$_____ no later than _____. Buyer shall apply for financing within 7 days of acceptance of this offer.

By comparison, this is a version which might develop from buyer agency:

> Sale is subject to Buyer obtaining a commitment for a   mortgage in the amount of $\$$_____ no later than _____, and not to exceed an annual interest rate of _____% . Revocation of mortgage commitment for reasons not caused by Buyer shall not be construed as Buyer default.

It might well be that, for strategic reasons the buyer might actually want to specify the type of mortgage, but then finding a different but still attractive financing package would give the seller the option to back out. The seven-day application requirement may be reasonable, and the buyer may willingly offer it as a seller inducement; however, putting this in a standard form makes it an obligation and not an option for, practically speaking, the buyer cannot really cross this one out, or change it to, say, fourteen days.

The most obvious differences though, are in the interest rate ceiling and the commitment-revocation instance of the second version. A sudden upturn in interest rates could send monthly mortgage payments beyond a buyer's ability to pay while literally dropping property values. There is a ceiling above which both buyer and seller would agree is unreasonable.

Regarding the commitment revocation, it does occasionally happen. Bank mergers, administrative changes, and failings, or even a job layoff could lead a bank to back out of its mortgage commitment, leaving the buyer out in the cold without the house and without his/her earnest money deposit. One might argue by noting that it's not the seller's fault either — *but this is the buyer's offer!* Moreover, in such rare circumstance, the seller would still have the house, and the buyer may have only that deposit money.

It's relatively unimportant which party bears transaction costs

ONE VERY CLEAR DIFFERENCE that will appear between offer forms developed by sellers' agents and buyers' agents is in the matter of transaction costs being borne by either buyer or seller, or shared between them. At first look, it might appear that the preference on each side would be to have the other side bear the cost. That loses sight of two fundamental truths:

- the value of a property is the amount of money it commands for the right to have it;

	10 Crest Drive	306 King Road
Price	$210,000	$212,000
Buyer Fees	$10,000	$5,000
True Value	$220,000	$217,000
Seller Fees	$6,000	0
Seller's Net	$204,000	$212,000

Table A

Table B

	10 Crest Drive	306 King Road
Price	$204,000	$217,000
Buyer Fees	$16,000	0
True Value	$220,000	$217,000
Seller Fees	0	$5,000
Seller's Net	$204,000	$212,000

- even if the money passes through the seller, the buyer is the one who must come up with it.

The **true value** is not just the official "price", but the total of everything a buyer will pay to own something. Consider the two homes illustrated in Table A, above, with maximum price and fees buyers are willing to pay. The Crest Drive property is the higher valued home, since buyers are willing to pay out $220,000, even though it is the lowest priced. If the buyer of the Crest Drive property and the seller of the King Road property each agreed to pay all fees, adjusting prices accordingly, as shown in Table B, it would make no difference in true value, cash outlay of the buyer, or the seller's bottom line (net return).

Everything is paid for by the buyer, some of it through the price, some directly out of pocket. The one advantage of paying it through the price (eg. King Road) is that it simply makes the deal possible, because it is one way of financing the fees. It never has to work against the seller in any way at all.

Real difference would appear in fees or taxes that are based upon price, as in the case of excise stamps. However, a price expanded to cover seller payment of fees, can also encompass any incremental costs to the seller. A particularly tacky listing agent might be tempted to base the King Road commission on the raised price, but not if he/she wanted to be able to look ethical colleagues in the eye.

It is the buyer, and not the seller, who should be resisting the transfer of fee payments through the price to the seller. The seller walks away with cash determined by the "bottom-line", while the buyer pays not only the one-time price-based increases (eg. excise tax) but lives with ongoing charges like higher mortgage payments and value assessment over the many subsequent years of taxation.

All traditional conventions about who pays what are no more than conventions. The buyer's offer is based on the buyer's need, and any competent seller's agent will focus the seller's attention solely on the *bottom-line* difference between competing offers. Allowing for lender restrictions, the buyer should:

first, determine a basic offering price which encompasses fees local convention assigns to the seller;

second, reassign fees to buyer and/or seller according to the *buyer's* need;

third, adjust the price, increasing it by the cost of fees added to the seller's expenses, and decreasing it by the amount of conventional seller fees to be assumed by the buyer. Adjustments should also include incremental costs or savings.

THE FINAL STEP in this process is to make sure the listing agent is aware of what has taken place and what the bottom line is. Conventions and traditional hang-ups aside, listing agents understand "bottom line", and can generally be relied upon to explain it to the seller. If there are any doubts about the listing agent's ability or willingness, then a condition of the offer should be that the buyer and/or buyer's agent present the offer directly to the seller.

Assure seller gets the point

A REAL ESTATE CONTRACT has three dimensions. The two most obvious are the money going in one direction, and the property in the other direction. The third dimension is *time;* like the other two dimensions, time can have different implications for buyer and seller. For agents, "yesterday" is always best, so the commission is in-hand *today.* For either or both of the principals, it might be a whole different matter. Time may or may not be of the essence.

The time issues

When "time is of the essence" and so-stated in the contract, then either party has the right to declare the other in default when a specified date has not been met. Putting that phrase in the offer may be unnecessarily giving the seller an option to back out if the buyer's lender is a little slow. On the other hand, the buyer may want to prod the seller to move it along before interest rates climb. It is something to be considered strategically; whether time is to be declared "of the essence" should not be a matter of whether it is or is not on a standard offer form.

A two-stage process for the agents, not the clients

THERE IS A FINAL TWIST on this business of an offer and acceptance in certain parts of the country. In some locales, a process has evolved in traditional brokerage in which the **Offer and Acceptance (O&A)** is merely a temporary agreement to subsequently write a more fully detailed **"Purchase and Sale Agreement (P&S)"**. The standard offer in such a case usually further specifies that the P&S will nullify and take precedence over the O&A.

Why would anyone sign an incomplete agreement obligating them to sign another agreement they have not even seen? Perhaps even more puzzling, why would they do it for something with the stakes as high as in a real estate transaction? And finally, why would a buyer actually put up money for such a "privilege"? The answer is that they have been assured by the professionals that this is the way it's done — essentially that the second stage isn't really a big deal, but a simple mechanical process of working out routine details.

But still, if it were a matter of a simple mechanics and routine details, then why not put them all on the table before getting the signatures? In fairness to traditional agents, the "rewrite-the-whole-deal" approach did not develop as a scam to do buyers out of what they secured in the first contract; it was hardly needed, since only one side was truly represented in the first place. Rather, this two-stage process seems to have evolved as a convenient way of "closing the deal" — i.e., of tying both buyer and seller into something that will at least generate a commission, lesser details relating to client benefits to be worked out later.

It is actually in the new era of two-sided representation, that the obvious second-stage opportunity to renegotiate or clandestinely re-write people out of already-obtained rights becomes truly dangerous. Because both buyer and seller are threatened, we might apply the "two-edged sword" metaphor; but it is even worse than that, for more than two sets of interests are involved. We've seen above that the territorial and commission issues of agents have a way of finding their way into the business between buyer and seller *(see box)*, and I have personally viewed one-sided P&S "adjustments" of covenants fully agreed upon in the O&A.

> ee also the MLS study revealing traditionalist disincentives for buyer agents bringing buyers (pages 63–64, 90–92) and the clear imposition of agent interests into the buyer's offer by Standard of Practice 16-16 (pages 142–143).

Market exists to serve customers, and not the market professionals

THE TWO-STAGED PROCESS was ill-advised in the first place, being sloppy procedure at its best. Today, it is absolutely inconsistent with the fundamental concept of the customer quality revolution, i.e., the definition of "quality" as conformance to customer specifications. The buyer's offer is exactly that, the customer's specifications; the role of the buyer agent is to explicitly develop those specifications, so both buyer and seller know exactly what is at stake. The seller is free to reject it, counter-offer, or turn to other buyers. The buyer having an offer rejected, is free to redefine the specifications and re-offer, or turn to other properties. Full consumer buyer *and* seller awareness of all options is the key ingredient of a free and dynamic market. That's good news for market professionals working in the consumer's interest, and bad news for those who think the market exists in their own interests.

To summarize and emphasize the message of the last several pages:

- *The offer belongs to the buyer* and is a statement of the buyer's half of a purchase and sale agreement; i.e., the "customer specifications."

- *It should be unclouded* by extraneous items like restatement of obligations to other parties already documented elsewhere (such as agent employment agreements).

- *It should also be complete,* stating all expectations, concessions, and conditions in such a way and in proper legal form so that, upon acceptance in all particulars by a seller, it becomes a full and valid purchase and sale agreement.

The signed purchase and sale agreement seals the consequences of quality or non-quality agency. It all comes together here. A contract is a meeting of the minds of buyer and seller. It defines "one mind" for which both agents now work and, at least theoretically, all conflict, negotiation, and issues of counterposed interest should be over. If the contract has been competently written, and if the parties are committed to abide by it, the remaining tasks are a matter of teamwork between both sides.

The "catch" in this optimistic scenario is reflected in the twice-repeated "if", calling for pre-contract and post-contract vigilance. If-#1 (competency) is best assured by the clients themselves making the right choice of agents, reinforcing their judgment with the information in this text on agency and one other more specific to buying and or selling (specific suggestions below in Chapters 10 and 11), and by having competent legal counsel review the contract before signing. Given the right agent and the right contract, and a good attorney, the risks in the if-#2 category (abiding by the contract) are greatly minimized.

CHAPTER 7

The Revolution Revisited

I T I S T I M E for a brief departure from real estate into certain dynamics of the quality revolution. The goal here is to show what quality on an automobile assembly line has to do with the quality of real estate agency service, and why change is so inevitable.

When quality goes up, price goes down

One of the big lessons of the quality revolution in both industry and services was the discovery of how far off-base were traditionalist assumptions about the so-called "cost of quality." Put simply, the idea was that quality costs money, and that the more effort that went into the quality of a product or service, the higher it would necessarily be priced. Thus, according to the traditional thinking, there had to be a compromise on quality, a reasonable trade-off between excellence and cost. A certain amount of defects were acceptable within tolerable limits (eg. 1% or 2%). It was that attitude that Peters and Waterman were criticizing in the 1982 *In Search of Excellence* passage I already quoted above:

> [The traditional approach] has arguably led us seriously astray.... It doesn't command that we overspend on quality, overkill on customer service....*

*page 101

Overspend? Overkill? These words grabbed attention and raised eyebrows, but also made people think. In traditional American business thinking, Japanese automakers and electronics manufacturers were doing exactly these things; but instead of Japanese production costs going up, they went *down*! — and so steeply and consistently that their low-priced high-quality products nearly destroyed their American competitors.

Quality is free. Nonquality is expensive. IT WAS SURPRISING only to those who didn't get the message when Philip Crosby published his 1979 wake-up call, with the then-radical title, *Quality Is Free.* How can you overspend on something that is *free*? In both the title and the text, Crosby showed that effort given to achieve *zero defects* paid for itself many times over by avoiding the costs of *non-quality*! The very real *non-quality costs* accumulate in rework and repair, returns and replacements, back-up inventories and systems, legal expenses, repeated efforts, and colossal time expenses.

"Zero defects" has since become one of the slogans of the revolution, adorning walls from shop floors to executive offices. Defect tolerances such as 2%, 3%, or higher were cut to 1%. But 1% created a problem, for improving on it meant expressing the rate as less than one defect in 100 pieces (i.e., talking in awkward terms of less than a single unit), so the reference was changed to defects per 1,000 pieces. That old pseudo-wise slogan of the status-quo — "If-it-ain't-broke-don't-fix-it" — was scrapped in favor of the new concept of *continuous improvement,* and typical expressions of defect rates went to defects per ten-thousand, then per million, and today in terms of *billions* and higher! The result was the tumbling of business costs, dramatic increases in product and service quality, and the salvation of many companies and many more jobs.

The first places where this all happens — where the revolution takes place most readily — is where non-quality costs are recognized as primarily costs to the business (necessarily transferred to price) and as a factor in the competition for customers. Where there are physical products or physical services which require inventory, rework and repair, or replacement, non-quality costs are the most obvious and provide near-immediate savings as an incentive for making changes. In wage-labor (see box) intensive areas, personnel time also translates to massive in-house costs for repeat procedures, back-up systems, and continuing effort for problems which could have been prevented. Here too, the internal numbers force acceptance of change.

I n day wages or salary, payment must be made regardless of company income. Excluded are volunteers and those paid by commission or any other function of company income.

Passing nonquality costs to the customer

THE ATTENTION GIVEN to these *internal* non-quality costs that actually show up on the books of the business sometimes takes focus away from the *external* costs of non-quality which quietly pass as a residual to the customer with the low quality product or service. We can appropriately call these the *Customer's Residual After Purchase* (CRAP), examples of which would include extra stops at the gas pump, breakdowns and repair bills, and both the pain and expense of poor medical care. One example of the post-revolution reduction of such CRAP is a comparison of my own current fuel-efficient second car, now pushing 250,000 miles, with the short-lived gas-guzzlers of pre-revolutionary Detroit.

Quality enables price lowering and market advantage

THUS, THE REVOLUTION MOVES FASTEST where there are significant non-quality costs in the business process and, consequently, improvements in process-quality mean imminent dollar savings. The savings can be taken as an instantaneous increase in profits, or be used in whole or in part for a price drop which will, in turn, increase unit sales and profits. Improved **customer-quality**, as opposed to **process-quality**, is almost a *secondary* benefit with the customer getting a better product or service with a reduction in CRAP. Of course, CRAP reduction produces a long-term market benefit to the company, i.e., the invaluable reputation for quality. The point is that it often doesn't begin with desire to produce better customer quality. The long-range market position produced by improved customer quality is the "bird in the bush". Short-range financial return or price advantage produced by improved process quality is the "bird in hand" and the stronger incentive for business people so-focused on the "now" that they are blind to the inevitable.

REAL ESTATE DIFFERS from those sectors of the economy where the quality revolution has been in high gear, but only in those elements that relate to its getting off the starting block. There is plenty of non-quality in the real estate business, but traditional operations convert all non-quality costs to CRAP, i.e., literally dumping it all on the buying and selling customers.* Thus, process-quality improvements may not save the company anything in the short-run. Furthermore, where customer awareness has not yet connected post-purchase costs to service quality, there is no need for concern over long-range consequences. By the time CRAP begins plaguing the new homeowner in property problems, high monthly payments, surprises about neighborhoods, communities, schools, or taxes, the agency has long since collected the commission. Such is also the case with discomfort or financial adversity to a former homeowner or heirs resulting from selling at the wrong time or wrong price. Totally invisible are "opportunity costs" — opportunities lost because low-quality service failed to produce best price, best home, or most affluent willing buyer actually available.

CRAP happens — but only after the transaction is history and the agents have been paid. In the view of successful** traditional agencies, the system "ain't broke, so it won't be fixed." Thus, the quality revolu-

Internal incentives for quality reform absent from real estate

*All **clients,** including sellers, are also the customers of their agents.

**"Success" being a function of commissions accumulated, not customer satisfaction.

tion in the real estate sector would not be something easily initiated or enthusiastically supported *internally*. But the *external* initiatives have begun.

External incentives are present

Historically, there has always been some external activity in response to perceived non-quality in the form of **FSBOs** on the owners' side, and on the part of buyers responding to FSBO ads. However, there is a difference between rebellion and revolution; because each FSBO exists as an individual case and disappears with a sale or at the hiring of a listing agent, FSBOS have not created true ongoing organized competition, as Japanese competition did to (and *for*) the American auto industry.

People have to remember though, that for a very long time, the American auto industry was also fully insulated from competition and enjoyed a captive market. What a joke it seemed in the early seventies when a "motorcycle" manufacturer (Honda) from a place renown for the production of *junk* actually shipped *cars* to the USA. That first little car reaching the California shore was like a spark hitting the brush country, and consumer awareness like the Santa Ana winds swept the fire of quality revolution across the continent.

The spark has hit the dry brush of traditional real estate practice. The traditionalist fire apparatus is coming out to smother the flames which the winds of awareness have already carried beyond them. Creative sales pitches* and desperate legislative ploys** are like buckets of water that may drown a blaze of consumer light and heat here and there, but cannot save the dry-

*Above, pages 18–19, 37, 44, 52

**Below, pages 191–194

brush agencies that fail to sink their roots deep into the fresh water of quality reform.

Returning to earth from my writer's "metaphoria", the experience of a thousand or more business areas will be repeated in real estate. The customers will no longer accept the CRAP, simply because they do not have to. They are no longer captive to one set of providers. Both seller and buyer agencies will do two things:

- Give clients exactly what they want (i.e., no mixed services) and

- Divest themselves of non-quality activities and costs (i.e. things clients will not subsidize).

Those surviving will be more efficient, more specialized, and more skilled in buyer or seller service. They will also realize more profit: gone will be the horde of *amateurs*, which inflated agent ranks far beyond consumer need and spread commissions so thin that fees had to be proportionately inflated. Competition and flat fees will bring the fees down, but the frequency of transactions for surviving full-timers will probably bring net incomes up.

CHAPTER 8

Traditionalist and Opportunist Reaction

A.
THE TRADITIONALISTS' DILEMMA

double agent: *n.* A spy who pretends to work for one government while actually working for another.

double dealing: *adj.* marked by duplicity ; treacherous. *n.* Deceit.

*Webster's II New Riverside Dictionary. Berkeley, NY: 1984.

I SUGGESTED earlier that "double agent" is a more accurate term than "dual agent" for sellers' agents deceiving buyers in the wwʙ and woʙ modes.* The dictionary definition of "double agent" indicates that, by applying it to such real estate agents, I am giving spies a bad name. A spy, at least, is expected to be deceptive and not play by the rules.

*Above, pages
16–17, 38–39

Still, there is a clear parallel between a double-agent and a listing agent who leads a buyer to think he/she is the beneficiary of confidentiality and loyalty that is really owed to the seller. In the current age of consumer quality, three elements combine to expose such duplicity when it occurs:

- **laws of agency:** based in three centuries of common law, provide clear rules of the game;

- **disclosure:** (the most recent rule) makes sure everyone knows who the players are;

- **consumer advocates:** (including buyers' agents) now insure that consumers know the rules and when someone isn't playing by them.

These three elements — laws of agency, disclosure, consumer advocates — might seem to be a pretty effective formula for putting an end to double-agentry. They are in fact the three indispensable supports of consumer quality reform in real estate which, like a tripod, will not remain standing without all three legs in place. The challenge, therefore, to those who would defeat the **"customer quality tripod"** would be to figure out which leg is the most vulnerable, and then unite all die-hard traditionalists in a concentrated effort to cripple it.

IT WASN'T quite that diabolical or creative. For one thing, the defense method of first choice for most traditionalists is *denial*; and it is very difficult to kick at the legs of anything while your head is in the sand. Slowly, there was some flailing at the disclosure leg with the "no-real-difference" pitch, and some attempt to chip away at the advocate leg by sabotaging buyer agent commissions. However, neither of those legs is really very vulnerable. There is no publicly acceptable way to openly argue against disclosure, and increasingly aware consumers won't long be fooled by the "no-difference" fantasy. The advocate leg is equally secure since listing agents neither control buyer agent commissions nor can take other measures to limit buyer agent activity without running afoul of restraint of trade laws.

First denial...

...then under-cutting

EVENTUALLY, traditionalist desperation would lead to striking at the third leg, the one that would seem to be the *least* vulnerable — *the very laws of agency*, rooted in centuries of common law. Ironically, it is exactly there where those conspiring to maintain the profitability of double-dealing have found their most promising target!

Let's apply a little "game theory".

IF:

> *i.* the rules of the game (laws of agency) prohibit a gameplan that enables you to rig the game;
>
> *ii.* the players must wear uniforms (disclosure) so spectators and referees will know who's breaking the rules, and
>
> *iii.* the referees (advocates) keep the rules public and use public exposure to keep the players following the rules;

THEN:

> The only way to keep rigging the game is to rewrite the rules! While you're rewriting to allow your gameplan, add a rule that allows you to put on the uniform of your choice.

Lobbying the lawmakers

ABSURD? Certainly, to those readers who have arrived at this point in the book, as well as to others who understand real estate agency, consumer quality, and the traditionalist self-interests resisting consumer reform. The problem is that others do not understand;

among them are lawmakers who must rely on the industry professionals for that understanding. Unfortunately, within the current professional population are far more traditionalists than reformers, all well trained in making themselves look like "friends" of the buyer. As a legislative lobby, they can appear to the legislators, the rule-writers, as "friends" of the consumer. Without honest information exposing the propaganda of the double-agent lobby, responsible legislators can be fooled. Fortunately, given the facts, wise legislators can also see the difference between consumerism and trade association protectionism, and between a fair deal and double dealing.

For the reader to see how these things come into play, it is necessary to again review real estate agency operations, this time in light of common law and how it safeguards the welfare of clients.

I EARLIER NOTED some listing agencies claiming to provide exclusive buyer agency through one agent and exclusive seller agency via another.* Under the common law, that is deceptive because *one and only one* broker in the firm, the "**principal broker**," is actually *the* agent of all the firm's clients. All other agents, whether licensed as "brokers" or "salespersons", work only in that principal broker's name and authority. Any listings obtained by anyone in that firm belong to the principal broker, and that one principal broker is *the* agent of the owners of those properties. Likewise, the same principal broker is the *one* agent of all buyer-clients of the firm, regardless of who obtained them.

Common-law structure of agency is for client protection

*Above, page 22

Since all agency-services in a given firm are provided through one person — i.e., one agent — no firm with both buyer-clients and seller-clients can claim to be providing exclusive buyer agency or exclusive seller agency, no matter how the work assignments are distributed.

"Common law" has more in common with "common sense" than a shared adjective. The common law which undergirds the system of contracts and agency in English-speaking nations evolved from the common experience of people repeated over many centuries. As a result, it operates in very close harmony with human reality; i.e., with what people hold to be good common sense. Thus, agreements are made and agency obligations formed in line with meanings and expectations verified in a long history of commonly-shared experiences and contexts; i.e., a sense of communication and shared understanding — a "common sense."

The deception of mixed agency

THUS, WITHIN THE COMMON LAW, the concept of "principal broker" evolved, simply reflecting what people commonly know to be the way any office operates. There is always someone in charge, and an organized philosophy and interdependent interests that make it an *organization* rather than a mere collection of people who happen to be working in the same place. Common sense says it is pure nonsense to assert that the buyers' agent at one desk has no personal interest in property sales that could provide income to his/her boss and the sellers' agents at the surrounding desks. An organization does not exist without *interdependent* interests organized under some central coordinating authority. The common law of agency simply identifies that central authority and holds it accountable in the person of the principal broker to the clients! By common law and just plain common sense, a buyers' agent in a mixed-representation agency cannot divorce him/herself from interest in the well-being of either seller-agent colleagues or a boss whose income rises and falls with sellerside income. The same is, of course, true for a sellers' agent among buyer-agent office mates. Thus, there can be no truly "exclusive buyers' agent" nor "exclusive sellers' agent" in an agency that has both sellers' and buyers' agents.

But, how important is **exclusivity**, i.e., an agent's always representing either buyers or sellers, and not having some of both among his/her clients? Does it matter at all if a buyer-client and a seller-client of the same agent (or agency) aren't actually involved in the same transaction?

INVOLVEMENT IN THE SAME TRANSACTION is not required for conflict of interest; to the contrary, sometimes the conflict prevents transactions that should occur. It is not being in the same *transaction* that sets up the conflict, but being in the same *market*. An agent can represent house sellers and car buyers at the same time because they are in two different markets. There's also no conflict in representing both residential sellers and commercial buyers. But such "apples and oranges" distinctions cannot be made within the residential market. One can argue that $50,000 houses and

Conflict of interest

"Mr. and Mrs. Buyer, believe me. You can trust me not to be influenced by the fact that my boss and my coworkers make much more money if you buy a home listed with this agency — or by the fact that our commission structure rewards us for keeping prices up. You can trust me because I will be your buyer's agent!"

$500,000 houses are not in the same market, and see no conflict in representing sellers in one "market" and buyers in the other. The flaw is that *agents'* interests span the full price spectrum; no agency could keep the two price-level "markets" from overlapping by requiring listing agents and buyers' agents to turn away clients outside their designated dollar boundaries.

Conflicting interests do not arise out of *transactions*. Like transactions (or even the non-occurence of transactions) they arise out of *market interests*. These interests come into conflict the instant an agency has one buyer-client and one seller-client in the same market. The seller's interest is for *any* qualified buyers the agent can find. The buyer's interest is in being brought to homes selected exclusively on the basis of the buyer's needs. One's contract says, "make every effort to convince any capable buyer to offer on my house before he/she finds a better buy somewhere else". The other says "don't let me jump into buying one house if there's a better choice for me somewhere else." Fidelity to one interest inherently betrays the other.

This might be unfamiliar ground to the reader, and consequently seem a bit complicated. Actually, it only gets complicated when agents (or agencies) cross the line and try to be agents to both buyers and sellers. That is why traditional agents didn't do it before they saw their profitability threatened with the recent coming of buyer agents. In fact the underlying principle is so uncomplicated and so fundamental to the common sense of even ages past that Jesus Christ offered it as an undisputed premise to a higher level spiritual teaching. Christ's premise and the common law and common sense principle:

No one can serve two masters!*

THIS SCRIPTURE was quoted to me and other new Realtors® at our indoctrination training in 1977 by no less than a Past President of the National Association. It was invoked as a sacred business teaching and ethical principal. In any given market, good Realtors® served one master — and in non-investment markets *(see box, next page),* that master was almost always the seller. Exceptions would be when an agent's friend or relative wanted help in buying a home, but that was always regarded as an unfortunate circumstance, one of those

*Mt. 6:24. Premise to the spiritual teaching against serving both God and Mammon

Mainstream historical rejection of mixed agency

rofessional investment buyers, as I had been, sometimes engaged agent expressly in their own service. That was unheard of in non-investment real estate in those days.

realities of an imperfect world. Such buyer connections were always regarded as conflicting interests which had to be disclosed to sellers *(see box below)*. Never raised was the idea that buyers (other than those the agents personally cared about) ought to have their own representation.

Today, many buyers have the option of their own representation; and it is evident that the number of both buyer agents and buyers turning to them will expand at a very great rate. In the past, despite the attraction of independence from agents (indicated by the persistence of FSBOS):

- *most buyers* came to sellers' agents because they were the sole access both to the great bulk of properties for sale and to guidance through the process. But today, both are now available through buyer agency with the added benefit of true agency protection.

- *most owners* turned to sellers' agents because that was where the buyers were. But today... and tomorrow?...

isclosure to sellers of dual or conflicting interest was always a priority among ethical agents. Disclosure to non-client buyers is another matter.

ACCORDINGLY, the business problem facing traditional agencies is not just the loss of buyers, but the potential loss of *sellers*. If it were just a matter of buyers now coming through different doors, the agent workforce could adjust accordingly, with some of them joining buyer agencies. Even in the traditional system, commissions were split between buyerside and sellerside; so buyer agency in itself would, at worst, cost listing agency owners only that fractional bonus they get on the occasion of an in-house sale (1.5% on an even-split 6% commission*). Cost efficiencies gained from no longer dividing work activity along "both sides of the street" can actually offset the firm's loss of the in-house increment. But, if firms don't have the listings, there will be no share of the commission whatsoever.

The real threat of buyer agency

*See above, page 60

It actually isn't buyer agency that is causing the real problem for listing agencies, but the fact that, without buyers as bait, traditional listing agencies may in truth have little of real value to offer sellers. In this modern age of computers and the Internet, there indeed may be more effective and economical ways of bringing a property to market than through traditional listing agency methods. In Chapter 9, "Flat Fee Seller Agency," we will look at a non-traditional solution to the dilemma — the actual provision of **quality** seller service. By definition, however, non-traditional approaches are not routes traditionalist agencies will willingly take.

Traditionalists are people who identify themselves with the things they do in life, assuming the value of these things to be worthwhile because they have "always" done them! Hence, they psychologically derive their own sense of personal value from the things they do, and are personally threatened by people and events which would change such things. Unlike traditionalists, **"operationalists"** are people who see the things done in life as mere operations aimed at accomplishment of some valued output or purpose. The customer quality revolution is a major turn away from the internal focus of traditionalism to the external focus of operationalism.

Operationalists do value tradition, but for its stabilizing effect on operations and output, and not as an end or output in itself. There is a difference between traditionalism and true respect for tradition. Tradition does not form in history, but in the present; it begins with people facing up to their "today" and grows through the practice of subsequent generations living their present, not their past. *Tradition* is the light from history that gives us bearings as we move ahead even through darkness. *Traditionalism* is plain and simple fear of the dark, a hysterical delusion of safety gained by closing the eyes.

Tradition-alists were champions of the one-master principal

As I POINTED OUT, prior to the appearance of buyer brokerage and disclosure requirements, there was no interest among traditional agents in changing the fundamental laws of agency. On the contrary, the profession's most esteemed spokespersons went to the extent of invoking sacred scripture in defense of providing representation to one side only. Actually, it was a separation that would leave buyers out in the cold with no representation, for the near unanimous, very clear, and conspicuously righteous call was for purity in fiduciary service to the *seller.*

Now, this is not to suggest that business people should not change their minds, nor even that it is ignoble to do that for financial gain. It is to be expected that when a business breaks new ground, exposing new sources of income (new customers or clients), other businesses will move into those new markets. Many currently successful and high quality buyer agencies began as traditional seller agencies, sticking to the ethical "one master" principal when they made the transition. In some there might have been a period of adjustment, and even some wrestling with the temptation of not letting go of listing income. There is nothing wrong with following the profit motive, including creating competition for those without competition because they were first into the new area. Their reward for pioneering the new market is a head start over competitors, not a monopoly over captive customers. For the customers, the competition is what keeps prices down, and quality up.

There's that word again — "quality" — the business of giving informed customers exactly what they are looking for. Note the word, "informed." Profits can be made by selling uninformed people what they don't need, but think they do. That is selling *junk* (product or service), not quality. This is not to say product or service providers are to decide for customers what they do or do not need, but to acknowledge that all customers agree they need accurate and not inaccurate information. That is why the definition of **quality** is conformance to specifications by an informed customer. That is why the customer quality tripod* is all about keeping the customer informed; it is the obvious purpose of disclosure (Leg #1), the heart of advocacy (leg #2), and inherent in the "common understanding"** that is the essence of the common law (leg #3).

*Above, pages
168–169

**Above, page 172

To summarize the dilemma facing traditional agencies:

1. Common sense and common knowledge of workplace reality say it is impossible to properly represent counterposed interests of both buyer and seller within the same workplace, i.e., that "no one can serve two masters."

2. The laws of agency (tripod leg #3), based in common law built upon centuries of common experience, reflect the reality. These laws place all agency representation in the lead agency person as one agent, a "principal broker", who becomes legally defined as dual agent when contracting with both buyer and seller interests. These laws exist in most states and were enthusiastically supported by traditional agencies before facing competition from exclusive buyer agents.

3. The law of disclosure (tripod leg #1) requires such dual agents to disclose to clients that they are dual agents and cannot provide the full service and undivided loyalty of an exclusive buyers' or sellers' agent.

4. Traditional agents tempted to skirt the law of disclosure or obscure it with "no-difference" pitches, are disadvantaged by buyer agents and other consumer advocates (tripod leg #2) who can point to the laws and their clear definitions of responsibility.

5. The inability to attract buyers may deprive traditional listing agencies of their greatest attraction for *sellers.*

6. Fully informing clients of agency representation reality is now:

> **(a)** *inherent in quality agency and the quality tripod;*
>
> **(b)** *profitable for buyer agencies;*
>
> **(c)** *a threat to the profitability of traditionalist listing agencies;*
>
> **(d)** *required under common law which traditionally was supported by traditional agents and still the law in most states.*

Listing agencies and agents are now at that point where they must heed the wisdom of Yogi Berra:

> **When you come to a fork in the road, take it!**

They have come to the end of the old long lone stretch of "seller-only" road, reaching the fork and it's choice of either seller agency or buyer agency. The operationalists among them are those with a functioning steering wheel; they will simply steer toward the future, respecting the rules that still apply, but recognizing that

the terrain is changing. The traditionalists, with their
steering wheels bolted according to the past will try to
force the road ahead back onto the old course.

Travel along the old road had three distinct features,
one of which will be excess baggage on the road ahead.
The difference between operationalists and traditionalists is which feature they will move to unload:

1. the process of inviting both buyers' wallets and sellers' homes directly into their agencies;

2. commitment to the common-law concept of providing quality service to one master;

3. making money.

Everything covered up to this point should make it
clear that holding on to both 1 and 2 will mean the loss
of 3 — and the reader knows well that feature 3 will
not willingly be sacrificed. Operationalists, however
comfortable with traditional methods, will hold the
output of quality service (2) more important than
hanging onto outdated procedure (1), and will either
become exclusive buyer agents, or develop non-traditional ways to attract and serve sellers.

Traditionalists, on the other hand, put importance
of process (1) second only to income (3). While their
speech professes noble values, most highly valued is
security, which they equate with stability, i.e., avoiding
change in the activities that have been profitable.
Ironically, the one thing that stands most in the way of
their clinging to their "tradition" of luring both buyers
and sellers is the one thing that is truly a "tradition" in

the full cultural sense of the word.   It is *the common law* evolving from the common experiences, senses, and understandings of people over many centuries — the very common law *the traditionalists extolled* when it suited their purposes.   But extolling is, after all, only talk — and business is business.   Revealing that their public veneration of the common law was so much lip service, traditionalist lobbies in many states now promote legislation which relegates the "one master" rule to the scrap heap of no-longer-profitable principles. Clearly exposing the traditionalist intention to kick out the common-law leg of the Consumer Quality Tripod* is the clause in such legislation recommended by the National Association of Realtors® which blatantly provides that wherever the statute is inconsistent with the common law, the common law is *superseded*!

*Above, pages 168–170

    Tradition, no.   Heresy, yes!

LICENSING OF REAL ESTATE AGENTS is a state function; accordingly, changing the "law" is really a matter of changing fifty distinct sets of laws, one at a time.   The states themselves are in varying degrees of readiness for such a campaign; and the first step in a state change-the-law campaign is somewhat of a "catch-22" — to enlist the support of the local traditionalist establishment which, by definition, is inherently disposed *against* change.   Of course, this change is all about obstructing the bigger change of genuine exclusive buyer agency.   The trick for the national traditionalist strategists is to get their local counterparts to take buyer agency seriously; and I have already pointed out

The national state-by-state legislative campaign

that traditionalists first react with *denial,* using things like the "no-difference curve" to explicitly avoid taking it seriously. It is easy to maintain the illusion that buyer agency is not a threat to current practice in those locales where buyer-agency has not yet emerged. But, even in those places, it's coming.

Local denial aside, to the traditionalist mentality it is a national threat requiring a national campaign; for the freedom of communications and movement in the United States makes real estate a national market. Through both the media and people relocating from other areas, local buyers will know they deserve better representatives than sellers' subagents. Thus, the traditionalist campaign against the true consumerism of genuine exclusive buyer agency has to be national.

The buyer-friendly mask

STILL ANOTHER DILEMMA faced by the national traditionalist interest is that the wake-up alarm to local traditionalists cannot be that "the enemy is coming." Such publicly adversarial reaction to buyer agency would only broadcast contempt for a buyer's right to representation — effectively alienating buyers (tomorrow's sellers) and maybe create job openings for former listing agents in businesses which make FSBO signs. Thus, the national campaign to preserve traditionalist practice was obliged to put a positive spin on buyer agency as a "good thing", pitching it as something that would not end the traditional practice of playing both sides of the street. Suddenly, buyer agency is portrayed as just another service that can be provided by a listing agency. Of course, to call this particular pitch a "curve" is a gross understatement; the directional change is no less than a U-turn — a full turning back from a near-century of pious fidelity to true agency.

THE TASK OF national campaign management unavoidably falls on the National Association of Realtors® (NAR), the largest professional association of real estate agents in the country. NAR's duty is to represent all legitimate types of real estate agents, for nearly all exclusive buyer agents are also Realtors® (i.e., members of NAR); but their voice within NAR is dwarfed by the overwhelming mass of seller-agent members, most of whom were hardly aware until recently of even the existance of buyer agents. NAR is so dominated by the mindset of its traditionalist membership that it virtually disregarded the buyers' need for agency throughout its history and, in classic traditionalist denial, all but ignored the existence of buyer agency for most of the last decade. Not until November of 1996, and two years after some of its member Realtors® who were *genuine* exclusive buyer agents joined in setting up their own professional association (the National Association of Exclusive Buyer Agents — NAEBA), did NAR put itself in the buyer agent association business.

It did not do that by sitting down with its exclusive buyer agent members and building an organizational division to advance the professionalism of full exclusive agency for buyers in accord with its long standing principle of pure agency. Rather, it simply *purchased* the privately-owned Real Estate Buyer Agent Council (REBAC), essentially a commercial training entity spe-

Rewriting a history of ignoring buyer agency

cializing in training and certification of buyer agents, exclusive and *otherwise*. With NAR's own long experience in training and certification of real estate professionals, and genuine exclusive buyer agents in its membership, it already had the organizational resources to set up its own buyer agency division without the purchase of REBAC. What it did *not* have was a *history* of being in the buyer agent business and, in particular, a history of double-agency apologetics to obscure the U-turn it was about to take.

Buying a place in history

REBAC was formed in 1988 by pioneering Denver buyer-agency operator, Barry Miller, as a legitimate for-profit venture centering on buyer-agent training, certification and newsletter publishing. The next year, Miller established Buyer's Resource, a national buyer agency franchise operation *(see box below)*, making REBAC part of that enterprise. By 1992, REBAC had 450 members, a modest operation, but diverting administrative effort from its prime function of support to the franchisees; so it was sold to entrepreneurs who would aggressively promote its training and certification products to an industry growing increasingly aware of their commercial value. Miller estimates that at the time of the 1992 sale of REBAC for about $20,000, 80% of its members were true exclusive buyer agents,

B uyer's Resource is the first of two national buyer-agency franchise operations founded by Miller. The other is Only Buyers America Real Estate, 1996.

reflecting the prior focus of its exclusive buyer agent owners upon the advancement of buyer agency. Then, a new focus upon the market for REBAC products recognized how very few buyer-only agencies and how very many listing agencies there are in this country; the road to profit was not to tell potential trainee customers in listing agencies that they cannot be buyer agents. Thus, REBAC's definition of an "exclusive buyer agent" does not include the common law, common sense, and NAEBA prohibitions against working in a listing agency. Moreover, REBAC adopted definitions of several other types of buyer representative, making the label of buyer "agency" accessible to virtually every traditionalist operator. It worked; REBAC membership was at least 5,000 by NAR's acquisition in November of 1996; credible reports are that the sale price included a cash payment of $300,000 with increments based on membership growth, putting the full price around $900,000. Whatever the price, the value was now even more than the cash return for its products for, with it, NAR *purchased* (a) a history it never lived, and (b) rational precedences for positions it not only never held, but piously opposed.

BY OBSCURING THE PAST, NAR and its state organizations can now project images of something more than the voice of merely the real estate agent profession, but of sellers' agents *and* of buyers' agents — a self-declared source of "balanced" advice on legislation from either perspective. Instead of appearing as a front for the seller-agent establishment trying to deny buyers their right

Obscuring the past

*Diverse
REALTOR/REBAC
Web sites, 3/6/98

to exclusive representation, NAR/REBAC can claim to be "the largest association of real estate professionals focusing on all aspects of buyer representation" *

Sound impressive? Consider that those "focusing on all aspects of buyer representation" would include its darkest enemies. Specifically because REBAC does not limit membership to those committed to full and genuine exclusive buyer agency, it officially boasts of more than 7,500 members at the time of this writing with unofficial word of a current count exceeding that by many thousand. These include not only those meeting its loose definition of "exclusive buyers agent", but those who work as buyer "agents" at their convenience even while personally representing sellers and taking listings.

The REBAC membership application actually invites agencies who are

> "interested in integrating buyer agency services into their day-to-day real estate operations to provide a full menu of services for both buyers and sellers"

Thus, ninety-nine listing agents in an agency with *one* buyer agent (exclusive or not) will now have bait-and-switch at their disposal:

> *Yes, we do offer buyer agency if you think it really makes a difference. I can set things up for you with our buyer agent when he's around. In the meantime, I can show you a few houses we have that probably won't be on the market for very long...*

They can also tell *sellers* that they have buyer agents as one of their ways to attract buyers (without, of course,

mentioning that steering the buyer to them is a violation of buyer agency).

NAR and REBAC are doing for buyer agency what
American settlers did for Mexico's northern territory of
Texas. Traditionalist agents committed to the old way
of working both sides of the street are emigrating into
the "buyer agent" business with about as much loyalty
to buyers as Sam Houston had to Mexico. Mexico at
least had other states after the loss of Texas; but once
the concept of true buyer agency is brought under the
dominion of traditionalist interests, buyers will be back
where they were without genuine agents. The
NAR/REBAC abandonment of the common law and
common sense definition of agency enables NAR to
masquerade traditionalist members as buyer agents,
and itself as their advocate in the lobbies of state
legislatures.

THERE, IT THROWS ITS POWER behind new legislation,
the alleged purpose often expressed as a sudden need
to "clarify the duties of real estate brokers" — a need
not recognized in all the years prior to disclosure laws
when sellers' agents had absolute control. In truth, the
problem for traditionalist sellers' agents has not been
any lack of "clarification"; on the contrary, the real
problem is that the enactment of disclosure laws has
indeed provided consumers with clarification about
what has really been going on. The clarity was
enhanced with common law language distinguishing
"single agency" from "dual agency", "client" from "customer", and defining common sense concepts of agent

**A sudden
need to
"clarify" a
century-old
structure**

duties and conflict of interest. The arrival of exclusive buyer agency provided the other missing element (along with disclosure) in a new and very logical order for the business of selling and purchasing property.

"Old order" replaced by "new order"

IN THE **old order** of things, two things vital to a "fair deal" were missing: (1) buyers often did not know the professional working with them was really not their agent, but the seller's agent; and (2) even if they knew, they couldn't find a buyers' agent because none existed. The **new order** simply introduced the missing elements — disclosure and buyers' agents — and a fair deal to both buyers and sellers. However, the new order was less of a profitable deal for sellers' agents who had things their own way under the old order.

Displacing "new order" with disorder

WHILE SOME TRADITIONALISTS might yearn for the old order, the bright ones know they can never return to a day without disclosure or buyers' agents. Perhaps it is more accurate to say that they cannot return to the day when they didn't have to give at least lip service to disclosure and buyers' agents. Mere words can always be redefined and, with the help of misguided lawmakers, written into legislation. As in the overworked screenplay plot where the blind person cuts the lights to even the odds with a seeing opponent, people who are blind to the opportunities of progress have only one way out — to retard the progress by making murky what has become clear and by replacing order with disorder.

B. LEGISLATED DISORDER

WITH ACTIVE ENCOURAGEMENT and guidelines from the national organization, state Realtor® associations have successfully lobbied for new statutes castrating the client safeguards under the common law, replacing clarity and order with disorder and redefinition, the combination providing cover for traditionalist agencies to continue working both sides of the street. Traditionalist self-interest state legislation may involve one of four ploys (or some blend of the first three): (1) legitimizing dual agency, (2) disguising dual agency under new labels, (3) eliminating the principal-broker protection to clients, or (4) stripping the consumer of all rights to agency.

Ploy #1 — Legitimatizing Dual Agency

In some places the traditionalists masquerade as reformers, and actually legislate out of existence the institution of subagency, perhaps going so far as to denounce it as unfair to buyers. Subagency was unfair in all the decades before real buyer advocates exposed it, doomed anyway as buyers inevitably see a far better alternative in the buyers' agent.

One way the new gimmick operates is to require by law that all people seeking the service of real estate agents be offered the "choice" of hiring the agent as a seller's agent, a buyer's agent, or a dual agent. Of course, any buyer or seller already has these options under common law; and in states requiring disclosure, the consumer would know what those choices mean (assuming the agent *obeyed* the law). The difference now is that the law backs up the agent's pretense of ability to actually *be* a buyer's agent one minute and a seller's agent the next.

Lumping the three options together, the law raises dual agency to equal status with full buyer and seller agency. Suddenly respectable, it replaces subagency as the income channel from both sides on the same deal. Agency automatically becomes dual agency when clients of the same firm enter into a mutual transaction. Thus, the agent's income tends to be highest when clients get the fewest agency benefits.

Unless the buyer signs an exclusive buyer agency agreement with this agent also representing sellers, the buyer still has one major problem that existed under subagency, and without the protection that subagency gave. Client or not, the uncontracted buyer is still **high-risk*** to the agent, mitigating against the agent's obligation to recommend against a less-than-optimal purchase. And because the so-called buyer's agent is not the *seller's* agent, the buyer will have no recourse against the seller for the agent's actions.

*Above, pp. 66

Ploy #2 — Relabelling Dual Agency:
Genuine respect for tradition provides clarification, giving us the words — the labels — already established in common understanding. However, when something other than clarity is intended, a useful tactic is to *avoid* traditional terms, especially one as fully defined as "dual agency". Thus, the new legislation masks what is still dual agency with terms like "limited agency,"

"designated agency," "transaction brokerage" and "appointed agency". Such labels present a facade of something new, an illusion reinforced with plastic guidelines for allegedly appropriate "disclosure". Since the "new" thing is just dual agency by a different name, what is really attempted is change in the disclosure rules without being caught in the act. These new "disclosure" requirements can be satisfied by double agents seducing agreement from buyers and sellers with far less information than meets common law standards for *informed consent.*

Ploy #3 — Elimination Of Principal Broker: By allowing designation of so-called exclusive buyers' agents and exclusive sellers' agents within a given agency, this legislative tactic denies what both common-sense and common law recognize, that interdependent interests are inherent in the very definition of organization. Neither the firm nor its supervising individual is "agent" to the client, for neither bears fiduciary responsibilities to either buyer or seller. The "agent", if any, will be the individual agent who signed-up the seller or buyer, and is irrationally presumed to be independent of surrounding interests adverse to those of the client. There is in effect no longer any "principal agent" or "principal broker", no individual standing in for the whole firm and obligating the agency as the client's agent. If either "client" thinks that the "agency" is his/her agent, then both are in a position of a buyer in the days prior to disclosure.

Neutralizing disclosure

IN EFFECT, ploys #2 and #3 mean that firms still committed to working both sides of the street will have two legal approaches to avoid telling a buyer that they owe **fiduciary** (i.e., full agency) responsibility to the seller:

- Firms that are big enough to assign some agents exclusively to buyers and others exclusively to sellers will be able to tell buyers they have an "exclusive buyer agent" for them. It won't be true in the common sense of what agency is (after this, for sellers as well as buyers); but it will be *legal* because the legislation abrogates common law and makes common sense irrelevant.

- Just as before, firms will be able to drop fiduciary responsibilities from their services. They won't have to tell a buyer they owe loyalty to the seller because, as a dual agent (however they paint it), they'll owe neither side such agency service.

It is important enough to repeat that the chief evil of both these double-agent approaches is sabotage of the full-disclosure principle. The *first* approach simply would never work if the full truth were told; neither informed buyers nor informed sellers would accept the fairy tale of a so-called "exclusive" agent amidst the interdependencies and conflicting interests of such a firm. The *second* approach could be feasible for certain buyers or sellers who do not need full agency representation, but disclosure means they'd know the difference; those needing full agency would go elsewhere and those accepting the partial service package would not pay a full package price (See Chapter 9).

Under the old order,* only buyers got the truly unfair deal, denied not only agency, but even awareness of the non-agency. The **new order** meant dealing the same cards — agency and awareness — to both sides. The new order brought fairness and equity, and the two things are not the same. Consider the old joke about the man who was not prejudiced because he hated everybody. This double-dealing legislation is not inequitable because it deals the bad cards of inadequate representation and non-agency to seller as well as buyer. Of course, it is still a good deal for the dealer.

*Above, page 190

> The *fourth* ploy — eliminating consumer rights to agency — is relegated to the end of this chapter for reasons cited there.

TRADITIONALISTS' SUPPORT of this legislation stems from the mistaken notion that they are the dealers. The truth is that they will be lucky to even stay in the game. What they hope for is a return to the old order, with both sellers and buyers walking in through their doors. What they will get is far more than they bargained for.

Traditionalists being duped by false allies

Up to now, I have been discussing two forces; **traditionalists** and **operationalists**. There is a third group, the real dealers in this legislation, who are simply "*opportunists*". They align themselves with the traditionalists for their political support, but with no concern for either tradition or status quo. They are more like the operationalists in terms of knowing how to subordinate process to what they seek at the end of an operation. Unlike either operationalists or traditional-ists, they respect neither tradition nor even the stabil-ity of operations, one of the reasons they can blatantly engineer disorder.

Big firms to benefit at expense of smaller ones

Instability in any market destroys competition and eventually settles down, leaving those who've survived with improved position, usually the *big* firms. The cards are stacked in favor of only the biggest double-agent firms, this opportunity being the prime catalyst for this legislation. Nevertheless, while they are the cat-alyst and the real dealers in this matter, the *force* is the traditionalist mob, giving its numbers to the legislative effort and even reducing its professional association to a protective trade lobby.

Traditionalist fears are being exploited for a cause not in their interest. The target is market share, and not the market share inevitably going to dedicated buyer or seller agencies. Buyers and sellers attracted to **dedicated** agency will not be enticed by the now-legal-ized gimmicks. The target is the traditional market—those service customers remaining comfortable with mixed agency firms. Irrespective of how large or small that market will be as consumer awareness develops (despite the orchestrated disorder), the competition for share is only between mixed-service agencies. This leg-islation will give market advantage to large dealers at the expense of small and medium mixed service agen-cies lured into supporting its passage.

The typical small agency with the familiar "Agent On Duty" sign will have to change it to the plural "Agents On Duty", to cover one agent for buyers and another for sellers. The masquerade of full agency to both sides will require round-the-clock agency divisions with incompatable revenue profiles spawning jealousy as one division outdoes the other. Worse, bitter internal conflict is certain when an internal "exclusive buyers' agent" leads a buyer toward the listing of another firm or, worse, away from the listing of the agent at a neighboring desk.

Firms unable to staff both "exclusive buyer" and "exclusive seller" divisions might offer limited-agency or dual-agency, but certainly not at the full agency price. As already indicated above,* And expanded upon in Chapter 9 (next), partial services and component fee structures are inevitable. Those *claiming* full agency will include the large double-agency firms, but also those that *actually deliver* genuine exclusive agency, i.e., the *dedicated* buyer firms and sales firms. While limited/dual agency firms will be those without the resources for full agency claims, full-agency firms will also be in the limited service competition. Small firms trying to work both sides of the street will be overwhelmed.

*Above, pages 26, 73, 104, 155

Both as a result of technology and some limited service packages, time spent with individual clients will be less than in the past. There will not be more clients, so fewer agents and agencies will be needed. Small traditional firms trying double agency before finally changing to dedicated agency will be crippled financially during the double agency trial, and then find no room in a small market dominated by competitors who got there first.

Mixed agency (big and small) doomed in tomorrow's market

Long range survival of even the biggest opportunists will depend on their readiness to transition to dedicated agency when the legislated double agency schemes ultimately fail. Legislators who passed the laws can repeal or rewrite them, and deceptions cannot hold against the ever-swelling tide of consumer awareness. Consumers will turn to dedicated buyer or seller agency, no matter what charades the law allows mixed agencies to play; and profit conscious agents will respond to consumer choice. Profits will come only with maximum quality at minimum cost, rather than desperate and transparent deceptions aimed at restoring the forever-lost monopoly.

Ironically, and tragically for traditionalists and opportunists alike, in their obsession with undercutting buyer agency, they may be all the more unprepared for the quality offensive about to take place on the *seller* side of the business. In this legislation, they have blundered into dealing themselves a bad hand for the new game coming to town.

They forgot that their best card is the one that makes them licensed *agents,* enabled to act in full fiduciary capacity for clients. Chapter 9 will reveal the market value of licensed agent status in offering new-order quality as sellers' agents, as Chapter 6 did in the case of buyer agency. However, the legislative chicanery foolishly devalues that asset, openly promoting the notion that the fiduciary obligations of full confidentiality and total loyalty to the client's best interest don't mean very much. Hungry for money of both buyers and sellers, the pitch to each is that the in-house presence of the other's agent is no threat -- since agents are simply advisors or facilitators rather than dedicated and empowered workers in their clients' specific interests. In truth, both sellers and buyers need full agency service, and that means legitimate and healthy profit for both buyers' agents and sellers' agents. That's not enough for those who just don't get the fable of the goose and the golden eggs. Wanting it all, their greed could lose it all. Their short-sighted legislation sacrifices the very thing that gives them *unique* market leverage over providers of seller non-agency services which simply do not require a license.

SUCH LEVERAGE is *legitimate*, for the consumer need for agency is real. However, in their own security needs, traditionalists lose sight of consumer need. Well after the above passages were written, and just as the final version of this book was going to print, something happened in one state to underscore how traditionalists undervalue the consumer right to full agency protection. In March of 1998, this state's traditionalists not only *devalued* agency, but abandoned it! Thus, "ploy #4", the ultimate betrayal, had to be added here.

The ultimate betrayal

Ploy #4 — Eliminating consumer rights to agency. For traditionalists, the problem is consumer choice. Detroit's problem in the late '70s would have gone away if Congress simply denied Americans the choice of buying foreign cars, i.e. simply outlaw the high-quality, low-cost imports. Congress could never be sold this bill of goods; but at this writing, the business-ahead-of-principle crowd actually pushed a bill through one house of a western state legislature to *outlaw agency* in real estate practice. Of course, such legislation outlaws *clients!* (Why bother masking or diluting the consumer benefits of agency — as in ploys 1–3 — when you can outright eliminate them?)

This is not reform legislation: the old "double agents" become simply "double dealers" who continue unreformed and secure in working both sides of the street — now relieved of the legal obligation to exercise loyalty, utmost care, disclosure, obedience, confidentiality, and accountability. Moreover, because these specific behaviors won't be outlawed, double-dealers can once again (as in the days before disclosure laws) privately imply them to both buyers and sellers; but now they won't have to deliver to *either* side. Those obligated by conscience (if not law) to these responsibilities won't be allowed to publicly declare that with the word meant for that purpose in common sense, common law, and common practice, i.e. "agency." The good guys will continue being good, but the bad guys — aided and abetted by naive lawmaking — won't have to fear any general public awareness giving consumers informed choice between good and bad. Of the four ploys described in this chapter, this will not pass in most states; in the few where it might, it most surely will never survive judicial review. As of this writing, this specific state's bar association persuaded legislators to put a hold on the second house's vote, but the threat of eventual passage remains.

CHAPTER 9

Flat Fee Seller Agency

WHILE BUYER AGENCY is in the forefront of the real estate customer quality revolution, the real heroes may well be *seller's* agents! Before the reader starts thinking the writer just made a U-turn, recall that all sellers' agents are not included in our definition of "traditionalist." By far, the greatest threat to the well-being of traditional sellers' agents is not the buyers' agent, but the *non-traditional sellers' agent* who believes sellers should get everything they pay for, and pay for only what they get.

However nervous buyer agency makes traditional agents, it won't put many of them out of the real estate business. It certainly dooms sub-agency; but that just means many current traditional agents will have to decide whether they want to be buyers' agents or sellers' agents. Many who made a good living "working

Inevitable: non-traditional seller's agents

with" buyers will put their skills to work *for* buyers; and they'll find welcome relief in no longer playing "guess-who-works-for-who." More importantly, the first to move into legitimate exclusive buyer agency will likely find it a haven from a real casualty-inflicting disruption soon to descend upon selling agencies.

Sellers, as customers of seller agencies, have been denied "customer quality"

RECALL THAT **"quality"** is all about conforming to customer specifications, and also that it applies as much to the customers of agency services (i.e., the clients) as it does to the customer of the real estate sale. Customer specifications of service need should vary as widely as the personal circumstances, abilities and personalities of individual clients (buyers or sellers); but sellers were never given that option by traditional agencies lumping everything in a blanket commission. Selling operations can easily focus on the thing being sold rather than on the person selling it (the owner), so individual needs were never recognized and individualized fee structures never happened. Buyer agency, on the other hand, by its very nature begins with specification of individual need. It is still evolving, and in an age of consumer awareness, so buyer agents will not be traumatized by the observations of Chapter 6 now repeated here:

> Work required of a buyers' agent will vary from one buyer to another .... Some buyers ... will have their financing in place. Others will have located their own property. Still others will require the agent to personally examine prospective purchases before taking valuable time for their own visits. Accordingly, a buyers' agent should have a schedule of charges which

vary with the nature and amount of service required. (pp. 97–98)

By CONTRAST, "a schedule of charges which vary with the nature and amount of service required" — i.e., *flat fees* — will be devastating to traditionalist listing agencies. Again, I specify *traditionalist* listing agencies, not progressive sales agencies. However, even if all traditionalist agencies and agents were to convert overnight to progressive quality-driven seller service, there would not be enough room for them all. The down side of the quality revolution has been *downsizing*, once the customer stopped being saddled with non-quality expenses, workforces were reduced by the number of people engaged in the non-quality activity. That meant a long-range upturn in productivity and quality jobs, but the short-range impact was a dumping of unnecessary activity and, with it, people who were unable or too shortsighted to move to safer ground.

Inevitable: downsizing and cutting of nonquality activity

Ironically, the most obvious non-quality activity, and the certain casualty of flat-fee reform on the seller-side, will be the very one given homage for its everlasting nature in the hallowed maxim of traditionalist wisdom:

*If you list, you last.**

*Above, page 49

No MORE! Listing is at long last, *lost* as the essential element of success. In the *Tampa Bay Business Journal* (7/28-8/3/95), Valarie Harring writes of a consistent multi-million dollar traditional listing agent who normally carried forty to fifty listings. Moving from the Chicago area to Florida, this agent confronted buyer

Aggressive listing is a nonquality activity

brokerage for the first time and agents outperforming her in transactions per week who *never took a listing*. For the agent, the story ends happily with conversion to a profitable buyer agency career.

Within seller-service firms, listing is non-quality activity because it does not directly serve those who are already customers (i.e., property owners). In fact, it even works against them, taking up the time of people who should be *selling*, i.e., procuring buyers, rather than more competing sellers. In all service businesses, some time must obviously be spent in marketing the service, getting out and hustling new customers (the customer of the service is the seller), but how much time is too much time? In the philosophy of **"customer quality,"** when capturing owners (listing) becomes more important than serving owners (selling), the point of "too much" has long been exceeded. There are two clear indications that this has in fact happened in traditional real estate:

- the "he-who-lists-lasts" maxim; and

- the judgment of the committed traditionalists of Benjamin County that time and effort spent procuring buyers was worth, at most, less than one-third of the full commission.*

*Above, pages 63–64

**Page 50

Recall also Robert Irwin's caution:

The last thing you want to do is list your property with an agent who "gathers" listings. * *

The major reason that the gathering of listings takes precedence over selling is the sheer number of agents in the business and that, in the past, they have all been listing agents. To take the eyes off listing would be to allow the competition literally swarming around to take all the inventory. That would be suicidal in the traditional system, the reason for the word "lasts" rather than "succeeds" in the maxim.

IN ADDITION TO listing activity, yet another non-quality activity from the standpoint of seller need is the *pre-contractual* "competitive market analysis" (CMA) which is too obviously a listing tool to be reliable, especially with many agents competing for listings.**

Inevitable: quality competition

**Above, pages 125–128

Part of the problem will be resolved by the situation illustrated in the case of the Tampa Bay agent. The number of listing agents will shrink as the legitimate opportunity of buyer brokerage is recognized. However, while the physical pace in the rush for listings may relax, it will be replaced by a different kind of competitiveness more in keeping with the new era of customer awareness and customer quality. The direction of this competitiveness will be determined by new seller attitudes developing from expanding awareness which cannot be clouded with legislated trickery:

- they will not be attracted by a selling agency's claim to a ready supply of buyers;

- they will not accept charges inflated to provide an agent with income for time not spent in their direct service;

- they will place low value on CMAS by parties who's income is contingent on a sale, and high value on independent appraisal;

- those tempted to flirt with the FSBO route will not be limited to yard signs and a short-run newspaper ad like their predecessors; they will use computerized listings and FAX machines (their own or commercial service) to bring their property to market.

These things mean that successful sellers' agencies will be those who compete first in the *quality* of service and, secondly, in the *price* of that service.

- **Competitive quality** means the listing agency recognizing that it actually provides the seller with only two services of unique value: agency representation and putting the property on the market. Attorneys can provide agency, and media and advertising specialists can provide market services, but only licensed agents can really combine the two. Competitive agencies will cultivate business, not by hustling listings in the old style, but by advertising and demonstrating their proficiency in bringing these two elements together on the seller's behalf.

- **Competitive price** means the listing agency must eliminate all directly charged non-quality costs (everything the seller doesn't want) and minimize all non-essential indirect charges. Simply put, it means delivering only what the seller agrees to pay for.

ADVERTISED AND SUBSTANTIATED *quality performance* at low fees will do more to garner listings than any agent hustling in the field. The saying in business where the quality revolution is established is "focus on quality (rather than the money) and the money will follow". Put another way, "... the *listings* will follow."

Selling agents will replace listing agents

Quality performance means selling homes quickly and close to the asking price. Legitimate appraisals by qualified objective appraisers mean realistic and *credible* asking prices, faster deals and streamlined lender approval. Traditional listing activity and CMA's each work in the opposite direction, taking time and costing money; agents must be compensated, so these things both push commission rates upward and slow the process down. Eliminating them provides both fee-reducing cost cuts and agent time to focus on the job of selling the property fast (made simpler by the assurance that the price is the right price).

The tasks of the seller's agent in the new-order will be to:

- master the technology and processes to get the property at peak selling shape to the broadest cross-section of buyers and buyer-agents,

and to then

- negotiate with the bidders.

Because the value is known and established in advance on the sellerside, and because purchase readiness has been assured by the professionals on the buyerside, things can proceed very quickly and trouble free.

**Quality
market
advantage
is there for
the taking**

THIS MAY SOUND a bit too idealistic; and if the response is that most agents simply won't operate this way, that response is correct. Most listing agents will not work this way — but some will, and they will be the ones who take away business from the others.

The question is, when (not whether) any sellerside agencies will begin offering flat fee services. Three things will make it sooner than later: consumer advocacy, technology, and credit cards...

- **Consumer advocates** (including but not limited to buyers' agents) will make the consuming public more acutely aware that the listing agency actually provides the seller with only two services of unique value: *agency representation* and *putting the property on the market*. Sellers will know that others have more to do with actually locating buyers than does the listing agent, even in the traditional system. They'll also know the real worth of CMA's, as opposed to formal appraisals.

- **Technology** involves computers and the internet, fax machines, video tapes, answering machines, cell phones, and beepers. Gone forever is the time when creation and maintenance of a homes-for-sale database (eg., the MLS) required a sophisticated network of agencies, centralized staff, and controlled distribution system. Today's technology makes it easy for both private sellers and various professional service providers to put a home on the market where any buyers' agent and many buyers (more every day) can effortlessly find it.

- **Credit cards** enable a client to pay for flat fee services (including appraisals, advertising, and Internet listing) independent of a mortgage lender or sale income (which will still pay off charges). Before credit cards, sellers short on cash were captive to agents who alone had the legal right to make fees for such services contingent on sale. With credit cards, that exclusive advantage held by agents evaporated.

SHORT-SIGHTED REACTION of traditionalists to inevitable dynamics may be self-defeating, neutralizing two current resources which could give them market advantage in the coming age of customer quality. The first is their market appeal as *agents*, something being crippled by their own ill-advised double dealing legislation (Chapter 8). Undermining the common law conceptions of agency by trying to legitimize double agents will only cater to the often-flawed notions of sellers that they really do not need any more agent representation than they can get from their lawyer. That is unfortunate, for market understanding is far different than legal understanding, and the team of both lawyer and agent is invaluable seller support. Ironically, the double dealing legislation is sacrificing seller-agent credibility in the hopes of getting buyers to trust seller agents — a hopeless objective in an age of increasing consumer sophistication.

Disorder legislation of seller-agent lobby is self-destructive

MLS must adjust

THE *SECOND* CURRENT RESOURCE traditionalists could be wasting is the MLS itself. MLS domination of the market can be maintained by listing properties on a competitive cost flat-fee basis; i.e., without exclusive listing and full service commission requirements. There is nothing proprietary in the simple database management techniques of the MLS, and competing listing services — even FSBO registries — are already emerging. Buyer agents have an absolute agency obligation to their clients to search all sources of properties; thus, the monopoly cannot be held together by the old control of listing agent over subagent. Holding out and refusing to provide low-cost flat-fee MLS access to sellers will not only destroy MLS's current competitive advantage, but eventually, its competitive viability.

That is not likely to happen any more than survival of the legislative double-dealing. Progressive selling agencies will simply see the writing on their computer monitors and beat the eventual stampede. Flat-fee seller agency is inevitable. So is the downsizing and career adjusting it will bring.

DIMENSION THREE

The Now

IMPORTANT!

Page references

In Chapters 10 and 11, page references in the book margins have added importance. Most of the content in these two chapters relates directly to previous observations. Page references are used as an alternative to restatement.

CHAPTER 10

The Now for Buyers

EW FIGURES have been as widely portrayed in American song and story as the gambler. From Old West saloons to urban smoke-filled rooms to casinos in Las Vegas and Monte Carlo, movie-goers have felt the high-stakes tension as bets are called and the cards turned. We never tire of the plot, perhaps because it is a romanticized metaphor for so many of the routine negotiations of real life. Still, while we may thrill in the risks of the on-screen gambler who just may have to depart through the nearest window, few of us really want to gamble in the important matters of our lives. And yet, in one of the biggest decisions most of us ever make — the purchase of a home — the metaphor of the professional gambler has several lessons.

Anyone who thinks a game of poker is a matter of drawing the right cards is an amateur. Everybody draws winning hands and losing hands. How much of a "gamble" the game actually is depends on how much one *knows*, relative to what the opponents know. The pro *knows* how to read the players as well as the cards, what to do with the cards that are dealt, and how to use the money he brings to the table. The catch is that the other players are playing the same game, and all doing their best to limit and even misdirect what the others really "know." They do that by keeping their cards covered, and by *bluffing*, i.e., sending the wrong signals. A pro playing with amateurs is not really gambling; neither is an amateur playing with pros.

The business negotiating table is not unlike the poker table; wise players take no suggestions from the other players about what moves to make. Your knowing what is needed for the right move is not among the ethical responsibilities of the other players in your poker game or house purchase. Informed choice is not something a genuine sale's agent willingly gives a customer.*

*Above, pages 34, 115, 133

Access to "the whole deck"

IN REAL ESTATE, the "cards" are the available homes. In poker, all cards should be available to all players — *provided the deck isn't stacked*. Your stake, the money you bring to the table, dictates what game you're in. Every property in your price range should be available for you to consider; but, what cards you ever get to see depends on who controls the deck. Sellers' agents bring their own deck of *listed* houses.

ONE WAY TO PLAY high-stakes poker is to hire a pro, i.e., literally "stake" a good player to play on your behalf. It is perfectly legitimate, provided the pro is not a "ringer", i.e. undisclosed to the other players. Home sellers traditionally hire stand-ins, so prior to disclosure laws, a typical traditional game put amateur players (buyers) against professional ringers with stacked decks.

Hiring a pro

DISCLOSURE LAWS have "outed" the ringers. Sellers' pros are still in the game; but it's not the same because you *know* it, and you *know* you too can hire a pro. The difference now, as I have said throughout this book, is consumer *awareness*.* From the old-order maxim of "let the customer beware" to the new-order disclosure requirement to "let the customer be aware", traditionalists have obviously never been great fans of buyer awareness, something made more than evident in the attempts to legislate disorder. ** In stark contrast, buyers' agents thrive on the development of customer awareness.*** While *property* is literally the stock-in-trade (the item sold) of the sellers' agent, *awareness* is the stock-in-trade of the buyers' agent.

Awareness is the buyer agent's stock-in-trade

* "Consumer awareness" is cited 36 times in the index.

** Above, pages 191–196

***Above, pages 72, 115

And yet, increased consumer awareness benefits not only buyers and sellers in the long run, but professionals on both sides. As well as more business for buyer agents, it means more profitability for enlightened *seller* agencies, once they dispose of non-quality procedures and costs.**** Thus, the inevitable future of real estate brokerage looks good for consumers and profes-

****Above, page 162

sionals — but where does that leave a buyer who wants to do business today?

Buyer is empowered now

THE ANSWER is that, for the aware customer, the future is here today! As I said in the first chapter, "the traditional system ... even as it now stands, has absolutely no power over those who know what is going on." *

*Page 27

In reading this book, you have already taken at least the first step to be one of "those who know what is going on". But what this book is, and its limits, should be kept in perspective. There are two distinct dimensions of the house-search and purchase process:

- the direct subject matter of property, from its physical aspects to dollar value, and the legal processes for transferring title;

- the market *system* itself, including the changes taking place within it, as well as the attitudes, relationships, and behavior of the system professionals.

Playing with the pros

As I SAID in the beginning, this is not a how-to manual for house-buying or house-selling; i.e., not about the first, but the second of these dimensions, about the system and the system professionals.**   Frankly, if they had their act together, you'd never need this book at all.

**Pages 27–28

In such an ideal-world condition, all you'd need is enough awareness of property, and of the mechanics and tactics of buying and selling, to enable you to hire the right agent with in-depth knowledge in these matters. Precisely because the current world of the agent is far from ideal, this book on that world becomes a prerequisite to any dealing with agents, your own or the sellers'.

The assumption underlying the rest of this chapter is that you *will* be working with real estate agents, and that you in fact do want one who is working *for* you fully as *your* agent — i.e., an exclusive buyers' agent who, by definition, works in an exclusive buyers' agency. Thus, the two remaining sections deal with the (a) "preliminary" stage before finding your agent and (b) what happens once you have found him/her. To the degree that you are confident of your own ability to proceed with less than such degree of professional assistance, you can easily adjust the substance to your own particular case. For me to proceed with any other assumption, however, would require cluttering the text with "ifs", "ands", and "on-the-other-hands"....

A. Preliminary Stage: Reading and Reconnaissance

With the right buyers' agent, you wouldn't need this book or any other, or to otherwise develop knowledge about real estate, law, or market practices. Of course, the "right" agent would have to be:

- a trustworthy professional steeped in knowledge fully applied on your behalf;

- a mindreader who will understand what you want and need even regarding things about which you have developed no understanding.

But, how would you select the right agent in the first
place without at least *some* prior perspective on the
subject matter? And even a mindreader could not read
what is *not* written on your mind, like your preference
between a pair of options you don't know exists.

The only way to have real assurance that the agent
knows what he/she is doing, and is fully representing
you, is to have some substantive knowledge of your
own about the areas in which you'll be enlisting an
agent's help. The best way to begin is to do just what
you are doing now — read! (This is, of course,
absolutely vital if you intend to proceed on your own,
without an agent.) In addition to this book about the
real estate system, I highly recommend to buyers the
following works on the details of buying and selling
real estate which should be available at your local
booksellers:

- *Trips & Traps When Buying a Home.* Robert Irwin.
  McGraw-Hill, NY. 1997. (A second Irwin work is
  Tips & Traps When Selling a Home.)

- *Kiplinger's Buying & Selling A Home.* The staff of
  Kiplinger's Personal Finance Magazine. Times
  Business (Random House), NY. 1996.

- *Not One Dollar More* Joseph E. Cummings, Kells
  Media Group, 1995.

- *100 Questions Every First-Time Home Buyer
  Should Ask.* Ilyce R. Glink. Times Books (Random
  House), NY. 1994.

- *Your New House.* Alan & Denise Fields. Windsor Peak Publishing, Boulder CO. 1994. This book deals with new construction.

- *Sonny Bloch's Inside Real Estate: the complete guide to buying and selling your house, co-op, or condominium.* H. I. Sonny Bloch and Grace Lichtenstein. Grove Weidenfeld, NY. 1987.

These complement the work now in your hands. No more than in the earlier chapters is the purpose of this chapter to teach the dynamics of housebuying — things covered by these recommended readings. The previous sections were about the system; this is about how *you* are going to encounter the system realities. The intent here is to bring the observations and lessons of the previous chapters together in a way that is useful for you as a buyer.

Remember, this is still *preliminary* to your actually searching out and choosing an agent. The idea is to maximize and organize what you do know regarding what is relevant to judging the suitability of a buyers' agent to your needs. The first part is to read; but the second part, still in this preliminary phase is an active *reconnaissance* of the local market making direct, but cautious, observations of properties, media, people, and customs.

13 buyer essentials

I'LL GET TO THE SPECIFICS of reconnaissance in a few pages, right after putting you through a necessary exercise — the itemizing of what you already know about what you will be encountering. After reading this far, here are the essentials you should keep in mind:

1: See pages 2, 7, 49, 85, 88, 109, 144–145

1. You are the customer, and it is your money that will be paying for everything, all costs, all profits, all commissions, all fees.

2: See pages 71–72

2. The customer determines the specifications for what he/she is buying (material or service), which includes not only the form, fit, and function of the purchased item, but the price and terms of purchase. Conformance to customer specifications is the very definition of **"quality"** and is enforced by a customer's awareness of purchase alternatives.

3: See page 34

3. Fiduciary obligations are not owed to you by anyone other than someone you expressly employ as your agent. It is most likely that any agents with whom you may be dealing actually do owe such responsibilities (e.g., confidentiality, loyalty) *to the seller.* As the customer, and not the client of such people, you are owed "fairness" but, practically speaking, that most often reduces to merely meeting specific disclosure requirements and avoiding tangible misrepresentation. What a buyer reveals to the seller's agent must, by law, be revealed to the seller.

4. Your buying power is a function of the knowledge and awareness at your disposal (yours and your agent's) regarding alternative choices, rights, and capabilities at every decision point in the process (yours and your agent's) regarding alternative choices, rights, and capabilities at every decision point in the process.

> **NOTE ON FIRST FOUR:**
> The first four items in this list of 13 "essentials" will also be referred to as the "key essentials" or "keys."

5. **Property purchase alternatives include all properties, offered for sale or not,** for which you might be willing to make a purchase offer. Among those for sale are those **listed** by real estate agents, and for sale by owner (FSBOS).

5: See pages 112, 174–175

6: See pages 122, 128–130

6. **From your perspective, the value of a property is the amount competing buyers are willing to pay for it.** If you want the property, it is the amount you have to meet before someone else does, or exceed if other bids are imminent. The **"value"** is not the same as its **"worth"** to you, nor is it set by the owner, by agents, by lenders, or the municipal assessors. It has nothing to do with its previous sale and purchase prices, nor with any work, time, effort, or dollars the owners may have put into the property. It is not even set by certified appraisers, though a certified appraisal is the best estimate of value. The best basis for judging value is to personally visit several properties either of known value (i.e., appraisal certified) or fully comparable to properties of known value; then compare the subject property to what you see there.

7: See pages
125–128

7. A competitive market analysis (CMA) by a seller's agent or any entity earning a commission based on the price or contingent on the sale is a completely untrustworthy indicator of value. Ultimate judgment of value of a given property should incorporate appraisal by a certified appraiser, and never rely on a CMA.

8: See pages
131–132

8. Buyers should expressly revisit and adjust their specifications as they grow in awareness of the market and their needs, and co-buyers should communicate that to one another. The **worth** of properties is based on these personal specifications independently of **value**.

9. Property should never be bought above worth, though a knowledgeable buyer may have personal reasons to buy above value, say, proximity to an ailing mother. Worth to a single buyer does not set the value of a property. For instance, if a property's value is $200,000 but a seller holds out for $250,000, and it is worth that to one buyer alone, the property's after-sale value remains at $200,000 because there is then no one for the new owner to sell it to above that price.

10. It is the job of sellers' agents and subagents to get you to reveal what a property is worth to you, and use that in the *seller's* interest. It is their job to cultivate your trust, and advise the seller against accepting any offer less than that worth. A wise buyer will never disclose (or let any behavior hint) to a seller, seller's agent, **subagent,** dual agent, or affiliate of such persons, that a property's worth is above value or any potentially successful offering price. It is a negotiating mistake to let any information regarding your motivation to buy, and especially of any need to buy, be conveyed to the seller or the seller's people.

11. **Dual agents may be ethically satisfied with a price that is above value and below worth,** telling themselves that both buyer and seller "came out ahead" — even though the seller may have been shown the true value and accepted a price at that level.

12. **Knowledge of your financial capability in the hands of anyone but your own legally-bound agent will almost certainly be used in the interests of others.** "Others" includes not only the seller, but the seller's agents, subagents, dual agents, and affiliates. People making their property available for your inspection and those expected to give serious consideration to your offer to purchase are entitled to assurance that you are indeed financially capable of delivering what you offer or promise, *but nothing more than that.* Involvement in a buyer's development of purchase financing is the usual method by which such persons gain excessive information regarding a buyer's personal financial affairs. Like revealing worth, any indication of buyer affluence motivates those on the seller side to hold out for a higher price; and some professionals may be motivated to steer you toward certain properties based

12: See pages 106–107

on your financial depth rather than your specified wants and needs.

13: See pages
139–145

13. **The "offer to purchase" is *your* offer.** It should say what you want to say, offer what *you* want to offer, and accomplish what *you* want to accomplish. The offer and acceptance is an affair of buyer and seller and should not be clouded by language inserted by agents to protect the interests of agents. The accepted offer should constitute a complete and valid contract, legally binding both parties to what they have agreed upon. Your offer inherently proposes a rationale for a seller's acceptance; and you have a right to be assured that such rationale is articulated fully and clearly to the seller, including responses to the seller's questions. That assurance may require the offer to be presented personally by you or your agent.

The "key" essentials

*Above, page 221

THE ABOVE THIRTEEN POINTS are the essentials you should be carrying from the prior pages as you begin your reconnaissance of the local real estate market and profession. I will occasionally refer to them as "Essential #1, #2 ..., etc." As implied in the note after Essential #4,* the first four — the "keys" —are of special importance; they are the keys to your control over the purchase process. The following summarizes these four "keys":

1. You *are the customer;*
2. You *set specifications;*
3. No one *but your agent has fiduciary obligations to you;*
4. *Buying power is a function of* awareness.

My semantic mischief in using the phrase "working ON buyers" as a spin-off of the traditionalist "working-with-the-buyer" charade may be harsh for some good people who, despite working both sides of the street, simply entered a professional system that was "the only game in town" and do provide at least the best service the system allows. The problem is that the system also allows a lot of things by a lot of people who are not going to be working in your interests. It is up to you to take control.

The four keys come down to:

1. *knowing who you are,*
2. *knowing what you want,*
3. *knowing whom you can trust,* and
4. *knowing what you know and don't know.*

In reality, these key essentials do not develop in this neat sequence. Knowing what agent you can trust (key #3) very much depends on how well you achieve keys #1, #2, and #4; and yet, part of the agent's job is to help you develop in these very areas.

Key #4 may in fact be seen as "the key to the keys", for it not only establishes the confidence you can put in your mastery of keys #1, #2, and #3, but also the reason for hiring an agent, i.e., to fill in the gaps you see in your own knowledge and abilities. This also identifies key criteria to look at in your choice of an agent, for the agent must have two specific competencies, encompassing not only what he/she knows, but also what he/she doesn't know. This is reflected in two general areas of performance you will be seeking in a buyers' agent:

- the agent's specific area of expertise, i.e., the local real estate market, including properties and their values, as well as the local real estate profession and its dynamics;

- critical areas beyond the agent's personal expertise, yet requiring the agent's advice, referral, cooperation and/or coordination regarding qualified experts (eg., attorneys, appraisers, inspectors, lenders, mortgage brokers, etc.).

Things to do before selecting an agent

THE AGENT CANNOT BE an expert in everything; but, beyond the primary area of real estate competence, he/she can at least be competent in the matter of using relevant experts. Thus, to facilitate your choice of an agent, you want to develop your own sense of the substance of each of these two competency areas.

Some minimum sense of what inspectors and appraisers do will emerge as prospective properties are visited and considered; and you will not need to select these people until after your search has narrowed to a specific property. On the other hand, it will serve your interests well to have your financing and legal representation in order prior to making your offer. Thus, the remainder of Section A is structured to help you develop awareness, before meeting your agent, in two areas: (1) the local real estate market and (2) attorneys and financial experts.

1. Local Market — Property, People & Practices: Complement your general study with reading local real estate advertisements, and with some cautious visits to open houses — the beginning of your reconnaissance — to begin developing a basis for your understanding of local value. Make that "open houses *only*": do not make specific appointments to see houses; do not visit listing agencies; and do not let listing agents escort you to houses; visit only during declared "open house" hours when the homes are specifically open for general viewing.

I used the word "cautious" because your visit to a home which eventually emerges as a purchase possibility could become the basis for a listing agent's claim to be the procuring cause of your interest and, therefore, entitled to the buyerside portion of the commission. While the *seller*, and not you, would have to pay that, it exerts obvious upward pressure on the seller's price demand. One way to protect yourself from this possibility is to look at homes you are sure you will *not* buy, such as those above and below your price range, and those in a style or location you know you don't want. Keep a looseleaf notebook record of all such visits. If possible, do not identify yourself to agents, explaining that you are only in preliminary stages of looking at the general market. Do not for one moment in your conversation with agents ever lose sight of Essential #10 (above). Politely tell sellers' agents that homes to be seriously considered will be those arising from investigation with a buyers' agent.

Caution

The agent's reaction to the mention of a buyers' agent will be part of your learning experience. Keep in mind that you or your agent may in fact one day be negotiating through this individual or one of his/her associates, so do not create barriers by debating opinions. Once out of the agent's sight, record both your declaration and the response in your notebook, along with whether or not proper agency disclosure was made, whether such disclosure was qualified by any of the "curves" described above, or whether the agent actually displayed an enlightened attitude regarding buyer brokerage. To the notebook entry, attach any descriptive material available along with brief notes of your own impressions of both the property and the neighborhood.

Notebook

Take your notebook task seriously. Keep the notebook (3-hole, 8½" X 11") in your car, along with a three-hole punch, a stapler, a role of tape, and plenty of blank pages. Use the sheets both for notes and for attaching small items; and staple together all items on the same property.

Focus on value and worth

IT IS IMPORTANT to not lose sight of your objective in keeping this notebook. What you are trying to do at this stage is develop a preliminary sense of property value and of worth. The properties should be kept in the book, not according to location, or listing agency, or asking price, but in order of their comparative values as you see them. The actual dollar amounts are not the criteria at this stage, just whether you judge one property as legitimately commanding a higher or lower price than another, and putting them in that order. Make sure the asking prices are in the record and, as events transpire, record price changes and sales prices — but keep them in the order of your estimate of relative value (remember essential #9, that a specific sale price doesn't necessarily denote value). As you keep up this exercise, you will start recognizing when certain numbers are out of line, and you will develop a perspective on the value impact of different communities and neighborhoods, and on the underlying reasons.

2. The "Others" — Lawyers & Lenders:

Here too, awareness begins with reading, and the recommended books on buying and selling have something to say about the roles varied professionals play in your search and purchase effort. Beyond such general reading, it will be helpful if your reconnaissance of the local situation provides perspective on the local players before you begin interviewing agents.

One of the thorniest early problems you will face is whether you should accept recommendations of agents, attorneys, appraisers, property inspectors, lenders, mortgage brokers, or other business people about each other. The very fact that they can refer business to one another sets up income interests which may or may not be in your best interest. There may even be referral fees *(see box)*, which should be dis-

> This practice is not to my liking, but it may be a local area practice in which an ethical agent or attorney passes on the benefit to clients as a fee reduction.

closed to you; and simply comfortable relationships can color the most well-intended perspective on one another's professional competence.

On the other hand, you do want a team who can work well together, and competent professionals know who the other competent people are. Moreover, the buyers' agent who is, by definition, a guide through the purchase process, necessarily compiles a list of professional resources specifically for client referral. In the end, the credence you will give such referral is a judgment call; how sound a call will depend on how well you cultivate your awareness.

Never lose sight of the fact that these people are in business, that they all have something to **sell,** and — one more time — you want to buy what you want to buy and not what they need to sell. You want to know what their services or products mean to you. If the agent's referral is a factor, then you also want to know what the service or product means to the agent, and whether the provider might want to please the agent more than you. Just like your buyers' agent, you employ lawyers and inspectors to dissuade you from making any purchase not meeting your quality needs (legal or physical) . However, practical reality dictates that their future income most likely depends more on pleasing the referring agent than pleasing you. An aborted sale pleases no agent whose income is contingent upon it; thus, purchasing through a sellers' agent can make every person you hire part of the *seller's* team and not your own!

WHERE THE DEVELOPMENT of a realistic local perspective may be especially critical is in the selection of your attorney. I cannot imagine any corner of this country where it is not a good idea to have an attorney in your corner in the purchase of real estate. You certainly want to be sure that the documentation is legally valid and properly recorded, and that you are fully protected in matters of liability or necessary recourse. However, the specific tasks attorneys perform in such assurances varies from state to state, and sometimes even between neighboring counties. Thus, you have some preliminary local shopping to do, at least laying some groundwork via the telephone, if not in a few face to face interviews.

In one state, attorneys actually perform and personally guarantee title searches, both of which are handled by title insurance companies in other states. In one county, lawyers alone write purchase and sale agreements, while in the next, agents do it. In some but not all locales, an attorney representing the lender manages the actual transaction in which property and money are conveyed.

Attorneys

THE PRACTICE OF THE conveyance session being managed by the lender's attorney can restrict your range of choices of an attorney. Since the lender legitimately passes all expenses along to the borrower (buyer), it is invariably cost-effective for the buyer to use the lender's attorney; and the lender will often allow the buyer to name the attorney from its approved list. The lender's interests almost perfectly coincide with the

Using the lender's attorney

buyer's in terms of the property sale, so if there has been no misunderstanding in terms of the loan agreement, the lender's attorney is free to provide full client representation to the buyer in the sale. Three problems can still arise:

- prior personal commitment to an attorney not on the lender's list;

- the lender represents significant future business for the attorney, and his/her focus on the lender's issues may distract from aggressive attendance to your interests;

- the list may be limited to attorneys with a traditional, old-order understanding of real estate.

These are all reasons to have lender and attorney selected before offering on a property. If a lender's list does not meet your needs, you may choose a different lender or accept the additional cost of a second attorney to represent your interests *(see box).* In some cases, the problem may simply be technical and cultural lag — a matter of your buyer's agent or his/her professional association updating the local bar or a specific attorney on buyer brokerage (What better tool for this than a gift of this book?).

This is not really a good idea if it is just a matter of a prior personal preference rather than a performance question. It then becomes just a case of an extra pair of hands to spoil the soup, two offices working many of the same documents, compounding costs and chances of error.

Whether your choice of an attorney is limited to a lender's list or extends to any attorney within range of your private jet, there are certain constants to consider regarding how well one might represent you in a real estate purchase. The practice of law covers many specialized areas, all encompassed by a lawyer's license, but not necessarily by his/her expertise. Moreover, the legal technicalities involved in a real estate transaction are distinct from the business dynamics taking place which are not inherent in a lawyer's license or training. As a practical matter, you want to know the attorney's claimed areas of expertise *before* you reveal what you are looking for. The search for an attorney is one endeavor in which word of mouth may not be reliable. People may have faith in Thurgood Darrow because he handled a divorce or some court case superbly, or maybe even the sale of their home; but even real estate law experience doesn't guarantee a grasp of the buyer's perspective. Accept no lawyer who has bought into traditionalist "no difference" pitches, or who sees no risks of conflict of interest in mixed agencies. You do want an attorney who can be part of *your* support team, a *buyer's* team, ensuring that your offer is legally sound and your interests legally protected, ensuring that the things for which you have bargained do become fully yours and legally recorded.

Most attorneys will not blatantly pretend an area of expertise or experience just to get your business. Nevertheless, you must insure against the few who will stoop to such behavior; and you also want to avoid those who unintentionally deceive because they miss the subtle distinctions of buyer representation. Telephone attorneys' and ask them or their staff to tell you in what areas of the law they specialize. If they respond by asking you what you're looking for, cross them off your list. Ask questions without tipping them off about what you regard as the "right" answers.

Lenders UNLIKE INSPECTORS AND ATTORNEYS, lenders provide a product (money) rather than a service; and while the product is necessary it does not make the lender (and probably not the mortgage broker) truly part of your team. That makes a difference in how you develop your awareness, particularly prior to selecting and hiring your agent. Preliminary preparation here is substantially more in reading than reconnaissance. While personal attributes are important in your team members, what matters with product providers are the attributes of the product (loan money) which includes its terms and its price (interest). You are the lender's customer, not his/her client; the lender may be a client of the mortgage broker. Whether you buy what they need to sell or what you need to buy should be a pure matter of numbers, and of clauses which translate into numbers; but they are salespeople with a product, and good salespeople will put the power of personality into the sales effort directed at you and those who might influence you — including both buyers' and sellers' agents.

Their sales tools aimed at agents might include the referral fees mentioned above, which agents should disclose to their clients (putting the obligation to tell you only on a *buyers'* agent). It will certainly also include intangibles which range from careful cultivation of personal goodwill and friendship to services which save the agent time, effort, or money.

Though such services, from credit checks to problem-free fast expediting of loan applications, may legitimately benefit you, those benefits must be weighed against the *numbers*, the real short- and long-range costs to *you* rather than what it does for the agent.

You want to develop your understanding of the numbers, and the language which still translates to the numbers, without the influence of the sales personalities. So, get your preliminary understanding from *reading* before your reconnaissance activity exposes you to pitches from the local loan industry. The following would be a profitable exercise for you to do after your basic reading and *before* talking to either lenders or agents: Find out where the local loan rates and terms are published regularly and use the explanations of terms and concepts in the recommended readings to understand the published comparisons between lenders. Watch for flawed reports which do not fully explain conditions or which do not compare the interest rates of competing lenders according to standardized criteria. *(see box).*

This exercise will prepare you to at least ask intelligent questions and to make informed judgments about the responses you get from lenders, mortgage brokers, or agents.

I do then recommend active general reconnaissance of the local lending sector — actual visits to lenders and mortgage brokers to hear what they have to offer, a simple information

A n advertised low rate for Bank A might be lower than Bank B's rate because Bank A also charges discount points which you pay up front. The **Annual Percentage Rate** (APR) is also known as the "true rate" because it accounts for such costs.

gathering tour, collecting brochures and business cards, and making no commitments or applications. After then analyzing all options, you may want to pursue application with a particular lender, especially if it does not involve significant expense or commitment.

Remember that this reading and reconnaissance of both the local market in the real local world is your preliminary work, intending to give you a comfortable basis of awareness before selecting an agent. Depending on how aggressively you attend to it, and your prior knowledge and experience (including whether you are relocating from outside the area), this phase can range from a few days to several weeks, but not longer for serious buyers.

Buyer agents

THE OTHER BIT OF RESEARCH that you have to do in this phase is a rather obvious one — finding who and where the buyer agents are. Of course, you first need to understand what an "agent" is, and then what a *buyers'* agent is. **You now know that anything less than an exclusive buyers' agent in an exclusive buyers' agency, or a single agent in precise conditions,* is not really an agent at all.** Thus, once you find those who say they are agents, you'll need to do some screening to separate out the real buyers' agents.

*pages 78–79, 242

There remains a problem. In some areas in these early days of buyer agency, the screening could leave you with *no* genuine exclusive buyer agents (EBAS). It might be worth your while at that point to try to persuade one of the wanna-be's to take the plunge and start as a full-fledged buyers' agent with you as his/her first client. Such an area might well represent an explosive market opportunity for its first buyer agency.

WITH NO EXCLUSIVE BUYER AGENCIES in the area, you may be obliged to settle for limited specialized services. I would avoid at all costs the non-exclusive agent who claims to be an exclusive agent; but an openly disclosed non-exclusive buyers' "agent" can provide useful specialized services to an aware buyer. The fact that such specialists might call themselves "agents" may not be important, and may mean only that they don't know what an agent is. It is not important because you know what the word means and won't let expectations of full agency lower your guard against adverse interests. Give the specialist no information you don't want sellers to know, especially about the *depth* of either your buying power or interest in a particular property. Arrange your financing outside the agency, independently develop your own perspective on area market values, and write your own offer with an attorney.

When an EBA is not available

All things being equal, non-exclusive buyers' *specialists* fall far short of the genuine exclusive buyers' agent in terms of meeting your needs; but, when the latter is simply not available, a competent specialist in buyer service can at least be better than the traditional subagent. Norm Braverman, CEO of *Best Agents*, a nationwide buyer-agent referral service (see below) recommends true exclusive buyer agents wherever they exist and, where they do not exist, their counterparts in "smaller independent firms experienced in buyer agency with a minimal number of listings to minimize the conflict of interest."

When a non-exclusive specialist is all you've got, state that you expect him/her to be working FOR you, and to disclose that to sellers, including those listed by anyone in the specialist's agency. The specialist's chief help to you should be in market access; spell out that "working for you" means bringing to your attention every property that potentially meets your specifications — *listed or unlisted* — and any holding back is cause for termination.

The next two pages contain a list of resources for beginning your search for a buyers' agent or (if none available) buyers' specialist in your local area. This is not an endorsement of those you locate via these sources, but merely an assist to put you on be the right track. It is up to *you* to determine if the professional you contact is indeed an exclusive buyers' agent — or the most suitable buyer specialist in those areas still beyond the frontiers of the consumer revolution. Take these sources for what they are. Those leading to true exclusive buyers' agents are specifically indicated. Publications are not responsible for how advertisers define themselves; referral services try to distinguish between agent types for your information, but still rely on the professional's self-definition; and the Realtor® organizations' (including REBAC) position openly encourages mixing of seller and buyer interests within agencies.

Sources

■ The Yellow Pages.

■ Newspaper ads in the real estate and business sections of your local newspaper. Watch for special real estate editions or supplements.

■ Local area real estate magazines.

■ National Association of Exclusive Buyer Agents (NAEBA)
(800) 986-2322
Established in 1994, NAEBA is the only national association of true exclusive buyer agents.
E-Mail: info@naeba.org. Web: http//www.naeba.org
7652 Gartner Rd., #500, Evergreen, CO 80439-5204.

■ National buyer agency franchisers listed here have toll-free numbers waiting for you to ask for the name and phone of their nearest local office, each of which is a true exclusive buyer agency. All will provide referrals beyond the locales of their franchisees. Each has its own website, giving more information about the organization than practical here.

◆ Buyer's Resource Inc., (800) 359-4092
Established in 1989. Currently in 20 states.
393 Hanover Center Road, Etna NH 03750.
E-mail: info@buyersresource.com
Web: http://www.buyersresource.com

◆ Fidelis, (800) 950-9003
Established in 1997. Currently in 9 states.
2247 San Diego Avenue, Suite 232, San Diego CA 92110
E-mail: fidelis@pacbell.net
Web: http://www.fidelisrealty.com

◆ Only Buyers America Real Estate. (888) 552-8937
Established 1996. Currently in 15 states.
3661 South Narcissus Way,
Denver CO 80237-1235
E-Mail: bmiller@onlybuyersamerica.com
Web: http://www.onlybuyersamerica.com

◆ The Buyer's Agent, Inc. (800) 766-8728
Established 1988. Currently in 28 states.
1255 Lynnfield, Suite 273, Memphis TN 38119.
E-Mail: rebuyragt@aol.com
Web: http://www.forbuyers.com

■ Buyer agent referral services: At no fee to the buyer, these services will
identify true exclusive buyer agents in exclusive buyer agencies, though
their referrals are not limited to such agents.

◆ Best Agents, (800) 962-1313
E-Mail: norm@bestagents.com
Web: http://www.bestagents.com

◆ Buyer's Homefinding Network, (800) 500-3569.
Buyer's Resource affiliate.
E-Mail: info@finderhome.com
Web: http://www.finderhome.com

◆ HomeBuyer's Champion Network, (888) 332-8937.
Only Buyers America affiliate.
E-Mail: pyarmo@onlybuyersamerica.com

■ Local and state Boards of Realtors® should be willing to provide you
with lists of members who are exclusive buyers' agents. Despite the organization's response to buyers' agents reflecting its overwhelmingly seller-
agent majority, buyers' agents do belong — especially where Realtor®
membership is required for access to the MLS. Use caution regarding a
Board's interpretation of who and what is a buyers' agent.

B. Working with an Agent who's Working for You

As a group, exclusive buyers' agents are among the most conscientious people I have ever met, and passionately dedicated to the customers' interests. Other people in most professions, including real estate sellers' agents can be just as conscientious and dedicated; but, at this early stage in the evolution of buyer agency, there is an obvious selective mechanism at work putting disproportionately more of the good guys on the buyers' side. These are the leaders in consumer advocacy in real estate, on the cutting edge of the customer quality revolution, taking on all the costs and risks that entails. For one thing this venture begins with the social cost of the resistance and even hostility of the traditionalists, no easy thing for people who inherently care deeply about others. All pioneering ventures entail risks, but this one has the added problem of highly organized sabotage of its income channels ranging from systematic "commissionectomy"* to deceptive legislation supported by a professional association to which most buyers' agents pay dues.** Such conditions tend to act as a moral filter, most often being overcome only by strong belief that what one is doing is "the right thing", a criteria relevant only to good people.

*Above, pages 90–92

**National Association of Realtors®. Above, pages 183, 185–189, 191

No question about it.... You'll find more good guys here than in most other places, at least until well after buyer brokerage becomes fully institutionalized as the usual way to buy a home, and the social costs and financial risks are greatly reduced. And because the good guys got in first, they'll be the established firms on the buyerside even after the latecoming opportunists (who are in every profession) also join their ranks.

Caveat DESPITE ALL THAT, I now have to tell you that being "good guys" should not be good enough for you. For most people, the purchase of property is among the biggest business deals of their lives. You need a good person who is also a good *business* person, and neither is guaranteed by the other. I have said that, all other things being equal, an exclusive buyers' agent is your best choice, and I will stand by that. However, the second-best choice is probably a small agency **single agent** who could sign on as your buyer's agent after establishing that you have no interest in the few listings he/she might have. But, suppose things are not equal, that your choice is between two clearly ethical people, one being a new exclusive buyers' agent and the other a well-experienced single agent...

Selection criteria YOU NEED TO BE SELECTIVE, and the preliminary awareness-raising activity in Section A* should help you make informed judgments as you visit with candidates for the position of your buyer's agent. You should be somewhat familiar with local property types and values, and how those things generally vary by community and neighborhood. You should also have

*Above, pages 217–240

some idea of local commission structures, and perhaps about attitudes toward buyer agents. And, of course you should have reviewed the thirteen essentials and feel that you have a firm grasp of the four keys. These are all things your prospective agent would normally discuss with a prospective client; and because of your experience with the subject matter, the quality of conversation should indicate how well your candidate both knows the area market and understands the keys to what you need in an agent.

BEYOND UNDERSTANDING, you want to know if the agent can deliver what you need. What does the agent's advertising and conversational claims say he/she can do for a buyer, and what evidence is there to back up the claims? Are there letters of satisfaction from satisfied customers, and past clients you can call? Does the agent have all the resources needed to carry out the job?

Past performance

A LACK OF RESOURCES can be a matter of just not having enough money, or a reflection of a lack of commitment or even task understanding. A new agency, as many buyer agencies indeed are, may be on a tight budget; but even here, you need to weigh the practical impact upon the service you are seeking. Perhaps you can live with an agent who has no cell phone, but certainly not with one who has no access to the MLS.

When the agency's resources belie its professed commitment to or understanding of the job to be done, then you want to move on to another candidate.

Resources

An agency claiming to be able to help clients with finding legal and financial services should be able to show you current physical lists of attorneys and lenders. If the agency claims (as any buyer agency should) to assist with active searching of all homes for sale, even outside the MLS, then let it produce not only the MLS documents or direct computer-connect, but the list and descriptions of current FSBOS, and explain how the list is updated.

Technology

LOOK AROUND THE OFFICE. Is it equipped and maintained as a modern professional business? Are there multiple phone lines, answering machine, fax, copier, and a computer? Moreover, can the agent who will be working as *your* primary agent in this office use each of these things, or will the computer or even the fax only be at your service during the hours the secretary or office "techy" is on the job.

The agent's technical ability is important, sometimes vital to the buyer's interest. Recall that the heart of buyer agency lies in keeping the client prepared, aware, and informed.* The "informed" part is tricky because *information* fast becomes mere historical data when it's received too late to act upon. Windows of opportunity for the right purchase open unpredictably and close the minute a competing buyer gets there with an offer. An agent's cell phone and lap-top computer can be the determining factor in who first learns of a property on the market and who gets the first appointment; and office-based equipment is an absolutely minimum requirement to even be in this fast-paced competition.

*Above, pages 115, 215–216

It is all about information and timing— even on the sellers' side. Properly informed sellers are those who know the market value of their property; often, only time (rather than the seller's agent) properly informs the seller as the property sits, attracting no offers. The common buying approach is to shop among the "sitters", to assume overpricing and make an offer below asking price, hoping the seller either anticipated a below-price offer or has gone through the time-informing process and is now resigned to true market value. Most homes are probably bought and sold this way, but when an asking price at market value appears on the market — either new or via the "sit-and-drop" process — it fast disappears because market value is by definition the price buyers are *willing* to pay. Buyers who are never in this competition, never able to capitalize on this opportunity, are those not in a position of instant access to the information nor set for instant action. Technology counts.

"Technology" is not limited to equipment, but includes the systems, procedures, and even materials the agency has put together specifically to serve buyer clients. Look for such systematic approach in the agent's description of how the agency works, and ask for examples of materials used. In the discussion on BAD Phase I, I discussed the first meeting with the agent and suggested:

> **The buyer should go home with all materials, most especially the unsigned agency employment contract, mull things over, and be sure he/she is**

*Above, pages
117–118

*fully aware of the whole process, benefits, costs,
and bail-out options before signing on. **

It is as much to the agent's advantage as yours to have
you commit to an agreement you fully understand and
know is in your interest. Along with the agreement the
agency will want you to sign, you will also want to
bring home a copy of a typical offer form of the agency.
To facilitate your review of these documents, the box
below contains a mini-index of the relevant text passages on each document issue. Take your time as you
review the forms, consulting the referenced pages as
necessary. Your objective here should be to develop
issues to discuss with the agent to tailor the agreement
to your needs. That does not mean the documents
must conform to my notions of a "good" document as
expressed in these particular specifics. It does, however,

Mini-index to
Agency Contract & Offer

underscore the often repeated message of this book that is expressed in the first two *key essentials:*

1. **You are the customer;**

2. **You set specifications.** **

**Above, pages 220, 224–225

These "keys" are not mere philosophical principles, but the straightforward *reality* which must be conveyed through clouds of traditionalist illusion. You need an agent who fully understands and commits to this, whose every word and action tells traditionalist listing agents that

- he/she is employed by you and by neither them nor their client, and also that

- both their client and they, or someone else, will be paid only for meeting your specifications.

KEYS #1 and #2 are the *alpha* of the thirteen essentials, with the *omega* being #13, i.e., that you the customer will set the specifications for any transaction with the seller in your offer.* Thus, these two documents — the agency agreement and the offer — encompass what buyer agency is all about. Make sure they both exactly reflect and fit your ideas about how you and your agent will be working together.

Examine the employment agreement and offer forms

*Above, page 224

With agreement between you and your agent about the specifics of the property search and purchase process, there remains only two issues before the two of you actually get to it; i.e, the matter of how you'll bail out of the process if it is not working and, of course, the fee. The rationale for "easy bail-out" is not complex, once considered: client retention by the agent is protected by *performance* in the client's interest, so a termination-at-will clause is appropriate with wording that protects against using it to avoid paying earned fees.*

*Above, pages 95–96

The ground has also been pretty well covered here and in Chapter 6 regarding the amount, and structure of fees. A final perspective is appropriate regarding the channeling of the buyer agent fee through a sellerside **conduit**. Remember that it is your paying the bills that gives you the right to call the shots, and that nothing in the way the business is conducted should be allowed to credit either seller or seller's agent (most especially the latter) as the bill-payer. The worst traditionalist habits, counterproductive to the interests of both seller and buyer (as demonstrated in the Benjamin County examples**), are fed by passing buyerside payments through the listing agent. For some, the mere "touch" of the money is both habit-forming and hallucinogenic, for they simply cannot break the illusion that the buyerside fee is something the *listing agent* pays according to his/her interests. The one cure is complete "cold turkey" withdrawal.

**Above, pages 63–66, 91–92

The offer form

***Above, pages 90–91

AT THE VERY LEAST, the offer form should never describe the buyer fee as a percentage of purchase price, which contributes to traditionalist images of a common pie and the temptation to finagle a bigger slice.*** Actually there is no reason to even use the seller as a conduit, for the disbursement of funds straight from the transaction can provide for direct payment to either the buyer or the buyers' agent. I am now convinced that an even better way to insulate both buyer and buyer's agent from the nuisance of traditionalist commission games is to not even mention the name of the buyer's agent in the offer or cash settlement schedule! Agency fees (on both sides) should be fully protected by the respective agency agreements; specification in the offer, purchase and sale, or even the settlement sheet is overkill.** The purchase and sale agreement and settlement distribution need merely provide that both principals receive enough cash to cover their fee obligations or reimburse their already-paid expenses (specifying the amount).

** Above, pages 89, 92, 142, 145

Accordingly, to the degree that the offer form provided by your prospective agent highlights *you* rather than the agency and avoids statements of *the agency's* rights (relying on its separate contract with you for that purpose), you *might* be able to infer the following about the agency:

- its focus is where it should be, on the interests of its clients;

- it is secure in its ability to perform and be profitable without overreliance upon legalistic devices;

- its procedures are forward-looking, designed specifically to accomplish the task ahead, rather than glued to paths of the past.

Fee structure

You MIGHT WANT to personally follow suit on the "forward-looking" angle. Do not close your mind to retainers and pay-as-you-go fee plans. The traditional practice of making agency commissions contingent upon sale and not due until closing may have a certain attractiveness, but not really be to your advantage. For one thing, a contingency fee is necessarily higher than a non-contingency fee; it is also meaningless if you know you are going to buy (you will be given access to everything available; see box below). For another, if you have the credit or cash to buy a house, then you have what it takes to pay the fee and/or retainer; the savings in fee reduction should far outdistance any credit charges from a legitimate lender or even a credit card. Brokerage fee rebates to the buyer can be for fees paid as well as fees due, thus providing payoff of the borrowed funds. If lender will not provide cash to the buyer, then the buyer agent can accept a fee and rebate to the buyer for earlier payment.

Specifying what you want

ONCE YOU ARE SATISFIED that you have found a fully qualified, committed and resourced exclusive buyers' agency, it then comes down to agreeing upon how this agency is going to work for you, and upon what *you* are

> **I**f the agency is a truly exclusive (dedicated) buyer agency. On the very day I write these words, my area's Sunday paper has a large agency ad with nearly 100 listings surrounding a boast of extending its services to include buyer agency. *Beware! Beware! Beware!* See pages 171–173.

going to do for your part in making it happen. Your part will involve two things:

- active time-consuming activity, and

- paying the agent for his/her part.

It follows that the more the agent does, the higher fee the agent merits. It also follows that the more you can do for yourself — *which does not add to the agent's time and effort* — the less fee the agent should expect. The agent may have a package price that is fair (hopefully not the traditional three-P* structure) for buyers requiring the full package of agency services. As an aware and self-prepared buyer, what you require is your choice, and the full package may indeed be best for your circumstances. Still, remember that the fee is negotiable, and that you can do things to reduce the agent's costs and risks, even while serving your own interests to a higher degree.

While the major reason for developing market awareness before engaging an agent is to help insure the right choice of agent and agency agreement; such preparation should also have the effect of reducing the time an agent will have to spend with you. If you have also taken your own steps in terms of acquiring pur-chase money and legal representation** (accounting for the lender-lawyer relationship described above) that also represents a substantial savings in agent time. Time is money, *literally* in the case of an agent retained by the hour, and that can be a substantial savings to you — especially if you are prepared to move decisive-

*Above, pages 60, 89–91

**Above, pages 229–236

B U Y E R　N E E D S

		Finding Money	Finding Attorney	Acquiring Property
F U N C T I O N S	Advice	Yes	Yes	Yes
	Research	On file	On file	Yes
	Escort	No	No	Yes
	Representation	No	No	Yes

Table: Agent Functions and Buyer Needs

ly toward purchase. Even with an agent who does not work by the hour, a prepared buyer means a time savings and a dollar savings; so use that in negotiating the agent's fee.

Use and misuse of agent time and effort

LET'S LOOK AT THE AGENT'S PART in your joint work effort. Carrying over from traditional real estate practice, buyers' agents typically provide assistance in three areas: finding mortgage money, finding an attorney, and finding and acquiring property. In each of these areas, assistance may take the form of one or all of four functions: research, advice, escort, representation (standing-in). The table indicates where the agent's efforts are best and most economically spent in the buyer's interests. The "No"s do not mean "Never", but that it is not generally the most cost effective use of an agent's time to be escorting buyers to lenders and attorneys, nor to be standing in for the buyer in dealing with these people. On the other hand, the buyers' agent should have updated files on attorneys, loan sources and interest rates for your reference. In addition, his/her advice on these matters can be invaluable, and not take a great deal of time. Thus, while it is a good idea to have laid groundwork toward lender and lawyer selection, it is usually wise to avoid committing to either until after hearing the advice of your agent.

The real message of the table is not terribly profound. The string of "Yes"s in the last column says it:

if you want to get the most for your money from a real estate agent, then put him/her to work in real estate!

That, of course, is the message of the third column; but what this series of "Yes"s does not show is that the relative amount of time needed in each of these individual activities will vary from buyer to buyer. Buyers relocating from distant areas may need escorting more than those who are native to the area. Buyers with demanding professional responsibilities may require the agent to examine the homes and report back (research) before they will take their time for a visit.* *Above, pages 97–98

You need to know what the best mix of services is for you, and to make sure a clear statement of service expectation, price, and method of payment is part of your buyer agency employment agreement. Whatever you decide about the distribution of tasks between yourself and your agent, you should know at every point in the process exactly where you each are and how well you are being served. Recall that the *purchase*

Sales Process	S1. Find and qualify prospect (buyer)	S2. Show and sell property.	S3. Convey property and liabilities
Purchase Process	P1. Prepare buyer.	P2. Find and qualify prospect (property)	P3. Acquire property and benefits.

The Sales and Purchase Processes

process is not a *sales* process, as clearly shown in the Sales and Purchase table comparison above (repeated here from page 105). Because it reflects *your* objectives and not those of the seller, it establishes the basis for *your* management and assessment of the process according to what you want to get out of it.

It is also the structure of the discussion of buyer agency on pages 104–157. Again, we want to avoid rehashing material that's only a few page flips away; but another "mini-index," on the next page, should be helpful for a quick brush-up on any point needed for clarity.

Agent's role — and yours

THE PROCESS IS NOT SO TIGHTLY STRUCTURED that it will not allow for you and your agent to follow any agreed-upon approach. The business of your financial preparation (mini-index, B1) provides a case in point. The text on this aspect of the process (pages 106–111) is not about the mechanics of financing, financial analysis, the laws and procedures of lending, or the various types of loans and lending institutions. There is no reason to duplicate things adequately covered in the recommended readings (as well as in any conventional book about buying real estate); and there are many professionals right there in your area (including your agent) available to advise you and even actively guide you through every step of financing your purchase. This text is about the broader issues arising *prior* to the mechanics of arranging financing, involving system pitfalls, matters of whom to trust, and questions of optimal use of time, effort, and money. Using the right agent — whether as simply an advisor (as recommended) or as active finance chaser — the mechanics will fall into place.

The text on Property Search and Qualification* does include some specific activity sets which your agent may or may not be set up to do as I have

*Above, pages 111–134

Mini-index to the Purchase Process

Sales Process versus Purchase Process: 104–105.
B1. FINANCIAL PREPARATION: 106–111.
B2. PROPERTY SEARCH & QUALIFICATION:111–134.
    Buyer Awareness Development (BAD): 116–132.
        BAD-I — Disclosure: 116–118.
        BAD-II — Profiling: 118–122.
        BAD-III — Value: 122–131.
        BAD-IV — Tailoring: 131–132.
    Quality Purchase (logic, not emotion): 132–133.
    Due Diligence and Stopping the Sale: 134.
B3. ACQUISITION (Offer): 134–157.

described. They may simply not fit with a system your agent already has implemented. What matters most are the objectives these procedures are intended to achieve. At the least, the approaches described here provide a framework for discussion between you and your agent, and for comparative judgments leading to under-standing and agreement about what you want to accomplish and how you're going to do it.

*pages 116–132

The entire Buyer Awareness Development* (BAD) process of Dimension Two is about expanding your awareness, something you can largely accomplish on your own without interfering with the agent's efforts.

**pages 118–122

***pages 131–132

Profiling (BAD-II)**, for example, is simply a matter of coming to self-understanding; and *Tailoring* (BAD-IV)*** is a continuance of that. The agent's objective perspective, as well as his/her experience in the process with other buyers, should be invaluable but not essen-tial. Recall that this expanded profile displaces a source of agent headaches directly attributable to the conven-tional approach acquired from traditional real estate, so it should be welcomed.

Respecting your agent's role

****Pages 122–131

THE "SPECIFIC ACTIVITY SETS" (above) most likely to challenge some agents are part of the *Development of Value Perspective* (BAD-III)**** One of these is the "drive-by" element, and any unescorted activity of buyer-clients within the "pouncing range" of other agents. Both law and the Realtors® Code of Ethics pro-tect contracts between parties from interference by third parties; the classic example is one agent coaxing the client of another to terminate or violate the contract. By-and-large, traditional agents respect the integrity of *listing* contracts, but some, in classic denial, cannot grow beyond old order mindsets formed in a time when only property was put under contract and buyers were "fair game". Thus, in some areas, buyers' agents who allow their clients to tour the market unescorted might rightly worry about traditionalists who simply cannot comprehend the legitimacy of *buyer* contracts. In such areas you can both ease your agent's anxiety and protect your own interests with simple precautions:

- Do not deliberately contact other agents.

- When inadvertent contact does occur, *immediately* disclose that you are contracted to a buyers' agent, perhaps even giving the other your agent's business card, and promptly report all such contacts to your agent.

- Do not deal with other agents at all without the presence of your agent and even then, only in strict accord with the advice of your agent.

- In general, neither request nor acknowledge information, and refer all information requests to your agent; express no potential interest in any property; acknowledge no advice or recommendations.

Respect your exclusive buyer agency contract and the protection it gives you as well as your agent.

*Above, pages
65–66, 92–93

Remember the high-risk, low-return sellerside philosophy, and that your protection against that is the
agent's exclusive contract with you. *

The Buyer's Market Analysis

Also within bad-III, the procedural detail of the
Buyer's Market Analysis (bma)** might prove daunt-
ing to some agents, or simply not fit into the existing
operating procedures of others. Agency efficiency —
to your benefit — is facilitated by a certain amount of
standardization of the services provided to its various
clients, so the agent may have good reason for not tak-

**Above, pages
128–130

ing on the detailed tasks as specified here. There may
already be an internal system in place, or perhaps even
the use of an external value-estimating service. Even
with total agreement with the method, it may not be
possible to set up a "base list" with "anchors", "variants"
and "location factors"*** in time to apply to *your* prop-

***Above, page 129

erty search. Nevertheless, the philosophy is right, and
simply formalizes the value comparison process both
agents and buyers intuitively perform. So, mere discussion of the bma process between you and your
agent, involving any relevant properties in the agency
file, may at least accelerate your local value perspective
development. Without complicating the agent's work,
and based upon understanding of bma, you could still
organize your own notes as you look at properties; that
organization, however informal, should still provide:

> *a value perspective that is more organized that*
> *the one carried [intuitively]... and more trust-*

****Above,
page 130

> *worthy than the one being sold by the sellers'*
> *agents.* ****

Right up until the moment the property is located, every step you have taken in the purchase process can be regarded as your personal preparation. The preparation is over the moment the offer decision is made; you are at the point of Essential #13, the "omega",* where the inevitable becomes the *"now."*

*Above, page 247

It is not the end of the purchase process, of course. That comes with acquisition, but it is pretty much the end of things to say about your dealing with your buyers' agent (the actual subject of this book). The overriding issue of buyer agency is that

> *everything that takes place after this point must be determined before this point i.e., in the decisions that you make regarding your specifications to be presented in your offer.*

The decision issues are of two types, the broad process issues covered in the section on acquisition**, needing no expansion here, and locality-specific issues which cannot be covered here. This is the time not for dealing with the buyers' agent, but for the buyers' agent to do the dealing.

**Above, pages 134–157

CHAPTER 11

The Now — for sellers

Crazy! You'd say I'm crazy, if I dared to suggest that someone seeking to sell his or her home might want a good buyers' agent...

— Very first words of this book.

B Y   T H I S   P O I N T, I have pretty much established that some of my best friends are buyers' agents, *but.....*

Let's face it, you do not want to hire a buyers' agent — or a buyer agency — to *sell* your house. A word of caution: in self-defense, a *seller* should define "buyer agency" to include *all* firms promoting buyer agency as a regular service. That means especially those double agent firms pretending to fully serve both sides. The fact that **dedicated** buyer agencies would never accept such a firm as a legitimate buyer agency is no reason for you to now accept it as a legitimate *seller* agency.

Understanding agency and nonagency

Now, that doesn't mean that you necessarily do not want to do any business with such firms. You certainly do not want to (a) retain as an agent someone who has agency obligations to adverse interests, or to (b) retain limited agency service from someone charging you a full agency commission — but it might benefit you to (c) be a straightforward *customer*, paying for a specified service that is useful to you. These assertions (a, b, and c) may require some expansion and review of earlier text:

(a) Adverse Interests: Full fiduciary (agent) service by one entity to both buyers and sellers in the same market is by definition impossible. Any organization (eg., a real estate firm) is a single entity in which members are bound by powerful social and financial interests, bringing their individual ties to external opposing interests (eg., buyers and sellers) into internal conflict. By *law* in most states, this must be disclosed as **dual agency.**

(b) Limited Agency (& full commissions): Dual agency constitutes less than full agency service, *disabled* by the very definition of certain **fiduciary** duties from full provision of them all. Eliminated by definition is *undivided loyalty* and, thus, help with positioning for advantage in the give-and-take of buying and selling. The duty of *full disclosure* to each client is limited by the duty of *confidentiality* to the other. Reduced agency service would seem to call for a reduced agency commission.

(c) Specified service customer: If you are not looking for "agency" from *the* agency, then a specific service (eg., MLS) for a fee might be appropriate.

"Oh, come on, Mr. and Mrs. Seller. We haven't changed everything just because we now do buyer agency as well as seller agency. Yes, it is true that we can no longer give you undivided loyalty. And yes, we also cannot pitch your house to our buyers if we can get them a better deal elsewhere... but we still haven't changed everything. After all, we are still charging you the same commission."

Seek a dedicated agency

Agency is just one of the services a real estate firm can provide to a seller, but just calling a firm an "agency" does not guarantee that service. It is not well-advised to look for legitimate full seller agency in any firm marketing itself as a provider of both buyer and seller agency. Seek trustworthy seller agency in **dedicated** *exclusive* seller agencies; i.e., those providing seller

A legitimate full-seller agency meets all six fiduciary responsibilities of undivided loyalty, utmost care (due diligence), disclosure, obedience, confidentiality, and accountability.

agency and only seller agency. Note that such firms do include *some* traditional agencies!

The obvious logical approach is to look at the full menu of services each firm provides, and the costs and benefits of each. The trick, it seems, is to understand what *agency* — the fiduciary package — gives to you as something separate and distinct from other services of the firm. Other services might include (and not be limited to) publishing availability of the property (eg., MLS, newspapers, the Internet, even a yard sign), provision of needed forms, value estimate, and/or procedural advice. Such things are all quite natural for an agent to provide along with agency; but they are not agency, and can be provided by people other than real estate agents.

You hire people to do things you want done, but you either cannot (or choose not to) do on your own. More than simply having something done, agency creates an extension of yourself, empowering someone to not only act and speak, but see and hear on your behalf and in your interest. The agent is not simply someone you hire to perform, but someone through whom *you* will perform. What your agent speaks and mispeaks, *you* speak and mispeak; what your agent sees and hears, *you* see and hear. You are the principal, the *doer*, with all the agent's abilities and knowledge added to yours and subordinated to *your* interests.

What is it that you cannot do, that you now need the function of agency to accomplish? What is it you

O nly licensed agents may, under the law, charge fees contingent upon the sale of the property.

will not get done, by using your own abilities, and then simply hiring the needed non-agency services?

The answer is to **sell** your property, i.e., if you want your property *sold* in the sense of someone actively *selling* it, aggressively and strategically moving it on the market for the highest price, in the shortest time, and at the best (for you) terms. Accomplishing this requires combining the "non-agency" services with strategic persuasive interaction with prospective buyers by either the seller or someone fully empowered to act on the seller's behalf. If you want active *selling* of something of significant value of yours by someone else, then you want that someone to both have the knowledge, resources and skills to do it effectively, and the clear-cut fiduciary obligation to do it in maximum fidelity to your interests. That is the benefit of agency.

You will *get* genuine agency only from dedicated exclusive seller agencies, including those traditional agencies which do not extend their invitations to buyers to lengths that bring them into implied dual agency. It safely includes traditional agencies which make full lawful disclosure without adding the "no-difference curve" and without carrying the "working *with* buyers" pitch to the point of dual agency. It also includes *non-traditional* agencies which remain dedicated to representing sellers and only sellers.

SINCE THE BENEFIT of agency is that it supports aggressive **"selling"** in the full sense of what that word means, it follows that you would forego the cost of

Hire a sales agent

Your choices

agency if either (1) such "selling" is not what you are looking for, or (2) you could effectively sell it yourself.

(1) To "sell" or not to "sell":   The "Bought, not Sold" theme of this book might hint that I would advocate against "selling". Such is not the case. I do advocate open-eyed affirmative *buying* so that, after the transaction, the buyer will know the property has been bought for all the right reasons, because it is right in every way for him/her, and not because it was *sold* over and above practical reasons for not buying. Such active *buying* is made necessary by the unavoidable and legitimate reality of affirmative selling. I advocate the use of *purchasing* professionals for two reasons: (a) to counterbalance sophisticated selling techniques of *sales* professionals, and (b) to supplement the buyer's knowledge of the complex and largely unknown aggregate he/she will be getting from the transaction (i.e., the property).

Likewise, I strongly advise open-eyed affirmative *selling* so that, after the transaction, the seller will know that the reason for selling (rather than giving) was because the right price was paid, and not because the buyer or commission-earning agents *sold* him/her on the idea that the price was right.

(2) To sell it yourself or go with a pro:
Will professionals *net* you more money than you'd get on your own?   If not, will sparing you any effort, time, or stress in the process be worth the cost?   Today, the process is far more complex than in days past, in terms

of legal liability for disclosure and social responsibilities toward protected groups and the environment. Also, the advent of buyers' agents now adds reason for you, like buyers, to counterbalance the professionals on the other side.

However, what you will get from the transaction (i.e., money) is far less complicated than what the buyer will get (the property), and does not require anything comparable to the buyer's need for investigation of property details. You do want to be certain that you get what you should get, but the professional who can most impact that is not the agent, but the *appraiser*, who will show you what price to accept* Also, your interests regarding legal aspects of the transaction should be the focus of your *attorney*.

*Above, pages 125–127. Listing agent is not a reliable authority on property value.

THESE ARE THE ISSUES you must weigh in your decision of whether or not to use an agency or go the "FSBO" route.** On the other side of what you have to gain is the cost — i.e., the fee which you should be willing to negotiate — and the risks. The risks are of two types: (a) to your own interests and (b) to the interests of others who may hold you legally liable. Beyond basic competence, the first risk issue relates to the level of *trust* you can put in the agent to truly serve your interests; the second (which we'll deal with first) is that of *liability*.

Gains, costs, and risks

**Above, pages 45, 209–210

Liability

*See page 82

AN INDIRECT RISK of agency is the *liability* you assume for the actions of your agent, and the traditional system actually extends that risk through the network of sub-agency*.   Recall that the agent of your agent — the subagent — is *your* subagent.   It is conceivable that with increasing awareness of how naive buyers are led to believe the subagent is *their* agent, that court action might be brought not only against deceptive subagents, but against their principals — and that could include you. This neither calls for abandonment of the sub-agency system, nor for your own refusal to use sub-agents, but you do want statements in your contract with the listing agent to the effect that:

(1) the listing agent will clearly instruct subagents to make open, honest, and uncompromised disclosure;

(2) the listing agent will confirm that such disclosure is understood by the buyer;

(3) the listing agent will hold you harmless from (i.e., accept complete responsibility for) inaccurate representations made to buyers by him/herself and/or subagents; and

(4) the listing agent has and will maintain a current "errors and omissions" insurance policy which will cover such damages (you might want to examine the policy).

THIS "FOUR-POINT SOLUTION" to the problem of sub-agent liability is far superior to the **"seller's customer-agent mandate"** (SCAM) approach described earlier * i.e., mandating that co-broking agents enter into a buyer-agent contract with the buyers. In that approach, making the co-broker the *buyer's* agent relieves you of the subagent liability. The SCAM approach fully deserves the openly contemptuous acronym, for the very purpose of agency is to serve clients, not to create a cover for the sabotage of their safeguards!

Of course, you, as the seller, do have to protect yourself from the event that an over-eager subagent makes some claims you never intended. However, full protection is provided by the straight-forward above board four-point solution described above. Think about this very carefully:

> *Why would you as a seller ever sign a contract to be the client of an agent who would advocate creation of an agency contract explicitly designed to shortchange a client?*

Now, it also should be noted here that this nevertheless highlights one advantage the seller does derive from buyer-agency. If you should sell to a buyer legitimately represented by a buyers' agent, then you in fact will not be liable for mistakes made by that agent. Moreover, to some degree, *some* oversights made by you or your agent may in fact be mitigated by the fact that the buyer had professional representation. This is not an excuse for misrepresentation, for the days of

Reject SCAM and those who advocate it

*Above, page 82

caveat emptor (let the buyer beware) are over; but a potential charge of taking advantage of a "naive" buyer carries far less weight when the buyer has the personal service of his/her own purchasing professional. Of course, the reality is that the presence of a competent buyer's agent actually means a far less likelihood of successful misrepresentation.

Finding a trustworthy agent

I STATED THAT LIABILITY is the *indirect* risk issue of agency, rising from disservice or damage to the interests of *others,* actually an indirect risk to *your* self-interest. Self-interest is, of course, your very reason for hiring an agent and placing trust in him/her. The *direct* risk of investing trust in another is that of it being placed in the hands of the wrong person, one who will put his/her interests above yours. There are certain tests you can make of an agency's trustworthiness:

Trust Test #1: *Does the agency have adverse interests in its client population?*

1: See pages
172–175

Mixed service agencies as described here actually *invite* adverse interests into their client base.

Trust Test #2: *How does the agency treat other clients?*

One treatment test is closely related to Test #1. Given that some clients can accept the reduced agency level of a mixed-service agency, are they still being charged full agency fees?[2*]

2*: See pages
262–263

Another case in point, already noted, is that of converting a subagency customer into a client for the express purpose of limiting his/her recourse (i.e., SCAM).[2**]

Still another case in point —the following true scenario, as testified to by a buyer regarding conversation with a seller's agent:

2**: See page 82

> *The agent told the buyer that he was sure the owner would accept an offer below the asking price.*
>
> Buyer: *"Are you supposed to tell me that about your client?"*
>
> Agent: *"Why would you care? A lower price is better for you."*
>
> Buyer: *"What's best for me is to deal with people I trust. Your client can't trust you, and neither can I."*

Trust Test #3: *How does the agency treat non-clients?*

Focused on his own self-interest, the agent in the above scenario tripped himself up because he assumed all others are the same. The same blind spot may be operative when you ask agents about how they handle buyers. Will they let buyers think they are the agents' clients? Will they make the required disclosure (Did they do it with you?), or will they try to mitigate the disclosure with distortions like the "no difference" pitch? You cannot trust someone to be honest with you who will deceive buyers. Moreover, if the agent actually believes there is no difference between seller and buyer interests, then this is not the person to sell your property.

Trust Test #4:   *Whose interest is reflected in the agency's commission splitting?*

*Above, pages 51, 63–64

Remember the Benjamin County listing agents taking twice as much of the commission as they gave to co-broking subagents.* If they are really pushing to *sell* your house, shouldn't the incentive be out there for people to bring in the buyers? While 50-50 may be the norm, wouldn't high selling motivation be indicated if the lion's share went to the subagent?

Trust Test #5:   *Is this a selling or a listing agency?*

**Above, pages 49–50, 62–66

There was adequate discussion earlier of the pitfalls of engaging a listing agency rather than a selling agency.** As implied in #4, the commission split can be revealing.

Another way is to simply find out how many listings the agency has and how many full- and part-time agents. An agency will generally take pride in telling you how many owners use its service and how big its staff is. Divide the number of listings by the number of full-time agents (count four part-timers as one full-time). Be aware that ten listings per agent does not mean four hours of a forty-hour week are devoted to servicing each listing (i.e., finding buyers), for inventories are built by chasing *list-*

ings, not buyers. Assuming equal time between listing and selling, the service per listing is thus
reduced to two hours, less what it takes to go to the
bathroom and other diversions. Of course, equal
time *cannot* be assumed in an industry with the slogan: "If you list, you last"*; nor will it exist in an
agency with commission structures which make the   *Above, page 49
collecting of listings "high-reward, low-risk", and
servicing buyers a "low-reward, high-risk" waste of
time.**

**Above, pages
65–66

Trust Test #6:   *Do they simply tell you what they believe you want to hear?*

All sellers want to hear that what they have to sell
is worth a lot of money. Remember that there are
more reasons for an agency to list your house than
to get it sold, that your $100,000 house advertised
for $150,000 will attract $150,000 buyers who can
be sold something else. You can and should know
the market value of your house before talking to
agents. A real appraisal from an unbiased and certified appraiser will usually cost less than $200 or
$300 and be the best single investment you can
make to insure a timely sale. Knowing the real value
also gives you a basis for testing to see if the agents
will cater to your suggestions of putting it on the
market at a ridiculously inflated price.

Trust Test #7: *Will they use lip-service to your interests or subordinate your interests in service of their own?*

One clear example is the shaving of dollars for themselves off compensation to subagents and buyer agents. Will they use diminished commissions to restrain buyer agents from bringing good offers?* Will they argue that it is in *your* interest to hold back commission shares, but not turn over the savings to you?**

*Above, pages 65, 86–87, 91–92

**Above, pages 86, 91

Likewise, will they tell you it is in your interest that the commission you pay to them include any buyer-agent fee; and will they dare to require that in the listing contract? Recall that a buyer-agent fee is set between buyer and agent (as the seller agent fee is set between you and your agent) and that the buyer's offer will likely include money for that fee and stipulate direct payment, making no difference in what you net from the sale. Deleting or modifying the stipulation voids the entire offer and risks any ultimate deal solely for the interests of the listing agent.

Trust Test #8: *How truthful are they in explaining the reasons for certain policies or actions?*

What do they say about their fee policy? Fees are negotiable and not set by law; moreover, *they may not be set by any association or agreement between agencies (spoken or unspoken) — price fixing is against the law!* If any law or regulation or Standard of Practice is cited as a reason for not agreeing to something, pick up a pencil and ask what the specific authority is. Do not bluff; write it down and check it out.

Remember that *you are the employer* and your agent will be your employee, and the listing contract is the employment agreement. It is not his/her "policy" which defines the job description, but *your service specifications*. Even before you become a client, you are at least a customer, the object of a sales pitch for client services. Remember that quality is all about conformance to customer specifications, not about the agency's "policy". What makes the quality revolution work is *you*, the customer, knowing what you want, setting your specifications, and exercising your option to reject any would-be provider who will not conform. You do not conform; the agency does. You do not bend your specifications to "policy" requirements set in the interests of the agency; you do not accept any listing contract which does not subordinate the agent's operating preferences to your specified needs.

SOME LISTING AGENTS easily run afoul of both Tests #7 and #8 in the matter of their "policy" on **buyerside** commissions; i.e., those earned either by subagents working with buyers or by buyers' agents. Rather than pay subagents well enough to create a real selling incentive, they keep the lion's share of the commission for themselves as in the Benjamin county case*. Regarding the matter of direct payment of buyer-agent commissions, either from the seller or the conveyance officer at the transaction, a not-infrequent listing-agent

Seller agent motives regarding commissions

*Above, pages 63, 91

reaction exposes the basest of motives. When a buyer's offer nets you a bottom line that meets your needs, no true "agent" acting in the seller's interest would require or even suggest rejecting the offer (as *any* change will do) to force the buyer's agent fee to pass through the listing agent's hands.

And yet, within the very week I write this, I hear from buyers' agents Ronn Huth in Massachusetts, Anne Cloy in Florida, and Gloria Arneberg in Minnesota of acceptable price offers being voided by deleting the clause that keeps the listing agent's hands off the buyer-agent fee. One listing-agent motive for hanging onto the job of paymaster can be purely monetary, for in the event the buyer-agent fee is lower than anticipated at the time of listing, the difference can be pocketed by the listing agent instead of the seller. Most often it is a matter of control, and of the reactionary politics of traditionalist resistance to buyer agency. What it is *not*, is an action in the interest of the seller.

What traditionalists cannot afford is for you, the seller, to see the reality exposed by the two separate payment channels for sellerside and buyerside fees. To witness that reality now, let us simply follow the money through several scenarios. Scenarios #1–#6, below, all are about a $190,000 property put on the market for $200,000. Listing commission is 6%, with the understanding that it might be shared with other agents working with or for buyers.

Scenario #1: Listing agent (LA) offers 3% to subagents (SA) who bring several buyers with competitive offers. Quick sale is for $190,000. The 6% commission of $11,400 is split evenly as promised.

NET: LA-$5,700; SA-$5,700; SELLER-$178,600.

Scenario #2: Listing agent offers only 2% to subagents, who are less motivated to bring buyers.* House sits a little longer on market and eventually sells for only $180,000. Commission is $10,800.

*Above, pages 65–66, 91–92, 272

NET: LA-$7,200; SA-$3,600; SELLER-$169,200.

In Scenario #2, *listing agent gets a bonus* of $1,500 over Scenario #1 *for costing the seller $9,400.* This practice occurs not only in Benjamin County,** but elsewhere simply because the reality is obscured by lumping the two commissions as one to the listing agent. One commission can result in only one entry on the settlement sheet at the conveyance session in which title and money are passed; payment of the second commission technically becomes a simple expense of the seller's agent, undisclosed, but for which the seller is ultimately liable.

**Above, pages 86, 91

Scenario #3: Buyer making acceptable $190,000 offer specifies direct payment to buyer agent (BA) of $5,700. SA agrees and reduces listing commission to 3% because it obviously meets spirit of the orginal agreement with the Seller, with the exact same financial outcomes as scenario #1...

NET: LA-$5,700; BA-$5,700; SELLER-$178,600.

Scenario #4: Same as scenario #3, but buyer agent (BA) fee is only $3,000. SA agrees and reduces listing commission to 3% because SA's effort is exactly as in Scenario's #1 and #3 and still in the spirit of the orginal agreement with the Seller. Lower BA commission benefits seller.

NET: LA-$5,700; BA-$3,000; SELLER-$181,300.

Scenario #5: Same as Scenario #4, but SA balks at direct payment and convinces seller to delete clause (thereby making counter-offer). Buyer accepts counter offer. SA collects full 6% commission of $11,400 and then pays BA fee of $3,000. Lower BA commission benefits listing agent..

NET: LA-$8,400; BA-$3,000; SELLER-$178,600.

Scenario #3 demonstrates that direct payment of buyer-agent commission in itself makes no difference whatsoever to the money outcomes for any of the clients or agents involved. All things being equal, it is exactly the same as Scenario #1, conforming to the understanding at the time of listing. Scenarios #4 and #5, show that while direct payment to the buyer's agent does not deprive the seller's agent of one cent of the full listing side share (3%), *it does keep him/her from pocketing the unearned dollars at the seller's expense!*

*Above, pages 86–91, 97–98, 144–145

As explained in Chapter 6,* the buyerside commission is set between buyer and agent, reflecting work required and not the sale price, and might easily (as in Scenarios #4 and #5) be below the anticipated 3%. The buyer agent's commission might also be *above* 3% if the particular buyer has made extraordinary requirements upon the agent. Thus, the following scenario is possible:

Scenario #6: Buyer makes $197,000 offer, expanded to cover direct payment to buyer agent (BA) of $8,000. SA agrees to reduction of listing commission to 3% because SA's effort is exactly as in Scenario's #1, #3 and #4 and still in the spirit of the orginal listing agreement with the Seller.

NET: LA-$5,910; BA-$8,000; SELLER-$183,090.

The above scenarios should create a framework for understanding what really takes place when an owner engages a listing agent, whether that is properly expressed in the listing contract or not:

- there are *two distinct sets* of activities involved: (a) maintaining and promoting the listing and (b) finding and coordinating buyers. (Traditional listing practice admits to this in the subagency commission share).

- An apparant market price established over many decades for **typical** services on each side appears to be 3%.

- Lumping sellerside and buyerside 3% commissions into a single 6% commission to be distributed by the listing agent invites agent self-service and seller loss. It is hardly more difficult to write out two commission checks than one, and doing so keeps control in the hands of the seller, i.e., *your* hands.

Reject one-lump fee structure in the listing contract

THE ABOVE SIX SCENARIOS are not offered here to imply that skimming commission shares from the buyerside of the table or pocketing savings belonging to the client is typical of listing agents; and only two of the six (#2 and #5) were such cases. Still, neither the opportunity nor the temptation would exist at all if the listing contract simply provided *one fee* for listing-ser-vice and seller representation, *plus an additional fee* if and only if the listing agent (or agent of the listing agent) produced a buyer. This would allow for the sell-er to find a buyer, saving at least that specific fee, or to accept a seller-benefitting offer from a buyer with an agent.   This common-sense approach is presented below as a new and specific type of listing contract.

Nevertheless, even traditionalists without the open-ly quasi-larcenous intent of scenarios #2 an #5 will still manipulate their clients into the one-lump commis-sion payment. Part of the reason is that the two-fee approach exposes something else to sellers: that the fees on the buyerside may *vary* significantly according to the service performed! In Scenario #4, buyer and agent may have set the fee of only $3,000 because the buyer arranged all financing and needed very little search assistance. In #6 ($8,000 fee), perhaps the agent did everything, plus arranging interim housing, furni-ture storage, day care, and anonymity protection. Such performance-based buyer fee variance sets an ugly precedence in the eyes of listing agents, for *sellers* would surely come to expect it as well. Take the following scenario as an example, an actual and recent occurrence:

Scenario #7: A New England buyer's agent escorted his client to a FSBO and an acceptable offer was presented. The owner was never fully confident about working without an agent and, seeing that the buyer was represented, expressed her anxiety before signing. The empathetic buyer and ethical buyer's agent reassured the seller that she was indeed entitled to her own agent. For her peace of mind, she then engaged a listing agent, accepted the offer, and sold the property. The listing agent's total role was to acknowledge that the offer was a fair price and preside over a transaction already made. For that minimal work, *she listed the property at the full commission rate for a deal done before she entered the picture.* The poor owner simply knew no better; the buyer's agent, though astounded, couldn't object on the owner's behalf without both risking his client's deal and being accused of interfering in the agency of others.

THE BUYER'S AGENT told me that the most perplexing thing was that the listing agent was not at heart an unethical person, but a good person who accepted the "ethics" of a traditional system. Such good people, however, instinctively resist changes in traditional systems, especially those changes which will give rise to questions about the real ethics of long-time practices. Thus, one change they cannot allow is for the reality of

Why good people do bad things

separate sellerside and buyerside duties to be reflected in separate fee payment structures; that would give rise to the frightening specter of sellers examining the specific performance factors upon which listing fees are based. In short, it is a certain step in the path toward the flat-fee seller agency described in Chapter 9.

Take charge

As THE EMPLOYING SELLER, *you* should be specifying the terms of employment, rather than be intimidated into accepting those embraced in the policies, traditions, and "official" *forms* of the employee. The listing agreement will likely sport the heading of the agency or its professional association. This is a *cultural curiosity*, not unique to the real estate profession, but functionally inconsistent with the fact that the client is the employer, and the agent the employee. It does, however, seem to be particularly true of real estate that the professionals get impressed with their own stationery and forget who is the boss.

It's you! And it is up to you make that clear at the time of hiring by insuring that the contract includes *your* terms. Let them keep their name on the top in big bold letters; just don't sign your name to the bottom until the *content* is what *you* require.

Standard listing contract

As ALREADY STATED, the employment agreement is the formal "listing" contract *(see box, top of next page)* and, historically, there are three general types of listings:*

*Pages 33–44

(1) exclusive right to sell (ERTS) — the listing agency is the only entity with the right to sell, and gets the commission regardless of who finds the buyer;

There is such a thing as "implied" agency, legally enforeceable; behavior, rather than specific agreement, leads someone into relying upon a perceived agency relationship.

(2)exclusive agency (EA) — the listing agency is the only *agency* with the right to sell, but the owner retains the personal right to sell (i.e., find a buyer) thus avoiding the commission;

(3)open listing (OL) — anyone who brings a buyer gets the commission agreed upon in the sales contract.

In ERTS and EA contracts, other agencies may participate as selling agents only as subagents of the designated agency. In practical terms, the owner always retains the right to sell, i.e., to find a buyer, but in the case of ERTS, the agency still collects the selling commission.

To understand where *buyer* agencies fit into this structure, note that these listing contracts deal with the right to *sell*; they govern only the selling process, *not the buying process*. Buyers' agents *do not sell!* Sometimes they buy, but usually they only advise the actual buyers. Thus, the buyer agent can be involved in all three types of sale as either a stand-in or advisor for the buyer. The only way a listing contract can exclude buyer agents would be to exclude *buyers*, for buyers necessarily bring along their right to have representation. This brings up an important principal:

Within the framework of these three listing types, when a buyer is guided to a property by his/her own agent, he/she has literally come on his/her own; i.e., the SELLER has found the buyer.

This dynamic has profound implications for your decision-making regarding the type of listing you might be
willing to grant:

- the *exclusive agency* (EA) contract suddenly becomes
  far more attractive to sellers and just plain ugly to
  listing agents. Before buyer agents, this listing type
  was little more than feel-good insurance for some
  sellers with vague hopes of finding a buyer on their
  own. Listing agent losses were minimal, but that
  won't be the case with buyers now engaging buyer
  agents in their house hunting.

- the *exclusive right to sell* (ERTS), the heart of traditional operations, does not fit in the new reality.
  Clearly, *two* distinct sets of fee-meriting services are
  performed — seller-service and buyer-service —
  and in a traditional co-broke, both the work and the
  single fee would be shared. Even when a seller produces a buyer, the listing agent still has to handle
  what the amateur seller can't do, so listing-agent
  compensation is still justified; but not fairly compensated for at least the buyer-finding, ironically, is
  the successful *seller/employer*, the reward inexplica-
  bly going to the unsuccessful *employee*. However, it
  is in a buyer-agent sale that the ERTS arrangement
  becomes a totally dysfunctional anachronism. The
  "right to *sell*", is simply an inapplicable concept,
  because the buyer-service performed is *not an act of
  "selling"*. The work does get done, so the listing
  agency need expend no more effort nor receive one

cent less than in a traditional subagency transaction. However, the buyer's agency *cannot* act or accept money as a subagency, nor can the amount of the buyer-agent fee be predicted or dictated by the listing agreement. ERTS is not geared to the unavoidable reality of buyers awakened to their own right to agency representation, and to their ability to *get* it. Its effect is to create opportunity and temptation for a listing agent's self-service at the expense of the client.

Proposed: A new kind of listing contract

I PROPOSE A SOLUTION — a *fourth* type of listing (alluded to a few pages back) which provides listing agencies with the protective attributes of the ERTS while giving sellers the the flexibility of EA:

- the **exclusive right to represent** (ERTR) would guarantee the right to represent the seller as listing agent regardless of who obtains a buyer. That means the agent will administer the listing and advise and represent the seller in dealings with buyers and/or buyers agents, along with associated responsibilities specified in the contract. It should entitle the listing agent to compensation commensurate for these responsibilities (typically about 3%, i.e., the traditional co-broke amount). In addition, *a second and distinct commission* can be paid to the listing agent if and only if the listing agent (or agent of the listing agent) produces a buyer. Thus, it would allow for the seller to find a buyer, saving at least that proportionate fee, or to accept a seller-benefitting offer from a buyer with an agent. An ERTR contract can also prescribe a fixed minimal fee to the agent for any additional work service due to a seller-procured buyer not having professional support.

Be advised that this is only my opinion of "what-oughta-be" and not "what-is". The *bad* news is that most listing agencies are traditionalists and, by definition, obsessive in their clinging to "what-is". The *good* news is that the EA listing (exclusive agency) and even the OL (open listing) *are* in the "what-is" category. Those are the options you — *as the interviewing employer* — can offer the stubbornly traditionalist agencies seeking to be hired by you. If a listing agency cannot see that ERTR protects its legitimate interests better than EA or OL, and every bit as well as ERTS, then shop on. There has to be one smart enough to work for you.

Get a lawyer!

AN IMPORTANT CAVEAT is needed here. What I have just given is *operational* advice — a strategy for dividing tasks and using money as both fair compensation and effective incentive. Close kin to such operational advice is *legal* advice, since the strategy requires agreements spelled out in legally enforceable contracts. And I here (and in other places) do give the one bit of *legal* advice that I dare to give: *get a lawyer!* By all means, get one who understands what you (as his/her employer) are looking for operationally; but do have one in your corner *before* you put yourself in any situations where you might be tempted to put your signature on any contracts. It may be especially important if you elect the ERTR route, for standard ERTR contract clauses will not be in the typical listing agent's sales kit; so your attorney will have to devise them. The trick is to make sure the attorney understands the concept — the *operational* concept — and determining that matter may in fact help you establish whether the attorney is limited by traditionalist dispositions or associations.

Promotion and advertising as criteria

IN DECIDING between ERTS, ERTR, EA or OL, consider how much value you put on *promotion* of your property, and of the potential impact upon promotion of different agency relationships. For obvious reasons there will be no agency advertising of an open listing, and decidedly *less* advertising by the listing agency if there is only an exclusive agency contract; certainly none that will help buyers and buyers' agents identify the property and directly approach you and bypass the listing commission. Under all but the most exceptional circumstances *(see box below)*, a listing agency cannot be expected to advertise your property without the ERTS or ERTR assurance of at least a listing side commission.

Advertising is in fact needed to reach many of the buyers house-hunting via traditional methods, some with no inkling of even the existence of buyers' agents.

> I t is possible that advertising your home may attract several buyers, not accessible with an agency's existing inventory. See chapter 3, pages 47–48.

*Above, pages
65–66

With traditional agency wisdom emphasizing listing over buyer service, even to the point of dismissing selective buyers,* buyers dealing with traditional agencies come to rely heavily on "this week's" real estate page. By contrast, among buyers signing up with buyers' agencies, promotion is of little value; their agents, who derive no income from listings, regularly and aggressively search the housing market for matches to buyer profiles. For such buyers, *just be on the list* at the right price and the right buyer will come to you.

Putting the essence of the last two paragraphs together (advertising *more likely* with the exclusive-right-to-sell or the exclusive-right-to-represent, and *more effective* with traditional buyers), ERTR or even ERTS might be the preferred choice if buyer agency has not yet become widely recognized in the area (which is inevitable, but maybe not today). As more buyers use buyer brokerage, exclusive-agency becomes increasingly a better choice, especially if area listing agencies remain intransigent in their insistance upon ERTS.

The best indicator of total fair market commission expenses for typical brokerage services on both sides is the historical going rate in the area for ERTS listings. Under an EA agreement, a buyer agency purchase will cut that cost to you in half, leaving the EA listing agency out in the cold. And you'll pay no commission at all if a buyer walks in off the street without an agent. Of course, what matters to you is your bottom line, and that depends to a far greater degree on the actual selling price. In an exclusive-agency listing, a **typical** $97,000 offer from a buyer with a buyers' agent would net you about the same as a $100,000 offer through your listing agent.

Property price

SELLERS' AGENTS will certainly encourage the highest offer they can (but the percentage commission makes a far weaker agent incentive than is commonly thought).* While buyers' agents will encourage the buyer to offer the *lowest* price they believe you will accept, they and their aware buyer will *know* market value** and try to outbid the market competition. If your property has had an appraisal (*not* a CMA), you will know the value of your property and how to judge the reasonableness of the offer.

*Above, page 60

**Above, pages 123–124

Going FSBO

IF IT IS YOUR INTENTION to retain the right to sell it on your own, then it is up to you to know all the dynamics and the pitfalls. Read what is suggested here, and more; and talk with your attorney. *You need to know three things: the selling system, what you are selling, and yourself!* To the degree that you do involve a system professional, the less you need to know about the system (just enough to know you have hired the *right* professional).

Hire an appraiser!

KNOWING TO A CERTAINTY at least one aspect of the property is crucial — the market value! Nothing so delays the sale of a property as the owner's inflated view of the value, and nothing so speeds up a sale and guarantees a loss as the owner's underestimation of property value. And nothing in the traditional listing process is so unreliable and untrustworthy as the estimate of value placed on it by someone with a vested interest in the value — i.e., specifically an agent who wants to list it, use it to attract buyers for other properties, and sell it for a commission. Hire an objective certified appraiser for $200 or $300; use a credit card if necessary, the properly-priced property will sell soon enough to pay it off before the charges mount.

To move the property yourself, you'll need to know it well enough to describe it to others, and you'd best do that on a form you can put in their hands. It is also a good idea to have done that before talking to agents, and especially if you chose to go the open listing or exclusive agency approach. In such cases, circulation of the property description among agents will have to be done by you. A property description form is provided at the end of this chapter.

Cost of delays

Knowing yourself means basically knowing what you need from the sale — after making a practical assessment of what you can realistically get (again, the *appraisal* and not a CMA) — *and when you want and need it!* You must come to an appreciation of *the time value of money.* Understand that a dollar in hand today is worth more than a dollar 100% certain at some later time. Money you will receive in a sale six months from now is worth less than the same amount put in your hands today; at the very least, you could bank it now and withdraw it in six-months with added interest. Thus, there is a loss occurring with the delay of a sale that accumulates with every passing day — and there is a rule of thumb you can use to calculate your monthly loss. Simply write down in whole dollars (no cents) the amount of money you would have in hand after a sale, and scratch out the last two digits. What you then see before you is a reasonable conservative approximation of what you are losing every month *(see box below)*.

It is time to bring together the many dimensions of dealing with agents and agency so that you can put together your own plan of action. What we have covered in this chapter is the following:

- the nature of agency;

- the purpose of a sales agency (to SELL);

- the question of whether or not to engage an agent;

- the risks of agency (liability and trust);

- finding the trustworthy agent;

- the optimal agency contract for you;

- what you have to know with or without an agent.

THIS IS PRETTY CLOSE to where I am going to leave you, knowing not all that is needed, but what it is that you *still* need to know. The one recurring theme I have pressed throughout this book has been consumer

Repeat: Get an appraiser

ationale: Average stock market return over many years has been about 1 percent a month. Even if you would not have invested that money in the stock market, it can be presumed that is because you have a better use for it — i.e., the alternative is worth at least that amount to you.

awareness. Consider the number of times I have said, "get an appraiser".

Consider a nontraditional sales agent

THERE IS ONE THING I have discussed only minimally in this chapter, though I describe it as the *inevitable* destiny of real estate seller agency, even put it in the title, and dedicated an earlier chapter to it — i.e., *flat fee seller agency*. I've let it go to this moment as a final reminder to you to return to that chapter as you seek ways to manage the marketing of your property. Also, as you consider the way a non-traditional flat-fee seller agent might work with you, an understanding will emerge regarding where you go from here...

If you are fortunate enough to have in your area a non-traditional flat-fee seller agent who believes in customer quality, then you have someone who will sit down with you (maybe for an honest dollar fee) and take you to the level of awareness you want, showing you what *you* can do, and what you can pay to have done.

How much study?

YOU CAN FOLLOW THAT SCHEME NOW, on your own. Study enough to stay *ahead* of the sales pitches of the professionals who profess to do what you need to have done. You need not know more than they — just more than they think you know when they make their pitches. There is nothing inappropriate about playing your cards close to your vest. And, of course, if you take the FSBO approach, your personal study should be all the more intensive (Final reminder, especially if you go without an agent, do *not* go without a lawyer). The following readings for sellers should all be available through your local booksellers or direct from the publisher:

- *Tips & Traps When Selling a Home.* Robert Irwin. McGraw-Hill, NY. 1997. (Irwin also wrote *Tips & Traps When Buying a Home.*)

- *The For Sale By Owner Kit.* Robert Irwin. Dearborn Financial Publishing, Chicago. 1995.

- *Kiplinger's Buying & Selling A Home.* The staff of Kiplinger's Personal Finance Magazine. Times Business (Random House), NY. 1996.

- *Sell Your Property Fast: how to take back a mortgage without being taken.* Bill Broadbent and George Rosenberg. Who's Who In Creative Real Estate, San Luis Obispo, CA. 1993.

- *Sonny Bloch's Inside Real Estate: the complete guide to buying and selling your house, co-op, or condominium.* H. I. Sonny Bloch and Grace Lichtenstein. Grove Weidenfeld, NY. 1987.

The property description form in this book

THE REMAINDER OF THIS CHAPTER (and the book for that matter) is devoted to the property description form promised above. It may or may not be suited to your particular property or area of the country, but you not only have permission to copy the form, but to cut and paste as you see fit for your own purposes. If you use a seller's agent, then this form is merely for you to take inventory prior to selecting the agent; your

agent should have a form suited to putting the property on the market in your area.

**Repeat:
Take charge**

TO SELL YOUR HOUSE without an agent representing
you, you will have to provide your own description to
buyers and to those bringing buyers to you (agents or
otherwise). Note that this form is expressly *not* an offer
to sell, and neither price nor date of availability is mentioned. Also omitted is a general verbal comment on
the overall amenities of the property. All these things
can be added directly or included in a cover letter, but I
advise against that until discussing the legal format, liabilities, and consequences with your attorney. Be sure
that you do not commit yourself to an agreement you
won't be ready to accept; and you don't want innocent-
ly intended words to run afoul of — for example —
consumer protection or anti-discrimination laws.

**Repeat:
Get a
lawyer**

THE JUST-STATED CAUTION should remind you that
despite all that has been said in this book about professionals poorly serving their clients, the value of those
dedicated to quality client service should not be under-
estimated. Just remember who it is that defines "quality" — by act of congress, by presidential proclamation,
and by the common wisdom of the worldwide quality
revolution it is *you!*[*] The message here is not to avoid
the professionals, but to be willing to use them because
you know *when* to use them, and *how* to use them, and
how to discern the useful from the users.

*Above, pages
102–104

OWNER'S DESCRIPTION OF PROPERTY

The following is as accurate a description as possible of the subject property, according to the best of the owner's knowledge and ability. However, it is not the work of a real estate or legal professional, and it is not presented or guaranteed as precise in every detail. This description is not in any way an offer to sell although the owner is open to reasonable offers as stated elsewhere. This description is merely a convenience to help one decide whether or not to give the property initial consideration as a potential purchase, and a starting point for inspection. Any offer to purchase must be, and will be understood to be, based upon the offeror's inspection and assessment of the property, whether by the offeror personally or by his/her designated agents. Real estate professionals (sellers' & buyers' agents) are invited to telephone for an appointment to view the property.

TOWN: _____ STREET ADDRESS: _____

VISITS BY APPOINTMENT ONLY. CALL: _____ PHONE: _____

PROPERTY TYPE: _____ AGE: _____ ROOMS: _____ BEDROOMS: _____
(1-fam, 2-fam.., farm, condo, mobile home...) (Number) (Number)

STYLE: _____ COLOR: _____ FLOORS: _____ FULL BATHS: _____ HALF-BATHS: _____
(Cape, ranch, cottage, 3-decker, etc.) (above basement) (Number) (Number)

GEN.EXTERNAL (✔)==> ___ In ground pool ___ Above ground pool ___ Storage shed ___ Barn ___ Stable ___ Tennis court
___ Paddock/corral   Other: _____
General Physical Environment (urban, suburban, rural, waterfront, woods, etc) _____
_____

FOUNDATION: _____ ft X _____ ft, OR _____ **LOT:** _____ **ZONING:** _____
(if rectangular)   (if not rectangular)   (acres)

GARAGE/CARPORT/DRIVWAY (describe)_____

BASEMENT: full? cement floor? finished? (etc)_____

ROOF (style? material? age? condition? (etc)_____

SIDING (style? material? condition? (etc)_____

(✔)==>**WIRING:** ☐ FUSES ☐ CIRCUIT BREAKERS   **ALARMS:** ☐ FIRE ☐ SMOKE ☐ CO ☐ GAS ☐ SECURITY

MONTHLY COSTS:

Txs $ _____ Wtr $ _____ Swr $ _____ Elc $ _____ Gas $ _____ Oil $ _____

(✔)==> **HEAT:** ☐ FHA ☐ FHW ☐ Steam ☐ Elec ☐ Other _____

FUEL: ☐ Gas ☐ Oil ☐ Elec ☐ Wood ☐ Coal ☐ Solar(_Pas _Actv) ☐ Propane

HOT WATER: ☐ Gas ☐ Elec ☐ Off boiler ☐ Solar ☐ Rental

A/C: ☐ Central ☐ Individual ☐ None   **INSULATION:** ☐ Full ☐ Partial ☐None

WATER: ☐ Private ☐ Public ☐ None   **SEWER:** ☐ Private ☐ Public ☐ None

OTHER COST ITEMS: _____

DIMENSIONS: KIT: ___'___"X___'___"   **LR:** ___'___"X___'___"   **DR:** ___'___"X___'___"

FR: ___'___"X___'___"   Enclosed Prch: ___'___"X___'___"   Workshp: ___'___"X___'___"

BDR1: ___'___"X___'___"   BDR2: ___'___"X___'___"   BDR3: ___'___"X___'___"

BDR4: ___'___"X___'___"   BDR5: ___'___"X___'___"   BDR6: ___'___"X___'___"

___'___"X___'___"   ___'___"X___'___"   ___'___"X___'___"

GENERAL INTERNAL ( )==> ☐ Washer ☐ Dryer ☐ Draperies ☐ Sauna ☐ Intercom ☐ Central vac ☐ Hot tub ☐ Humidifier ☐ Dehumidifier ☐

Atrium ☐ Foyer

KITCHEN: ☐ Eat-In ☐ Country ☐ Island ☐ Disposal ☐ Dishwasher

☐ Refrigerator ☐ Stove ☐ Microwave ☐ Adjoining pantry

SPECIAL KITCHEN FEATURES:

FORMAL DINING RM? ☐ Yes ☐ No Describe:

LIVING ROOM: ☐ Fireplace Other features

FAMILY ROOM: ☐ Fireplace ☐ Bar ☐ Wet bar Other

BATHROOM FEATURES:

BEDROOM FEATURES:

OTHER ROOMS (describe)

PORCH/PATIO(desc)

You are free to copy this form, change it for your own purposes, and use it as you see fit. See discussion on pages 293–294.

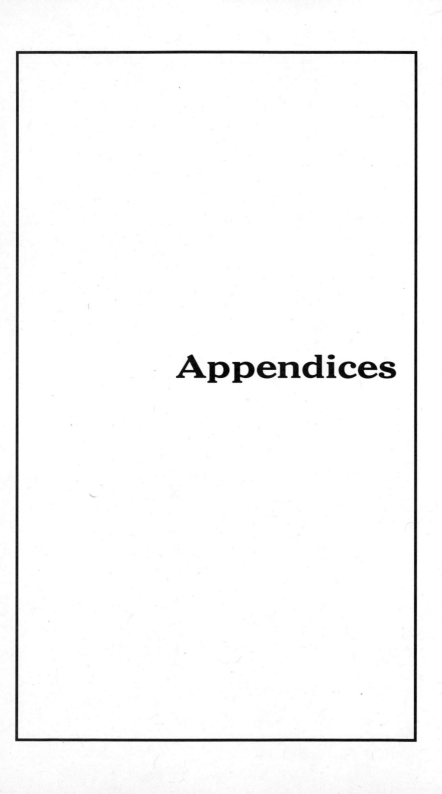

Appendices

Works consulted or cited

Bloch, H. I. Sonny and Grace Lichtenstein. 1987. *Sonny Bloch's Inside Real Estate: the complete guide to buying and selling your house, co-op, or condominium.* NY: Grove Weidenfeld.

Broadbent, Bill and George Rosenberg. *Sell Your Property Fast: how to take back a mortgage without being taken.* San Luis Obispo, CA: Who's Who In Creative Real Estate.

Carson, Rachel. 1962. *Silent Spring.* Boston: Houghton-Mifflin.

Crosby, Philip B. 1979. *Quality is Free; the Art of Making Quality Certain.* NY: New America Library.

Cummins, Joseph E. 1995. *Not One Dollar More: How to save 3,000 to 30,000 dollars buying your next home.* Oceanville, NJ: Kells Media Group.

Edwards, Kenneth. 1993. *Your Successful Real Estate Career.* NY: Amacom.

Federal Trade Commission. Report: *The Residential Real Estate Industry.* 1983.

Fields, Alan & Denise. 1994. *Your New House.* Boulder, CO: Windsor Peak Publishing.

Gabor, Andrea. 1992. *The Man Who Discovered Quality: How W. Edwards Deming Brought the Quality Revolution to America -the Stories of Ford, Xerox, and General Motors.* NY: Penguin.

Glink, Ilyce R. 1994. *100 Questions Every FirstTime Home Buyer Should Ask.* NY: Times Books (Random House).

Gooder Group. 1993. *AGENCY: Straight Answers About An Agent's Role.* Fairfax, VA.

Hopkins, Tom. 1991. *How to Master the Art of LISTING & SELLING Real Estate.* NJ: Prentice Hall.

Irwin, Robert. 1997. *Tips & Traps When Selling a Home.*NY: McGraw-Hill.

-2- 1997. *Tips & Traps When Buying a Home.* NY: McGraw-Hill.

-3- 1995. *The For Sale By Owner Kit.* Chicago: Dearborn Financial Publishing.

Kennedy, Danielle. 1990. *How To List and Sell Real Estate in the 90s.* NJ: Prentice Hall.

Kiplinger's Personal Finance Magazine (Staff). 1996. *Kiplinger's Buying & Selling A Home.* NY: Times Business (Random House).

Nader, Ralph. 1965. *Unsafe at Any Speed: the designed-in dangers of the American automobile.* NY: Grossman.

Peters, Thomas J., and Robert H. Waterman, Jr. 1982. *In Search of Excellence.* NY: Warner.

Peters, Tom. 1987. *Thriving on Chaos; Handbook for a Management Revolution.* NY: Alfred A. Knopf.

United States Department of Commerce Technology Administration, National Institute of Standards and Technology. *1993 Award Criteria -Malcolm Baldrige National Quality Award.*

Glossary

acquisition: 1. The act of acquiring. 2. The purchase process stage from first offer through taking possession.

adverse interests: mutually opposing interests where a gain for one interest is necessarily a loss to the other.

agency: 1. A legally obligating relationship in which an individual providing service (an "agent") owes certain fiduciary duties to another (the "client"). See: agents; clients; customers; fiduciary; 2. The business organization providing agent service to clients.

agency, single: See single agency.

agency disclosure: The requirement in several states that real estate agents immediately disclose to any and all potentially interested parties whether they are a sellers' agent, buyers' agent, or dual agent, and what that means in terms of obligations, loyalties, confidences, and due care for protection of the parties' interests.

agent: One who serves clients, acting on their behalf and meeting fiduciary duties which, in real estate, are enforced by law. "Dual Agents" are an exception, as defined below. See: agency; buyers' agent; fiduciary; listing agent; sellers' agent; dual agent; traditional agent.

anchors: Properties in a value stack which are actual properties in actual locations, fully documented with accurate measures and photographs. See value stack, variant.

annual percentage rate (APR): the annual loan charge rate adjusted to reflect all finance charges — a standard for comparison of differing loan and finance arrangements.

anti-trust laws: Laws designed to prevent conspiracy to limit or group boycott market competition, raise or maintain price levels, or allocate customers and/ or markets.

appraisal: A formal estimate of property value by a certified professional using disciplined technological method regulated by law and independent of financial or personal interest in the amount of the estimate.

APR: See Annual Percentage Rate.

BAD: "Buyer Awareness Development." The process of guiding buyers toward full awareness of all elements of agency, market, events, strategies, and options potentially relevant to their interests.

base list: A list of properties maintained by a buyers' agency with measured or reliably estimated values to serve as comparables for estimating value of potential purchases. Serves as base for constructing a value stack. See buyer market analysis, anchor, variant, comparable, value stack.

best price: 1. Highest price (if you are seller). 2. Lowest price (if you are buyer).

BMA: See buyer market analysis.

broker: 1. n. In real estate, a person licensed by a state to deliver full real estate services, including agency, in his/her own name and to collect a fee. 2. n. One who carries out the act of brokerage. 3. v. To carry out the act of brokerage.

brokerage: The act and/or effort rendered to bring together all elements of sales transactions, including the meeting of the minds of buyers and seller as well as all services and information needed for successful conveyance of title to and ownership of the item sold.

buy: 1. To acquire something in exchange for money (or other items of value). 2. Specifically here, to actively purchase, making cognizant selections from among investigated options, rather than being "sold" an article, product, or idea on the basis of the sales pitch. See sell.

buyer agency: The concept whereby a real estate buyer is entitled to agency representation just as has been the traditional case with sellers. See: agency; agents; clients; customers.

buyer market analysis (BMA): An approach to determining a buyer's guage of market value based on market activity of properties (comparables) with similar characteristics and amenities. See: comparable; competitive market analysis, base list, value stack.

buyers' agent: A real estate agent who represents buyers. Buyer is due full protection and rights as a client. Everything buyer reveals to the buyers' agent is confidential. Information revealed by seller or seller's agents must, by law, be used in buyer's interest — to obtain the best property, price and terms for the buyer. See: agency; agents; clients; sellers' agents.

buyers' broker: A broker designated as one serving buyers, i.e., as a buyers' agent but not necessarily an exclusive buyers' agent.

buyers' offer to purchase: The offer to purchase property, executed by an aspiring buyer to an owner, in writing, and open for the owner's consideration for a specific period of time. If accepted by the owner in all of its provisions within the specified period and prior to cancellation by the offeror, it becomes a binding contract.

buyerside: (also "buyer's side") Referring to activities or elements involved in working either for the buyer (eg. as buyer's agent, attorney, lender, contractor) or with the buyer as seller's subagent, or to compensation earned by such activity — as distinct from activities or compensation dynamics on the seller's side of the purchase/sale. See sellerside.

client: A special case of service consumer entitled to undivided loyalty, confidentiality, representation and obedience as well as other duties to be provided by agents; if purchaser of the service, the client is also the customer. See: agents; consumers; customers.

CMA: See competitive market analysis.

co-broke: For one agency to cooperate with another in brokering a property sale, one (the listing agency) placing the home on the market and being the owner's direct agent, and the other either (a) seller's subagent who procures the buyer or (b) buyer's agent who supports buyer in the transaction. Co-broking may involve commission sharing or two separate commission arrangements.

commission: The fee earned by a real estate professional for brokerage services.

commission split: The division of an overall commission between agencies or within an agency. It is usually expressed as a pair of numbers totalling 100 and representing the percent of the total going to each recipient (eg., 50-50, 60-40, 65-35).

comparable: ("comp:") n. A property used as a standard or item of comparison for establishing the value of another property — as in a competitive market analysis or in buyer market analysis.

competitive market analysis (CMA): A comparison of a seller's property to properties (comparables) on the market with similar characteristics and amenities as a means of estimating market value. See comparable.

conduit: A function assigned to the seller in a transaction in which the seller will serve as a channel for the conveyance of the buyer's brokerage fee payment to the buyer's agent.

conflict of interest: A condition which exists when the interests of a client are sacrificed, diminished, put at risk, or poorly served by an agent's self-interests, or by fiduciary obligations to a second client. Such conflicting agency relationships may arise out of implicit as well as express promises and agreements.

consideration: Something of value surrendered by one party to a contract as an inducement for the signing of the other; required in order for a contract to be valid. See valid.

conspiracy to fix prices: Communication and/or collaboration designed to set, raise, or maintain prices, rather than allow them to fluctuate according to free and open market competition.

consumer: One who uses (consumes) a product or service, either as a customer, client or non-paying user (eg. someone obtaining free information). See: agents; clients; customers.

contract term: See term of contract.

CRAP: Customer's Residual After Purchase. The residual costs of low quality which continue to be suffered by the buyer after acquisition.

curve: 1. A baseball pitch in which the ball is given a spin causing a trajectory intended to deceive a batter; 2. A verbal "pitch" (as in sales) in which words and ideas are given a "spin" intended to deceive a listener.

customer: A buyer of goods or services from sellers. See clients; consumers.

customer quality: As distinguished from process quality, or "quality" as it relates to the product or service actually delivered to customer. See quality; process quality.

customer quality revolution: A worldwide movement among manufacturing and service organizations, changing operational focus from traditional process considerations to "quality" service and product as defined by aware customers. See quality.

customer quality tripod: A metaphor illustrating the idea that quality reform in real estate is dependent upon three "legs": (1) laws of agency, (2) disclosure, (3) consumer advocacy.

dedicated: When referring to a real estate agency, it means the agency is comprised solely of exclusive buyers' agents or solely of exclusive sellers' agents. Antonym: mixed representation.

disclosure: 1. one of the fiduciary obligations of agency, requiring agent to make known to client all information relevant to client's interests. 2. requirement in several states that real estate agents reveal nature of their agency to buyers and sellers (See agency disclosure.)

discount broker: A provider of itemized real estate services, which may or may not include agency, on a flat fee basis. The word "discount" refers not to rate reductions, but to not counting charges for unordered or unused services in the billing. See agency; brokerage; flat fee; flat fee brokerage.

disorder: Referring to the sabotage of new order clarity and balance via deliberately disruptive legislation. See old order, new order.

drive-by: 1. A step in the property search process, a literal drive-by view of a property before deciding to schedule a formal visit; 2. a property so treated; 3. a system of providing clients of buyers' agents with a list of properties for drive-by viewing.

dual agent: Real estate "agents" who are an exception to the definitions of agent and agency here. They are openly declared to represent both buyer and seller, but more as mediators or facilitators than as sales or negotiation aides, and do not act on behalf of either party in dealing for advantage over the other. They cannot betray the confidences of either side and, by definition, give neither side undivided loyalty. Undisclosed dual agency is illegal. Consumer advocates generally do not endorse dual agents. Opposing concept is "single agency". See: agents; agency; clients; buyers' agents; fiduciary; sellers' agents.

due diligence: the obligation of an agent to proactively search out all factors potentially harmful to the interests of his/ her client in time to stop or modify the agreement or transaction process.

EA: See exclusive agency.

ERTR: See exclusive right to represent.

ERTS: See exclusive right to sell.

exclusive agency (EA): Type of real estate contract giving exclusive representation rights to one agent or firm. It limits options of the client, not of the agent. An EA listing gives only one real estate agency the right to sell the property for a commission, though it may employ sub-agents, but the owner retains a right to find his/her own buyer and pay no commission. In an EA buyer agent contract, buyer agrees to purchase only through the contracted agency.

exclusive buyer agency: 1. A real estate agency employing only buyers' agents and never engaging in agency for sellers. 2. Fiduciary obligation and service to buyers, independent of all obligations and inducements to adverse interests (eg., sellers, other agents, service providers).

exclusive buyers' agent: an agent who represents only buyers and neither accepts listings nor works in an agency which represents sellers or accepts listings, and who functions in conformance with definition #2 of exclusive buyer agency. See also exclusivity; single agency.

exclusive right to represent (ERTR): Listing contract in which an owner employs a sales agent would guarantee the right to represent the seller as listing agent regardless of who obtains a buyer, but at a commission rate encompassing seller-side and not buyerside activity. A second and distinct commission may be paid to the listing agent if and only if the listing agent (or agent of the listing agent) produces a buyer. See buyerside, sellerside, exclusive agency, exclusive right to sell, procuring cause.

exclusive right to sell (ERTS): Similar to an exclusive agency listing contract with the added provision that the commission will be paid regardless of who, including the owner, obtains the buyer.

exclusivity: Having only buyers or only sellers among one's clients. See exclusive buyers' agent; single agency.

FSBO: "For Sale By Owner". Pronounced fiz__bo. The acronym usually refers to a property being offered for sale in this way.

fiduciary: A relationship based in and investing trust in an agent by a principal. The six fiduciary duties owed by a real estate single agentG to the client are: undivided loyalty, utmost care (due diligence), disclosure, obedience, confidentiality, and accountability. A **dual agent** cannot provide undivided loyalty and confidentiality of each party prevents certain disclosure to the other.

flanking properties: Properties in a value stack between which an object property is inserted to develop perspective on its value. See buyer market analysis, object property, value stack.

flat fee: A fixed dollar amount billed as compensation for a specified amount or item of work, as opposed to a percentage commission.

flat fee brokerage: Real estate services on a flat-fee compensation basis, itemized according to customer specification, which may or may not include agency. See agency; brokerage; discount broker; flat fee.

going rate: A common phrase referring to the typical or most common price on the market for a particular commodity or service, irrespective of whether that rate has been set by illegal conspiracy or rose out of free and open market competition.

high-risk, low-reward: See risk and reward.

ideal deal: A sale at a price at real value above worth to seller and below worth to buyer. See worth; value.

listing: 1. The act of acquiring the agreement of a property owner to allow the placing of the property on a real estate agency's list of properties to be marketed. 2. A property so-listed. See sellers' agents.

listing agency: An agency whose member agents conduct listing activity. See: listing; listing agent.

listing agent: Real estate agents who contract with a property owner to place the property on the agent's list of properties for sale, and to promote and manage the sale of that property on the owner's behalf. See: agency; agents; sellers' agents.

location factor: A numerical multiplier applied to a property value in one location to determine the value of a similar property in another location.

low-risk, high-reward: See risk and reward.

mixed-representation: representing both buyers and sellers in the same agency, even if given agents may themselves be designated exclusive buyers' or exclusive sellers' agents. Antonym: dedicated.

MLS: See Multiple Listing Service.

Multiple Listing Service (MLS): A proprietary marketing service in which member brokers publish properties for sale, offering one-another co-broke fees for the procurement of buyers.

NAR: National Association of Realtors®. See Realtor®.

new order: Referring to the conditions of clarity and balance brought to real estate by disclosure laws and buyer agency. See old order, disorder.

object property: A property being considered for purchase and inserted into a value stack between properties of greater and lesser value to place its value into perspective. See buyer market analysis, value stack, flanking properties.

offer: See buyer's offer to purchase.

offer and acceptance: 1. The traditional steps of contractual agreement. 2. (O&A) The signed offer and signed acceptance of the offer in one combined document.

old order: Refering to the conditions of sellerside bias in real estate prior to the disclosure laws and buyer brokers. See new order, disorder.

open listing: A type of real estate listing agreement in which an owner gives several real estate agencies the right to sell the property for a commission, paying the commission only to an agency procuring a buyer, and retaining the personal right to find his/her own buyer and pay no commission.

operationalist: A person who measures the value of a procedure or activity by its accomplishment of some output or purpose (as opposed to **traditionalist**).

P&S: See purchase and sale agreement.

percentage of purchase price: See three-P commission.

primary market: The market for mortgage loans directly to borrowers (i.e., home-buyers). See *secondary market.*

principal: The person for whom an agent works.

principal broker: The licensed real estate broker in whose name all other licensed members of an agency operate as real estate salespersons (including some licensed as brokers).

process quality: As distinguished from cus-tomer quality, the degree to which a pro-duction or service process delivers prod-uct or service in full conformance to cus-tomer specifications. See customer quali-ty; quality.

procuring cause: the effort credited with causing the desired end result. In real estate, it is either the effort made made to bring a qualified buyer to a property or to locate a qualified property for a buyer — a matter of whether the property is "sold" or "bought."

purchase and sale agreement: (P&S) A con-tract between a property owner and a buyer, stipulating the price, terms and time of sale and conveyance of the prop-erty.

purchase offer: See buyer's offer to pur-chase.

purchase price percentage commission: See three-P commission.

purchasing support agency: An agency which exclusive provides support to cog-nizant selective purchase at the most favorable purchase terms, as opposed to the "selling" or promotion of a property for sale.

quality: The degree of conformance to standards determined by customer speci-fications of performance, utility and price.

quality revolution: See customer quality revolution.

retainer: A fee paid in advance of perfor-mance to reserve the services of an agent, sometimes credited against service charges.

Realtor®: A registered trademark of the National Association of Realtors®, apply-ing exclusively to its members. It is not a synonym for "real estate agent" though most Realtors® are real estate agents.

redundant: unnecessarily repetitive. See redundant.

reinvention: A term evolving from the cus-tomer quality revolution meaning the deliberate restructuring of something to more perfectly achieve its purpose according to the definition of quality.

risk and reward: In decision-making regarding alternatives for the investment of time or effort, the balancing of the possibility of damage or no reward against the amount of the potential reward. Options are ranked from "high-risk low-reward" (at worst) to "low-risk high-reward" (at best).

sales agency: A real estate agency employed by property owners to actively sell their properties according to the defi-nition of "sell".

salesperson: 1. One who sells professional-ly. 2. A licensed real estate agent who must work for a "broker" and acts only in the name of the broker.

SCAM: See seller's customer-agent man-date.

secondary market: The market involving the sale of mortgages from primary market lenders to cash-providing insitutions. See *primary market.*

sell: 1. To exchange something for money (or other items of value). 2. Specifically here, to actively promote, market, and cause another to accept an article, product, or idea and/or to carry out some behavior (including paying the maximally obtainable price for the sold item). See buy.

seller: The owner of a property which is either offered for sale, under an agreement of sale, or sold.

sellers' agent and subagent: Real estate agents who represent seller. "Seller's agent" is the one listing the property; "subagent" is any agent, other than a buyer's agent, referring or bringing buyers. Client of both is the seller. Buyer is their customer and not their client. Everything buyer reveals to them must, by law, be used in seller's interest — to obtain best price and terms for seller. See: agents; buyers' agent; listing agent; clients; customers.

seller's customer–agent mandate (SCAM): mandate by the seller or seller's agent that co-broking agent who is normally a sellers' enter into a buyer's agent contract with the buyer, soley to protect sellerside from subagent liability.

sellerside: (also "seller's side") Referring to activities and elements involved in working for the seller in the service of the listing agreement and general promotion of the property, or to compensation earned by such activity, — distinct from activities supporting buyer's property search, purchase capability, or offer, whether such buyer-support is given in the buyer's or the seller's employ and/or representation. See buyerside.

side: See: buyerside; sellerside.

single agency: The concept whereby a real estate agent or agency represents only one side in a purchase and sale transaction. The functional opposite of "dual agency".

single agent: 1. Technically, one who practices single agency. 2. In common professional parlance, one who specializes in providing single agency to both buyers and sellers, as opposed to exclusively serving either buyers or sellers.

subagent: See seller's agent and subagent.

term of contract: The specified period of time within which a contract applies.

three-P commission: Purchase price percentage commission. A fee paid to a real estate agent that is set as a percentage of the actual purchase price of the property.

traditional agent: Sellers' agent who draws buyers with promise of buyer-service, in addition to the product for sale (the property). Such service is often couched in offers to work "with" rather than "for" buyers — a subtle device tending to downplay their legal requirement to work for the sellers. See: agent; client; sellers' agent.

traditional system: The system of real estate sales in which real estate sales professionals contract, for a fee contingent on sale, to be the agents of owners in the promotion and sale of real property, and subcontract with other agents to act as the procurers of customers (buyers) for a fee-share upon successful procurement and sale. Buyers are attracted primarily through the advertising of property for sale, and with the inducement of "buyer service", usually downplaying that such "service" does not include agency representation which is exclusively committed to property owners (sellers). The commitment to obtain best price and terms for sellers and not buyers (i.e., the requirement of seller agency), is disclosed usually only to the degree required by law; and such disclosure is usually "softened" by distractions or qualifications implying that, in actual practice, it "makes no real difference" to the buyer.

traditionalist: As used here, not merely one who values tradition, but one who sees the value of a traditional production or service operation in what it does for the operators rather than in the definition of *customer quality*. Traditionalist reaction to consumer awareness of options begins with denial and redefinition, then moves to prevention with diversion and distraction and through limiting or eliminating the options.

transaction: The collective activities and proceedings in the conduct of the formal business of carrying out a real estate purchase and sale agreement, including property conveyance, money transfers and payments, documention completion and signing, and recording.

transactional agency: The system replacing subagency and automatic seller representation by defining agency responsibility within a given transaction as only seller, buyer or dual agency.

true value: See Value, #3.

typical brokerage: Brokerage arrangements on either buyer's side or seller's side, or both sides, in which all usual service elements are required, in the usual quantity, with no unusual elements or extreme demand (or near absence of demand) upon agent's time, effort, or expense, with payment for service contingent upon sale and due at closing.

undisclosed dual agency: Representing principals with opposing interests, with one or both sides unaware the agent represents the other.

valid: Legally enforceable — as applied to contractual agreements.

value: 1. The power of something to command a price to be paid in order to obtain it. "Invaluable": above and beyond all prices. "Valueless": not worthy of any price. 2. A dollar amount set for tax, insurance, or credit purposes. 3. "True value" is here set as the full amount of money it can command including price and all other acquisition costs.

value stack: A list of properties arranged in order of value as a guage for assessing the value of properties compared to it. See buyer market analysis, base list, object property, flanking properties, anchor, variant.

variant: Property in a value stack which is not an actual property but a variation of an actual property with an appropriately adjusted value. See value stack, anchor.

WFB (working for buyers) One of four modes of client relationship an agent assumes. Buyer's agent openly declares agency obligation to buyer so there is no room for seller to misunderstand. See also WFS, WOB, and WWB.

WFS (working for sellers) One of four modes of client relationship an agent assumes. Seller's agent openly declares agency obligation to seller so there is no room for buyer to misunderstand. See also WFB, WOB, and WWB.

WOB (working on buyers) One of four modes of client relationship an agent assumes. Sellers' agency simply adds "buyer agency" to its menu of services — despite continuing as agency to seller interests. See also WFB, WFS, and WWB.

worth: The degree of desirabilibity or usefulness of something, especially in terms of comparison to, exchange with, or tradeoff against other desirable or useful things.

Index

GIVE THE GIFT OF AWARENESS.

People you care about will be buying or selling a home.

WHY LET friends walk unaware of system pitfalls or newly available options as they approach one of the major financial and lifestyle decisions of their lives? The time to learn is before it all happens!

TO ORDER BOUGHT, NOT SOLD:

- CALL **1-888-732-3355** Toll Free (Have your credit card ready)
- or FAX this form to: **(413) 772-2450**
- or MAIL it to : Cogna Books, P.O. Box 1108, Greenfield, MA 01302

Your Name:_____

Street Address: _____

_____

City: _____State:___ Zip:_____

Telephone: (___) _____

Please Send: ____ books @ $14.95 each $_____

Sales Tax: add 5% for books shipped to addresses in Massachusetts:
$_____

Shipping and Handling: $2.50 for first
book, $2.00 for each additional book: $_____

                                        TOTAL: $_____

Payment: ☐ Check enclosed   ☐ Credit Card
☐ MC ☐ VISA
Card Number _____
Name on Card: _____
Exp. date: _____/_____/_____

COGNABOOKS®

GIVE THE GIFT OF AWARENESS.

People you care about will be buying or selling a home.

WHY LET friends walk unaware of system pitfalls or newly available options as they approach one of the major financial and lifestyle decisions of their lives? The time to learn is before it all happens!

TO ORDER BOUGHT, NOT SOLD:

- CALL **1-888-732-3355** Toll Free (Have your credit card ready)
- or FAX this form to: **(413) 772-2450**
- or MAIL it to : Cogna Books, P.O. Box 1108, Greenfield, MA 01302

Your Name:_____

Street Address: _____

_____

City: _____ State:___ Zip:_____

Telephone: (___) _____

Please Send: ____ books @ $14.95 each $_____

Sales Tax: add 5% for books shipped to addresses in Massachusetts:
$_____

Shipping and Handling: $2.50 for first
book, $2.00 for each additional book: $_____

                                        TOTAL: $_____

Payment: ☐ Check enclosed   ☐ Credit Card
☐ MC ☐ VISA
Card Number _____

Name on Card: _____

Exp. date: _____/_____/_____